ESKIMO ESSAYS

Eskimo Essays

YUP'IK LIVES AND
HOW WE SEE THEM

Ann Fienup-Riordan

RUTGERS UNIVERSITY PRESS   New Brunswick and London

Prepared with the support of the Alaska Humanities Forum and the National Endowment for the Humanities

Fourth paperback printing, 2003

Library of Congress Cataloging-in-Publication Data

Fienup-Riordan, Ann.
  Eskimo essays: Yup'ik lives and how we see them / Ann Fienup-Riordan.
    p.   cm.
  Includes bibliographical references.
  ISBN 0-8135-1588-2 (cloth)   ISBN 0-8135-1589-0 (pbk.)
  1. Yup'ik Eskimos. I. Title.
E99.E7F46 1990
979.8'004971–dc20   90-31331
                                            CIP

British Cataloging-in-Publication information available

To my parents,
Beth and Ken Fienup

Contents

List of Illustrations

Preface

ESKIMOS IN GENERAL AND YUP'IK ESKIMOS IN PARTICULAR
have been both understood and misunderstood by missionaries, scholars, artists, and the general public for hundreds of years. Eskimos
have been depicted as conservationists practicing waste-free management and consumption of scarce and limited resources; as being
peaceful and nonaggressive; as living free from law in a state of "contained anarchy"; and as lacking the concepts of leadership, territory,
and landownership.

This book addresses these and related half-truths, both individu-
ally and in concert. The reader may speculate on how these miscon-
ceptions have contributed to misunderstanding and stereotyping. I
attempt to suggest here how knowledge of Eskimo history and tradition can contribute to a fair representation of Eskimos past and present, as well as to an understanding of the preconditions that continue
to shape such representations.

Perhaps more than most anthropologists, arctic scholars tend to
lose themselves in the minutiae of their own field and to leave the
popular characterization of Eskimos to the generalists. We specialists
then criticize their misrepresentations from the sidelines. We often
prefer to discuss details with each other rather than trying to translate that detail into an accurate general conception of the diversity,
complexity, and richness of arctic life.

A prime objective of this book is to bridge the separation between
informed scholarship and popular concepts. The chapters that follow
are not intended as an encyclopedic compendium of the details of
Yup'ik life but rather as essays that address a central theme—the
intersection of Yup'ik and Western thought and cultural representation. As opposed to an edited collection, in which a variety of authors
offer different perspectives on a single topic, this book poses the same
questions about a variety of topics. I hope that the coverage stimu-
lates the student of anthropology as well as the general reader to
think about how indigenous peoples have been portrayed and how

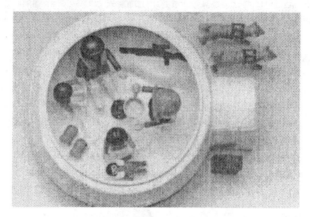

playmobil®

A child's image of Eskimos: plastic Playmobil toys.

we perceive them. I also suggest ways in which both natives and non-natives can use arctic scholarship to deepen their knowledge and understanding of the original peoples of the Far North.

The need for such a reconsideration is great. Eskimos are among the most overexposed peoples of the world, due in part to their phenomenal geographic distribution across the Arctic. Yet the same fascination that has driven research has relegated the Eskimo way of life to the status of culture-in-training, an understudy culture reminiscent of the composite American Indian of the Wild West. Such popular perceptions have had dramatic consequences, not the least of which is an attempt by modern Eskimos to depict themselves as what we have imagined them to be.

Eskimology traces its beginning to the pioneering work of Hans Egede (1745) and David Crantz (1767) in Greenland and to Ivan Veniaminov (1840), John Murdoch (1892), and Edward Nelson (1899) in Alaska. Subsequent students of the Arctic have focused largely on ferreting out the "facts" of Eskimo life rather than contributing to theoretical debates about how these details might best be represented. Over the last several decades, remarkably few articles about Eskimos have appeared in general anthropology journals such as the *American Anthropologist* and the *American Ethnologist*. Students of Marshall Sahlins, David Schneider, Clifford Geertz, and Roy Wagner, to name but a few, invariably head south to find "their people" and make their mark.

My concern in this book is as much with non-native intellectual history as with the details of Yup'ik Eskimo life, past or present. The roughly chronological organization of the essays emphasizes how the Yup'ik people have been objects of representation; non-natives in turn reflect this image back on the Eskimos, who then write their own history in part to create an image that they can use to represent themselves to non-natives. Within this circular framework three major issues of interpretation emerge.

The first is the way in which our inability to accurately see our own society continues to impede our ability to understand others. Westerners tend to view society as the gathering of separate individuals (Macpherson 1962) and in this Hobbesian mode elevate the self-reliant Eskimo to the position of ultimate individualist. Because Euro-Americans often imagine Eskimos to be a less sophisticated model of themselves, alternately noble and base, they all too often explain away Eskimo actions as functioning to unite domains of cultural activity that Western science has arbitrarily separated in the first place. Many non-natives see Eskimos as "naturally" peaceful until corrupted by civilization. They dismiss accounts of traditional bow-and-arrow warfare as myths rather than acknowledging them as historical narratives. They idealize the Eskimo hunter as the original ecologist; then they cannot understand why he does not readily adopt their rational plans for the management of fish and wildlife based on the concept of resources as scarce and limited rather than infinitely renewable.

The second major theme is the need to look at context to understand meaning. A mask, for instance, cannot be understood without comprehending its place in ceremonial dancing and the place of dancing in cultural activity generally. Similarly, ideology can best be understood as it is acted out in everyday life. The details of Eskimo cosmology have always fascinated and beguiled Western observers.

Yet disconnecting these details from the meaning people assign to their actions in particular contexts can lead easily to groundless speculation and error.

The third issue is that the present is incomprehensible without reference to the past. Each chapter poses different questions about the accuracy and validity of past Euro-American representations of Yup'ik Eskimo thought and deed and the effect of these representations on our present understanding. For example, current Yup'ik political alliances are impossible to understand without reference to traditional interregional alliances. In the same way the current testimony by natives on topics ranging from fish and game regulations to land claims is comprehensible only if one understands the traditional Eskimo view of animals as nonhuman persons.

Western observers have simultaneously naturalized Eskimos as paragons of simplicity and virtue and historicized them as the victims of Western imperialism. This process has been largely unencumbered by reference to Eskimo concepts of society, history, and personhood. An original assumption of similarity (that Eskimo society operates the way we think Western society does) has profoundly affected the current Euro-American comprehension of Eskimo history and action. Non-natives have taken an idealized Western individual, dressed that person in polar garb, and then assumed they understood the garment's maker. The result is a presentation of Eskimo society that often tells us more about the meaning we seek in our own history than its Eskimo counterpart. Moreover, modern Eskimos have risen to the challenge and to some extent have become what we have made them. The contemporary Yup'ik Eskimos' representation of themselves often is as much a product of non-native expectation as of their own history.

The first chapter in this book, "Eskimos, Real and Ideal," provides an introduction to the Far North and the variety of Eskimo peoples who make it their home. Both the natural surroundings and the way of life of the Yup'ik Eskimos of western Alaska differ markedly from social and environmental patterns generally associated with Eskimos. The fact that many non-natives do not recognize this difference is not surprising, as the image of the igloo-dwelling Eskimo of the Central Canadian Arctic was introduced by explorers such as William Parry and George Lyon over a century before most Yup'ik people began their direct encounter with the Western world. Although the Yup'ik Eskimos outnumbered their Canadian and Greenlandic relatives, delayed contact and limited commercial activity in western

Alaska meant that popular notions about Eskimos developed without taking Yup'ik reality into account. Arctic scholars have made substantial strides in correcting this imbalance, but the Yup'ik Eskimos remain simultaneously one of the least known and one of the most traditional of Native American peoples.

The second chapter, "The Ideology of Subsistence," I wrote in 1981 as the foreword to my first book, *The Nelson Island Eskimo* (1983). I included it as a brief introduction to my background and the experiences I brought to the field. It also introduces the reader to the part of the Yup'ik world that I know best and most often refer to for examples of the Yup'ik view of the world. In addition, the chapter provides a summary of the major findings of my work on Nelson Island, including the birth imagery and ideology of reproductive cycling that underlie a variety of social and ritual action on Nelson Island today. The theme of reproductive cycling is a central organizing principle in Yup'ik cosmology, although its expression in action has differed throughout the region. Its elaboration stands as an example of the kind of research required to understand the meaning as opposed to the functions of Eskimo social action.

The third chapter, "The Mask: The Eye of the Dance," was written in 1984 and published in *Arctic Anthropology* (1987). The chapter describes the system of symbols and meanings surrounding the work of the Yup'ik mask maker Nick Charles and the ways in which these meanings continue to connect both traditional and contemporary masks and masked dances to past and present aspects of Yup'ik ideology and culture. Whereas Chapter 2 details the broad themes of birth and rebirth and a dynamic cycling between the worlds of the living and the dead, this chapter describes the vision imagery, epitomized in the motif of the ringed center, that is one means of both depicting and effecting this movement.

The fourth chapter, "The Real People and the Children of Thunder," I wrote in 1988, and I have since expanded it in a biography of the late nineteenth-century Moravian missionary couple John and Edith Kilbuck (Fienup-Riordan 1991). Their experiences in western Alaska illustrate the process of cultural as well as religious conversion set in motion by the arrival of missionaries along the Kuskokwim River. The central thesis is that a comprehensive understanding of the missionary/Eskimo encounter depends on our ability to comprehend essential differences between the missionary and native ideas about the world in which they lived, including concepts of personhood, history, and society. Although fraught with misapprehensions, both humorous and sad, the process of cultural conversion was by no means one-sided. As the "real people" watched and listened to the missionaries, so too the Kilbucks' "thunder," though always a part of them, was modified by what they came to understand.

The fifth chapter, "*Selaviq: A Yup'ik Transformation of a Russian Orthodox Tradition*," details the origins and gradual elaboration of the cross-cultural and ethnically diverse celebration of *Selaviq* (Russian Orthodox Christmas) in western Alaska as well as contemporary non-native reactions to it. As it developed in western Alaska, *Selaviq* presents a classic case of the universal process whereby people make sense of new ideas and symbols in terms of what they already know. Since its introduction, the Yup'ik people have elaborated *Selaviq*, combining elements of Russian Orthodoxy and aspects of Slavonic folkloric traditions within a framework of Yup'ik interpretation and style. The creativity *Selaviq* demonstrates seems neither unusual nor unique but rather the norm for cultural and religious conversion. New "traditions" such as *Selaviq* never appear out of thin air; their origins involve a complex history of appropriation and creative transformation. In accepting the Christian message, the Yup'ik people were both performing a deliberate act of innovation as well as supplementing a familiar store of responses. In their celebration of *Selaviq* they have successfully transformed what was brought to transform them.

The sixth chapter, "Robert Redford, Apanuugpak, and the Invention of Tradition," was presented at the symposium "Along the Grease Trails" at The University Museum in Philadelphia in the spring of 1987 (Fienup-Riordan 1988c). The essay discusses a film project under way at that time in western Alaska and analyzes the discrepancies between Yup'ik history as it can be understood from the oral traditions and as both the film's scriptwriter and the Yup'ik Eskimos themselves chose to present it in the film. The scriptwriter used one of the most dramatic oral accounts from the period of traditional Yup'ik bow-and-arrow warfare as a vehicle for denouncing not only warfare but also the concepts of property and territory that lie behind it. Discussion of the filmmaker's reconstruction of the indigenous world leads to consideration of the anthropologist's reconstruction of a society as well as the natives' reconsideration of their own past. Insofar as the filmmaker's project coincides with the natives' creative reformation of their own history, the role of the anthropologist is not to insure "authenticity" in reference to a precelluloid past. Rather, it is to promote open dialogue between artists seeking new symbols to carry their culture's old meanings and a community seeking new meaning in the symbols of its past.

Chapter 7, entitled "Yup'ik Warfare and the Myth of the Peaceful Eskimo," was written in the fall of 1988 and presented at the Smithsonian Institution's "Crossroads of Continents" symposium in Washington, D.C. The fuller version included here was subsequently given as one of three keynote addresses at the Sixth Inuit Studies Conference in Copenhagen in October 1988 (Dahl 1989). The chapter deals with the disjunction between the stereotype of the peaceful Eskimo and the details of traditional Yup'ik bow-and-arrow warfare. A number of factors have contributed to the development of the Western conception of Eskimos as naturally peaceful. These factors include the relatively peaceful character of the Eskimo/Euro-American encounter; the extension of descriptions of Canadian Eskimos to all Eskimos; the tendency to extend observations on Eskimo interpersonal relations to intergroup relations; and our desire to see hunting societies in general and Eskimos in particular as an original, primitive image of ourselves.

The point is not to replace the image of the peaceful Eskimo with a violent one. To understand interpersonal violence and politically aggressive acts by Eskimos today, however, it is essential to understand the interpersonal hostilities and political alliances that were forged during the period of bow-and-arrow wars. Our representation of the Eskimo is especially important to understand because we have modeled our image of Eskimos, perhaps more than that of any other people, on an idealized image of ourselves.

Chapter 8, "Original Ecologists?: The Relationship between Yup'ik Eskimos and Animals," was written in 1987. It juxtaposes the Western view of fish and wildlife as finite and manageable and the Yup'ik Eskimo view of animals as an infinitely renewable resource, and it describes game-management conflicts in western Alaska that result from these different views. An appreciation of the Yup'ik concept of animals as nonhuman persons possessing an immortal soul and a special "awareness" is fundamental to understanding how productive decisions were made in the past and continue to be made to this day. Game management in western Alaska needs to take into account the fact that many Yup'ik Eskimos view the availability of animals, rather than their existence, as within the range of human influence. Here again the situation is complicated by the fact that the Eskimos are rising to our expectations and depicting themselves as the natural conservationists Euro-Americans expect them to be.

Chapter 9, "The Yupiit Nation: Eskimo Law and Order," was written in the spring of 1988 and presented at the annual meeting of the Yupiit Nation, a political alliance of nineteen Kuskokwim and coastal villages seeking confirmation of their right to govern themselves independently of both the federal and Alaska governments. I attempt to summarize what has been written about traditional Eskimo law and governance and to see where the literature coincides with the oral tradition of the Yupiit Nation members. In the literature, both past and present, the Yup'ik people are most often presented as lacking overt leadership and formal laws, their traditional system dubbed "contained anarchy" (Oswalt 1963a:54). On the contrary, although formal civil law and governance may have been lacking, the Yup'ik Eskimos had a detailed moral code and an effective system of social sanctions that were invisible to Western observers looking for a mirror image of their own legal system.

The concluding chapter, "The Invocation of Tradition," addresses issues of continuity and change in Yup'ik culture, including some of the new uses Yup'ik people are making of their history and traditions. Insofar as the non-native representation of Eskimos coincides with the Yup'ik conception of their own history, the role of the anthropologist goes beyond facilitating accurate representation. Students of Eskimo history can help bring into focus the unstated assumptions that underlie the ongoing conversation between non-natives seeking to know their own history by viewing "traditional" Eskimos and Eskimo people seeking recognition by non-natives of a new image of themselves.

This book aims primarily at debunking past stereotypes of Eskimos by detailing Yup'ik exceptions to the Eskimo rule. I hope to increase the reader's awareness of the context of past portrayals of Eskimos, thereby encouraging new thoughts about the consequences of these representations. Eskimos cannot be pigeonholed as either "primitive" white men or their fur-clad alter ego. Also, full recognition by the general public of cultural variability within the Arctic is long overdue. Many nonspecialists have tended to assume that the history and traditions of all Eskimos were directly comparable to those of their Canadian and Greenlandic relatives. The more we learn, the more we recognize considerable variation in the Arctic. Careful detailing of the origins and historical genesis of these differences will be critical to an accurate interpretation by non-natives of Eskimo action, past and present.

Acknowledgments

FIRST AND FOREMOST, I WISH TO THANK THE PEOPLE OF western Alaska for their continuing help with and interest in my work. Without their friendship and support the material for these pages could never have been gathered and its publication would hold no glory. For fifteen years, Yup'ik friends and colleagues have fed me, teased me, and told me not to talk so fast. I hope this book can in some measure begin to repay the debt I owe them.

I wrote the chapters in this book between 1981 and 1989. During that time I was fortunate to have had the interest and financial support of a number of organizations, including the National Endowment for the Humanities, the Alaska Humanities Forum, the Alaska Historical Society, and the American Association for State and Local History. Each grant, small or large, was a vote of confidence that I gratefully acknowledge.

This book owes its existence to the help and encouragement of many people. I especially would like to thank three teachers who have since become friends and who continue to inspire: Marshall Sahlins, who gave me anthropology to take to the Arctic; David Schneider, who got me to bring what the Arctic taught me back to anthropology; and, last but not least, Jim VanStone, who has read more manuscript material than is decent and always kept his sense of humor.

Both the individual chapters and the manuscript as a whole have profited immensely from the comments and criticisms of a number of friends and colleagues, including Lydia Black, Tiger Burch, David Chanar, Bill Fitzhugh, Gary Holthaus, Alexie Issac, Steve Jacobson, Sergei Kan, Susan Kaplan, Margaret Lantis, Harry Luden, Elsie Mather, Allen McCartney, Susan McKinnon, Steve McNabb, Phyllis Morrow, S. A. Mousalimas, Father Michael Oleksa, Wendell Oswalt, Ken Pratt, Irene Reed, Bill Schneider, Barbara Smith, George Wenzel, and Bill and Karen Workman. In listing their names I am reminded here, too, of debts I will find it difficult to repay.

Four of the ten chapters in this book have been published else-where. I would like to thank Alaska Pacific University Press, *Arctic Anthropology*, and the *American Ethnologist* for permission to reprint them here. I would also like to acknowledge my debt to anonymous reviewers who read and commented on drafts of these publications. I profited a great deal from their advice.

All but two of the chapters were delivered as papers at the annual meetings of the Alaska Anthropological Association in either Anchorage or Fairbanks. I am grateful both for the opportunity the association gave me to air my views as well as for the many helpful comments participants provided.

For the illustrations for this book I am indebted to a number of friends and institutions. Thanks go to James H. Barker, Don Doll, Suzi Jones, the Kilbuck family, Ted Mala, Matt O'Leary, Rosie Porter, Andris Slapinsh, and Paul Souders of the *Anchorage Daily News* for providing me with photographs and illustrations and to Ayse Gilbert and Karl Johansen for preparing maps. Photographs were also obtained from the Library of Congress, the Smithsonian Institution, the University of Washington Library in Seattle, the Moravian Archives in Bethlehem, Pennsylvania, the University of Alaska Anchorage Archives, the Alaska State Council on the Arts in Anchorage, and the Alaska State Museum in Juneau.

For help in the preparation of this book, I am particularly indebted to the word-processing and editorial skills of Dawn Scott and Judith Brogan in Anchorage as well as to Marlie Wasserman and the editorial staff at Rutgers University Press. It has been a real pleasure to learn from them how to make words say what you want them to in a clearer, cleaner style.

Last but not least, thanks go to my parents, my brother, John, and my sister, Mary, my husband, Dick, and our three children, Frances, Jimmy, and Nick. Without their love and support I could not do what I do.

ESKIMO ESSAYS

Introduction: Eskimos, Real and Ideal

Primitive Eskimos in Asia and North America had only themselves and their environment from which to make their living and from which to fashion a culture. Consequently they built their houses of blocks of snow and ice and skins. They subsisted largely upon sea animals, and used the fat or "blubber" of these animals for light and heat. Today they may have radios and cigarette lighters. (Cole and Montgomery 1967:201)

The primitive Eskimo eats fish and seal meat not because he is too stupid or too lazy to raise corn and cows, and not necessarily because he prefers wild to cultivated food. He eats fish and seal meat because his physical environment will not provide enough hay for cows and heat for corn. (Bradley 1968:37)

MANY PEOPLE WOULD PROBABLY VIEW THESE QUOTATIONS as accurate, if somewhat dated, representations of Eskimos. From childhood, we have heard about these fur-clad survivors of the polar regions. The "typical" Eskimo is an igloo-dwelling nomad who survives by capturing seals and an occasional polar bear, which he eats raw. During the long, dark winter, the smiling Eskimo mother tends her children by the light of a seal-oil lamp, while her clever husband repairs his harpoon for the morrow, when he will again risk his life to wrench from the frozen Arctic coast a livelihood for his happy family.

The parka-clad, igloo-dwelling nomads on whom these generalized images are based accounted for less than 5 percent of the approximately fifty thousand people who made the Arctic their home in the nineteenth century. Although the image applies only to the coastal inhabitants of the Canadian High Arctic, the extreme and exotic conditions under which these Eskimos lived continue to exert a strong pull on the popular imagination. Actually, Eskimoan peoples occupy a variety of environments across the Arctic and constitute the most far-flung aboriginal population in the world. Far from being dependent on polar bear and seal for survival, most Eskimos rely for their

FIGURE 1.1. Major Eskimo populations, A.D. 1800–1825 (from Burch 1988b).

Ocean

GREENLAND

EAST GREENLAND ESKIMOS

POLAR ESKIMOS

WEST GREENLAND ESKIMOS

BAFFINLAND ESKIMOS

COPPER ESKIMOS

NETSILIK ESKIMOS

IGLULIK ESKIMOS

CARIBOU ESKIMOS

SADLIRMIUT ESKIMOS

QUEBEC ESKIMOS

LABRADOR ESKIMOS

Atlantic Ocean

Lake Athabasca

Hudson Bay

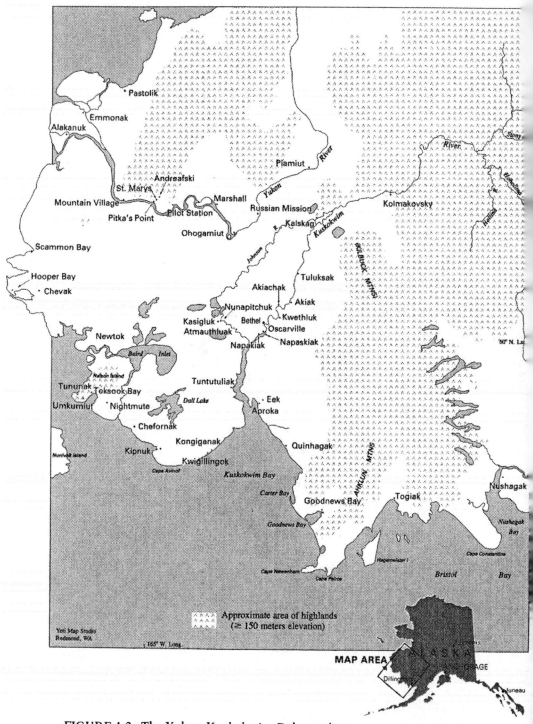

FIGURE 1.2. The Yukon-Kuskokwim Delta region.

sustenance on a seasonal variety of fish and wildlife, including the whales of north Alaska, the caribou of the Canadian Arctic, and the freshwater fish of the major river drainages of western Alaska.

Although these tremendous variations have been well documented during the last hundred years, the strength of the original romantic and enduring image of Eskimos set in motion by the arctic explorations of the sixteenth century remains undiminished. Perhaps no people in the world have simultaneously been so admired and so misrepresented as the Eskimos. Even our comprehension of their name is flawed. For nearly a century, both anthropological and popular sources, including the Oxford English and Webster's New World dictionaries, maintained that the name *Eskimo* derived from a proto-Algonquian root translating as "eaters of raw flesh." In fact the name originated in a Montagnais form meaning "snowshoe-netter" (Goddard, cited in Damas 1984:6). An original etymological confusion and the general public's continued willingness to see Eskimos as the ultimate "natural men" have combined to perpetuate the error. One does not easily dismiss a name that so succinctly embodies one's preconceptions, accurate or otherwise.

Ironically, belief by Eskimos themselves in the pejorative connotations of their name was a major factor in its replacement, at least in Canada and parts of Greenland since the 1970s, by the designation Inuit, meaning "people." This shift has proved satisfactory in the eastern Arctic. In western Alaska, however, the use of the term *Inuit* has created as many problems as it has solved, and the name has never taken root. The Eskimos of western Alaska are indeed members of the larger family of Eskimo cultures extending from Prince William Sound on the Pacific coast of Alaska to the Bering Strait and from there six thousand miles north and east along Canada's arctic coast and into Labrador and Greenland. Within that family, however, they are members of the Yup'ik-speaking not Inuit/Iñupiaq-speaking branch. Accordingly, the self-designation of the Eskimos of western Alaska has always been, and remains to this day, Yup'ik, from the base *yuk*, person, plus +*pik*, genuine or real, hence "a real or genuine person."[1]

Within the Yup'ik-speaking world, my primary focus is on the inhabitants of the Yukon-Kuskokwim Delta. Along with the native peoples of southern Norton Sound and Bristol Bay, the people of the Yukon-Kuskokwim Delta spoke the Central Alaskan Yup'ik language, which in the nineteenth century was one of five Yup'ik languages internally divided into four major dialects (Jacobson 1984:28). The other four Yup'ik languages of historic times were three Siberian Yup'ik languages and Pacific Yup'ik (Alutiiq), which was spoken around Prince William Sound, the tip of the Kenai Peninsula, Kodiak Island, and part of the Alaska Peninsula. Inuit/Iñupiaq-speaking Eskimos occupied the entire arctic coast, from Greenland west across Canada and northern Alaska as far south as Unalakleet on Norton Sound. Together the two language families—Inuit/Iñupiaq and Yup'ik—constitute the Eskimo branch of the Eskimo-Aleut (or Eskaleut) family of languages.

In both language and name, the Central Yup'ik Eskimos of the Yukon-Kuskokwim Delta (henceforth referred to as Yup'ik Eskimos) are decidedly different from their northern relatives. In fact, if we move point by point through the generalized image of the Eskimo, we find that Yup'ik Eskimos differ on every count (Lantis 1984; VanStone 1984b).

The coastal landscape into which the ancestors of today's Yup'ik Eskimos first moved does not resemble the glacial fjords of their Greenlandic relatives or the rocky coastline of the Canadian Arctic. Rather it consists of a broad, marshy plain, the product of thousands of years of silting action by the Yukon and Kuskokwim rivers. This vast alluvial prairie is criss-crossed by innumerable sloughs and streams that cover close to half the surface of the land with water and create the traditional highways of its native population. Except for occasional low volcanic domes, which break the surface on Nelson and Nunivak islands, along the coastline the sea is shallow and the land is flat.

Living as they do below the Arctic Circle, the Yup'ik Eskimos do not annually endure the frigid temperatures or seemingly endless winter nights of the arctic coast. December days are five hours long at the very least, and hunting and fishing can still take place in all but the coldest months of the year. Although wind chill can drive the temperatures to −80°F in winter, a sunny, windless July day can push temperatures to +80°F. Shore ice may extend up to thirty miles off the coast, but the sea is never frozen over. Polar bears find the maritime climate too tropical for their liking and rarely venture below Norton Sound. Indeed, spring comes to western Alaska by mid-April rather than mid-July as in the northern Arctic, and breakup typically occurs by the end of May. The summer season is also long by arctic standards, lasting up to three months.

The relatively long growing season of western Alaska supports a variety of vegetation, including numerous edible greens and berries,

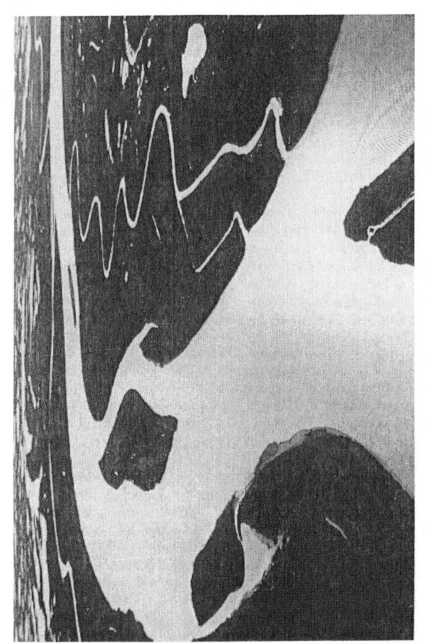

FIGURE 1.3. The topography of western Alaska (Courtesy James H. Barker).

which the local people harvest in abundance. Shrubs and trees, including willow and alder, crowd the shores of stream banks. The river drainages are forested with a mixture of spruce and birch from above Bethel on the Kuskokwim and Pilot Station on the Yukon.

Because their environment is soggy tundra and spruce forest as often as snow and ice, the Yup'ik people never used the famous igloos of the Canadian North. Instead, the spring floods of the mighty Yukon and Kuskokwim rivers supplied them with an abundance of driftwood, which they traditionally used to build semisubterranean, sod-insulated log houses that were both substantial and warm. These solid dwellings were constructed at large, centrally located, permanent winter sites that the delta's ample population returned to year after year.

Unlike their northern relatives, the Yup'ik Eskimos made their home in a rich and varied subarctic environment. Far from being scarce and limited, the resources of the land were immense. The place of the Yukon-Kuskokwim Delta environment in the development of Eskimo civilization was comparable to the place of the Nile or Tigris-Euphrates river valleys in Western civilization. As in the Near East, environment set the stage for cultural florescence. Rather than being a constraint, the environment of western Alaska acted as an impetus for the creation of a culture as complex and diverse as that in any other part of the Eskimo world.

As distinct from the coastal Eskimos to the north, the Yup'ik Eskimos never relied on the bowhead whale for their sustenance; the shallow coastline precludes the presence of this large sea mammal. However, the coastal waters of the Bering Sea abound with a variety of seal as well as belukha whales, walrus, and occasional sea lions. The thousands of miles of rivers and streams that criss-cross the delta lowland are richly endowed with fish, including five species of salmon, sheefish, several species of whitefish, northern pike, burbot, trout, blackfish, and stickleback. The nearshore waters also provide a productive fishery for halibut, flounder, and herring. Herring are harvested in abundance in early June and provide an important element in the coastal diet, as do whitefish and salmon inland and upriver.

In addition to fish and sea mammals, migratory waterfowl and birds, including geese, sandhill cranes, and whistling swans, flock to the broad coastal wetlands to nest and breed each spring and summer. Numerous ducks and seabirds, including pintails, old-squaws, and king eiders, are also taken. Traditionally they were harvested with blunt-headed arrows or with bird spears and spear throwers within sight of the hunters' homes. Now the noise of technology forces men to range far afield to fill their gamebags. Small land mammals including muskrats, otters, fox, and mink are also plentiful and were traditionally taken in both deadfall and spring traps and snares. Larger land mammals including brown bear, moose, and caribou are available inland and upriver and are as important as sea mammals along the coast. Though a late spring sometimes meant starvation in the past, fish and wildlife are generally readily available from the beginning of April through the end of November. Scarcity is not nearly as threatening as the popular representation of Eskimos allows (Fienup-Riordan 1986b).

The bounty of the Yukon-Kuskokwim Delta supported the largest Eskimo population in the world. As many as fifteen thousand people may have lived in western Alaska in the early 1800s, divided into at least twelve socially and territorially distinct regional populations (Figure 7.1). Each of these groups in turn was socially divided into a number of village groups, ranging in size from 50 to 250 persons and joined together by ties of blood and marriage (Fienup-Riordan 1984a).

The abundance of fish and game in western Alaska allowed not only for larger social groupings than were possible in most other parts of the Arctic but also for a more settled life. Like all Eskimos, the coastal Yup'ik people were mobile, yet their rich environment allowed them to move annually within a relatively fixed range. Each regional group demarcated a largely self-sufficient area within which people moved freely throughout the year in their quest for food. Typically, they did not need to travel between the regions, as they each had access to a complete range of resources. Dramatic fluctuations in animal populations and variable ice and weather conditions, however, often made interregional travel and trade expedient. A number of social strategies facilitated this movement, including the regular exchange of food, women, names, and feasts.

Interregional relations were not always amicable, and prior to the arrival of the Russians in the early 1800s bow-and-arrow warfare regularly characterized delta life. Although similar in many respects to warfare waged by north Alaska Eskimos (Burch 1974), the Yup'ik bow-and-arrow wars stood in sharp contrast to patterns of intergroup relations described for the sparsely populated Canadian Arctic.

At the turn of the century the bilateral extended family, numbering up to thirty persons, was the basic social unit in western Alaska, a rather large group by Eskimo standards. It consisted of from two to four generations, including parents, offspring, and parent's parents. Married siblings of either the parents or their offspring might also be included. The extended families making up a single community were joined by an overlapping network of consanguineal and affinal ties, both fictive and real. Members of a single residential group were probably related to one another in several different ways within four or five degrees of consanguinity. In larger villages, most marriages were within the group. Regular recruitment also occurred beyond the village, although normally within the bounds of the regional group.

Although small family groups moved out to spring sealing camps along the coast and summer fish camps along the river, families gathered each winter in permanent villages. Here the stereotype of the isolated Eskimo household consisting of noble hunter, wife, and child did not prevail. The Yup'ik Eskimos did not live in nuclear family units. Rather, communities of up to three hundred persons were residentially divided between a communal men's house (qasgiq) and numerous smaller sod houses (enet) in which resided four to a dozen women and children. In these enet women sewed skins, prepared food, and cared for the young children. At age five, boys moved to the men's house with their fathers and other adult male relatives. In this large structure the males of the community worked, ate, slept, bathed, conversed, and entertained visitors.

In the winter the men's house was the focus of community activity and the site of a number of elaborate ceremonial exchanges, including the Bladder Festival, the Great Feast for the Dead, and the Messenger Feast. The wooden masks and ritual paraphernalia produced by carvers for these occasions more closely resembled those of Northwest coast dwellers than those of the northern Arctic Inuit in complexity and artistic refinement. Some scholars have characterized the Bering Sea coast as "the cradle of Eskimo civilization," as it was here that Eskimoan culture achieved the highest degree of social and technological elaboration.

In sum, the Yup'ik Eskimos of western Alaska are as unlike stereotypical Eskimos as is imaginable. Our image of the Eskimo is a smiling, igloo-dwelling, parka-clad eater of raw meat, skillfully engaged in wresting a living from the most inhospitable environment in the world. The Yup'ik Eskimos, however, waged war, dwelt in sod houses, dressed in fish and bird skins as often as furs, ate prepared fish and fowl more often than raw meat, and all in all enjoyed the bounty of a rich and hospitable homeland.

Images of Eskimos

Given such pronounced differences between the Western image of arctic life and Yup'ik Eskimo reality, why has that reality remained so obscure and failed to affect the general image of Eskimos? How did it happen that the relatively meager population of the High Arctic commanded the attention of the Western world, while their more numerous and culturally complex southern relatives remained virtually unknown?

In fact, though Eskimos in general have long been the object of observation and speculation, Yup'ik Eskimos were largely ignored until the nineteenth century. The first Western explorers to encounter Eskimo peoples did so in the high Arctic on voyages and overland treks in search of a northwest passage between the Atlantic and Pacific. The Eskimos they met supplied the material for our original image (Neatby 1984; VanStone 1984a).

Aside from brief references to Inuit encountered by the Norse in the thirteenth century, the Western image of Eskimos had its beginning in the sixteenth century, when the first arctic explorers brought back descriptions of savages clothed in fur and given to eating raw meat. These exotic descriptions were followed in 1577 by the presentation to Queen Elizabeth I of an Eskimo man, woman, and child whom Sir Martin Frobisher brought back from his exploratory trip to Baffinland (Oswalt 1979:32).

Early descriptions presented Eskimos as neither docile nor smiling. Frobisher experienced a series of hostile encounters with inhabitants who were alternately described as "crafty villains" and "fierce and cruel" (Hakluyt 1589:220–222). An old woman who had been captured in a skirmish was described in something less than complimentary terms: "The old wretch, whom divers of our Saylers supposed to be eyther a devill, or a witch, had her buskins plucked off, to see if she were cloven footed, and for her ougly hew and deformity we let her goe" (Hakluyt 1589:220).

From the very first, explorers contrasted the raw fare of the Eskimos to their own cooked meat:

> They eate their meat all raw, both flesh, fish, and foule, or something per boyled with blood and a little water which they drinke. . . . If they for necessities sake stand in need of the premisses, such grasse as the Country yeeldeth they plucke up and

eate . . . like brute beasts devouring the same. They neither use table, stoole, or table cloth for comlines: but when they are imbrued with blood knuckle deepe, and their knives in like sort, they use their tongues as apt instruments to lick them cleane. (Hakluyt 1589:224)

In their dwellings, also, the Eskimos were depicted as animal-like:

Those houses or rather dennes which stand there, have no signe of footway, or any thing else troden, which is one of the chiefest tokens of habitation. (Hakluyt 1589:227)

Their winter dwellings . . . are made two fadome under grounde . . . having holes like to a Foxe or Conny berry. . . . They defile these dennes most filthily with their beastly feeding, & dwell so long in a place . . . untill their sluttishness lothing them, they are forced to seeke a sweeter ayre, and a new seate, and are (no doubt) a dispersed and wandring nation, as the Tartarians, and live in hords and troupes, without any certaine abode, as may appeare by sundry circumstances of our experience. (Hakluyt 1589: 300–301)

Another indication of their animal-like character was imputed cannibalism: "I thinke them rather Anthropophagi, or devourers of mans flesh then otherwise: for that there is no flesh or fish which they find dead (smell it never so filthily) but they will eate it, as they finde it without any other dressing. A loathsome thing, either to the beholders or hearers" (Hakluyt 1589:227). Ironically, this misinterpretation may have been mutual. At the conclusion of a skirmish during Frobisher's second voyage, a group of cornered Eskimos flung themselves over a cliff in lieu of allowing themselves to be captured by the English sailors "for they supposed us belike to be Canibals or eaters of mans flesh" (Hakluyt 1589:305).

In the end, the first-encountered Eskimos were appraised as lacking any "capacitie to culture": "But [they] are contented by their hunting, fishing, and fouling, with raw flesh and warme blood to satisfie their greedy panches, which is their only glory" (Hakluyt 1589:228). The bestial nature of the Eskimos was epitomized by the actions of a captured woman who healed her child's wounded arm "by continuall licking with her owne tongue, not much unlike our dogs" (Hakluyt 1589:305).

As the Europeans got to know the Eskimos better, they began to judge them more "humane and civill" (Hakluyt 1589:236). In their captives they observed the "civilized" virtues of grief, sorrow, affection, and even modesty: "Only I thinke it worth the noting, the continencie of them both [the captive Eskimos]: for the man would never shift himselfe, except he had first caused the woman to depart out of his cabin, and they both were most shamefast, least any of their privie parts should be discovered, either of themselves, or any other body" (Hakluyt 1589:307).

The accounts of Frobisher's encounters with Eskimos were, in fact, enlightened for their day in both their sympathy and detail. Moreover, the reader should recall that these early descriptions of Eskimos were largely accidental offshoots of the search for the Northwest Passage.[2] Happily, this "accident" was responsible for the most detailed accounts of Eskimos produced during the next 150 years of exploration.

In their arctic explorations, Frobisher and his contemporaries were understandably confounded by what they encountered. The Elizabethans understood Christendom to be composed of three races descended from Noah and were perplexed when they discovered what appeared to be people at the northern edge of the known world (Berkhofer 1978:35; Oswalt 1979:36). Were these creatures remnants of the lost tribes of Israel? Were they soulless people descended from another Adam or created spontaneously from the earth? Explorers would have been less surprised to discover nymphs, satyrs, or giants, given their view of the world. That they attributed any human qualities at all to the Eskimos they encountered is more remarkable than any presumed failure on their part to recognize such a link.

For the next three centuries, northern Eskimos continued to be visited, and numerous published accounts described their way of life (Collins 1984; Oswalt 1979). The European and American publics, avidly interested in the frozen tip of the world, eagerly received these descriptions, which in the beginning alternately represented Eskimos as sun-worshipping cannibals and scantily clad pygmies. Gradually, the fantastic images of Eskimos as cloven-footed savages, more animal than human, were replaced by more accurate accounts.

Although Eskimos had largely won recognition as hominids by the early 1800s, their character as human was still at issue. In the eighteenth century, Europeans viewed the newly discovered peoples of the Americas predominantly as defective members of their own species (Pagden 1982:17). Classical humanists as well as Christian theologians pictured the continuing degeneration of human beings after the expulsion from the Garden of Eden as a viable explanation for the otherwise inexplicable social and cultural differences that the New World discoveries presented. The "barbarous"—un-Christian and un-civilized—nature of the Eskimos was attributed to their long separation from their more fortunate (and as a result superior) European brethren.

Though the concept of degeneration remained a powerful explanatory tool for human diversity into the nineteenth century, the Age of Enlightenment produced alternate possibilities. One was articulated by Jean Jacques Rousseau in his *Social Contract* of 1762. Whereas Rousseau's predecessors, among them Thomas Hobbes, depicted "natural man" as brutish and self-centered, requiring reason and the restraining arm of society to control his animal nature, Rousseau eloquently defended the image of people as pure in a state of nature and subsequently corrupted by civilization. Although the Hobbesian viewpoint is reflected in Western thought to this day, so also is the image derived from Rousseau of the "noble savage." Time and context determine which view is in the foreground, but its opposite is never far away.

Depictions of Eskimos bear witness to the Western debate about human nature and Euro-American ambivalence concerning the encounter with non-Western peoples. Like the Indians of the American West, Eskimos were alternately depicted as Arcadians and as savages—simultaneously heroes and brutes; free of the constraints of civilization yet subject to extreme natural hardship and ordeal; idealized as healthy, vital, and noble and at the same time condemned as rude, ugly, and barbaric.

Accounts of Eskimos written in the late eighteenth and early nineteenth centuries vividly display this ambivalence. For example, David Crantz's (1767) descriptions of west Greenlandic Eskimos depicted them simultaneously as noble and base, condemning their "dark side" at the same time stressing their character as stoics, not savages: "The Greenlanders are not properly an untractable, fierce, wild, barbarous or cruel people, but rather a gentle, quiet, civil and good natured generation" (quoted in Oswalt 1979:95).

This ambivalent picture of Eskimos can also be seen in the journal accounts of the popular arctic explorers of the nineteenth century, including George Lyon (1824), William Parry (1828), John Ross (1819), Elisha Kent Kane (1856), and Robert E. Peary (1898, 1910). Each of these men, to differing degrees, pictured the Eskimos they encountered as admirable in some respects yet decidedly inferior;

their writings were permeated by an insidious and respectable racism. Peary, for example, repeatedly spoke in patronizing terms about the "fearless, hardy, cheerful little tribe of human children" who had helped him in his quest for the pole. In a brief ethnographic "sketch," he described the Smith Sound Eskimos:

> [They are] a community of children in their simplicity, honesty, and happy lack of care; of animals in their surroundings, their food and habit; of iron men in their utter disregard of cold, hunger, and fatigue; of beings of high intelligence in the construction and use of the implements of the chase, and the ingenious concentration of every one of the few possibilities of the barren country which is their home, upon the two great problems of their existence—something to eat, and something to wear. (Peary 1898:483)

Whereas English exploration had been motivated by the search for the Northwest Passage, American exploration focused on the search for a route to the pole, which Peary claimed to have conquered in 1909. The process generated a vast literature on Eskimos, both popular and scientific. At the same time that they increased their comprehension of the "reality" of arctic life, however, nineteenth-century Euro-Americans began to clothe Eskimos in a new, romantic image that they wear to this day.

The initial fascination for Euro-Americans was in the sharp contrast between the harsh, cold, primordial conditions of arctic life and the ultimately admirable human qualities and adaptive strengths attributed to its aboriginal occupants. Such adaptive strengths presumably enabled them to cope with the severity of their environment. The social Darwinism of the nineteenth century preached the survival of the fittest, a principle that was applied to all phases of natural development. What, then, was more admirable, more susceptible to idealization than a people who were apparently so perfectly fitted to their environment, masters of their natural domain? Typical of this characterization was the description of an Eskimo hunter by Eivind Austrup (1896:466), the first officer on two of Peary's polar expeditions: "As a hunter he has no equal—he reminds me in many respects of Fenimore Cooper's Indian chiefs. Nobody in the whole tribe could be . . . more free and independent, nobody stauncher in friendship or nobler in thought, nobody cooler in the hour of danger, or more astute during the hunt—in fact, he was a hero."

Just as nineteenth-century biographers concentrated on the heroic dimension of their subjects, repeatedly showing their ability to triumph against adversity, so descriptions of Eskimos in the exploration literature from this period presented them in the heroic mode. Their survival (like that of the explorers themselves) was proof that self-discipline, persistence, and the use of common sense could bring success. The explorers sought, among other things, to show how success depends on the individual industry and energy that we all possess. In their writings, Eskimos alternately appear as examples of people who exhibit such industry and adaptability (as in the glowing descriptions of the fitness of their skin-covered watercraft) and as examples of what transpires when such industry is lacking.

In sharp contrast to the initial representation of Eskimos as subhuman and animal-like, the twentieth century saw the emergence of an image of Eskimos as strong, noble, independent, and pure until corrupted by civilization. The arctic journals of men such as Parry, Lyon, Ross, Kane, and Peary, although presenting an ambivalent picture of the Eskimos encountered, provided the basis for a vast popular literature that reinforced and actively marketed this new and noble image. The Eskimos Peary brought back from his journey to the North Pole were housed along with the artifacts of Eskimo life at the American Museum of Natural History in New York City (Harper 1986). The publicity these arctic representatives received marked the progressive transformation of the image of Eskimos from subhuman to superhuman. Displayed along with their sophisticated hunting tools and wearing polar bear skins, these living specimens came to represent the ultimate survivors, intrepid and courageous individualists who through sheer cunning were able to best their rivals in the free marketplace of the arctic world. Happy, peaceful, hardworking, independent, and adaptable—these were the images most often used to clothe Eskimos in the twentieth century. The nuances of Eskimo reality dimmed in comparison to this dramatically staged representation, an image increasingly acceptable because of its incorporation of traits Westerners valued in themselves.

At the same time that Peary's Polar Eskimos were exciting public interest on the East Coast, Siberian Yup'ik Eskimos were housed in a papier-mâché "Eskimo Village" at the 1909 Alaska-Yukon-Pacific Exposition in Seattle. Complete with nearly one hundred Eskimo men, women, and children, the village was billed as the most "stupendous attraction" on the Pay Streak. Claimed the promoters, "These strange people, existing only on the products of the icy North, half civilized

FIGURE 1.4. The "Eskimo Village" at the 1909 Alaska-Pacific-Yukon Exposition (Courtesy Special Collections Division, University of Washington Libraries, photo by Nowell, negative no. 1766).

in their nature, knowing no god, having no laws, no government, unable to read or write, with no history of their antecedents, give continuous performances of skill, marksmanship, canoeing, dancing, singing and seal catching never before seen" (quoted in *Alaska Journal* 1984:14)

Here the double image of Eskimos is revealed: a "natural man," devoid of both history and culture, adapting and surviving through skillful marksmanship and individual prowess. Eskimos are remarkable as much for what they lack, from a Western point of view, as for what they have. Robert Rydell's (1984:199) discussion of the exposition neatly summarizes the Western vision of racial and material progress that determined, among other things, the turn-of-the-century vision of Eskimos:

When seen in conjunction with the federal government exhibits of natural resources on display in the Alaskan Building—which was built "to show the world that Alaska is no longer a place where only the Eskimo and Indian can live"—the Eskimo Village created the impression that for these people progress would be judged by their racial attributes and by what and how much they contributed to the economic growth of America's commercial empire.

If the explorer literature of the nineteenth century had introduced the Euro-American publics to Eskimos, and exhibits of living Eskimos consistently depicted them as being at a purer but lower stage of civilization, the early cinematographic representations of the 1920s and 1930s made them famous (Balikci 1984). In 1922 Robert Flaherty's documentary of Eskimos in the Central Canadian Arctic, *Nanook of the North*, opened to rave reviews and generated a veritable "Nanook mania," including the introduction of the ubiquitous Eskimo pie. *Nanook* was followed in 1933 by *Eskimo*, based on the novel of the same title by Peter Freuchen and filmed by MGM in Alaska, and in 1937 by *The Wedding of Palo*, filmed in Greenland under the direction of the Danish explorer Knud Rasmussen.

Each of these now classic films depicted small, isolated human societies that through ingenuity and fortitude were able to wrest from their inhospitable homeland a measure of dignity and sustenance. Whereas *Nanook* focused on the elemental battle between people and the natural elements, and *Palo* on the conflict between good and evil within people themselves, *Eskimo* took as its point of departure the conflict between uncorrupt "natural man" (Rousseau's noble savage) and the unwholesome influences of the "civilized" world. In all three, Eskimo heroes and heroines alternately conquered natural adversity and succumbed to the evils of civilization to a dramatic Western orchestral accompaniment. Whereas the exploration literature of the nineteenth century and exhibitions of the early twentieth century had been ambivalent in their representation of Eskimos, moviegoers were presented with an uncritical heroic image that haunts Eskimo peoples to this day.

The tendency of all three films to conflate diverse individual Eskimos into a single heroic stereotype was compounded by the persistent confusion of history with the present. As with the way of life of other indigenous peoples, Westerners viewed Eskimo culture as somehow changeless. Although they might allow Eskimos to acquire such modern accouterments as rifles, radios, and cigarette lighters, these were viewed as corrupting an original purity. Though Flaherty captured Nanook's quizzical reaction to the disembodied music of a phonograph, neither he nor his contemporaries were prepared to portray the complex interaction between the native and non-native

FIGURE 1.5. Ray Mala, star of *Eskimo*, the Clark Gable of Alaska (Courtesy Mala Collection, University of Alaska Anchorage Archives).

FIGURE 1.6. Mala and his sweetheart: the famous Eskimo kiss (Courtesy Mala Collection. University of Alaska Anchorage Archives).

worlds. Similarly, Edward Curtis (1930) carefully staged his photographic portraits of Nunivak Eskimos, using woven grass backdrops to conceal the impure traces of contact between his "noble savages" and the Western world.

The visual arts of the twentieth century were not alone in their tendency to romanticize Eskimos and deny them historicity. The perceived simplicity and "naturalness" of arctic life were eulogized by

FIGURE 1.7. The filming of *Eskimo* on location in Teller, Alaska, in the early 1930s (Courtesy Mala Collection, University of Alaska Anchorage Archives).

writers who sought in their encounters with Eskimos to experience themselves shorn of all culture. In Gontran de Poncins's *Kabloona* (1941) the "primitive" culture of the Eskimos served as the litmus test of civilization. In his self-examination de Poncins consciously challenged his acquired habits of Western cultural superiority to experience himself "not as a Frenchman, not as an individual product of heritage, place, environment, but as nothing other than, simply, a man" (Christopher 1988:266).

The French anthropologist Jean Malaurie (1982:19) echoed this attitude when he hailed his arrival at Thule in Greenland as "a return to the Stone Age" and acknowledged his debt "to these exemplary men, who obliged me to discover in depth my own identity":

> To know how the boreal hunter apprehends time and space can become a crucial element in our understanding of archaic thought processes. In watching the Eskimos live, in trying to grasp how they equip and organize themselves, . . . the ethnologist, no matter where he is from, is at the very roots of his own civilization. . . . The Arctic in 1950 was a living Lascaux. (Malaurie 1982:xvi)

FIGURE 1.8 "Maskette, Nunivak," photograph taken by Edward Curtis during his stay on Nunivak Island in 1927 (Courtesy Library of Congress).

As had Flaherty and Freuchen before them, de Poncins and Malaurie viewed the Eskimos as "essential men" whose daily lives epitomized the triumph of man over nature. They studied Eskimos, in part, "to understand how a primitive society dominated by an implacable environment can persevere" (Malaurie 1982:xvi). The other side of this heroic focus, however, was often the denial that such a "natural man" was capable of coping with the complexities of the modern world: "Unprovided in his natural rights as he is, . . . the Eskimo is unfit to meet the shock of intimate contact with an aggressive civilization built upon experiences totally different from [his] own" (Gordon 1906–1907:70). This emphasis on natural strengths may be more a curse than a blessing insofar as it undercuts the ability of contemporary Eskimos to present themselves as simultaneously modern and complex.

Although the Euro-American preoccupation with living groups as representations of earlier "uncorrupted" stages of civilization has abated, our fascination with the "perfect adaptability" and "individual freedom" of the Eskimos has not. Wendell Oswalt (1979:3) wrote: "The premium that they placed on personal freedom unfettered by rigid social constraints is important, as is the laxity of their sexual code. . . . Theirs was a simpler reality than ours, it required fewer social encumbrances, and it serves as a positive model for individual achievement, especially since theirs was such a demanding environment." Oswalt (1979:1) aptly concluded that Eskimos fascinate because aspects of their life-style stand in inviting contrast to those of all other peoples. He might have added that this contrast is a direct result of our need to see ourselves simultaneously opposed to and mirrored in a "primitive humanity." Eskimos continue to fascinate both because of their character as different and because we think we can see in them an original image of ourselves.

Yup'ik Eskimos in the Literature

In the development of the Eskimo image, the Yup'ik Eskimos were something of an anomaly. As the contradictory Western image of the Other changed from bestial and fantastic to adaptive and romantic, so did the image of the Eskimo. At the same time, because western Alaska was not a part of the "real Arctic" experienced by the early explorers, it was ignored. Lacking any real knowledge of the Yup'ik Eskimos, non-natives freely applied to them the image of the Eskimo derived from European experience in the High Arctic.

The first detailed reports of the Yup'ik Eskimos were produced not by Europeans or Americans but by Russians in the early 1800s, 250 years after the first English encounters with Eskimos on the northeastern coasts of Canada and Greenland. Exploratory reconnaissances were carried out in 1818, 1829, and 1842–1844 by Petr

Korsakovskiy, Ivan Vasilev, and Lavrentiy Zagoskin, respectively, to judge the merits of extending the Russian-American Company fur trade into western Alaska (Michael 1967; VanStone 1988). These explorers described the Yup'ik people in some detail, and their journals include accounts of the distinctive housing styles, elaborate winter ceremonies, dependence on fish, variety of technology, habits of dress, and unique language.

Unlike the navigators of the sixteenth century, the Russian explorers described the Yup'ik people they encountered in sympathetic terms. Korsakovskiy wrote of the *Aglurmiut*: "Few of them are ugly. . . . They have a kind and pleasant appearance. . . . Their clothing is simple and comfortable. . . . They are gentle, . . . and are very much attached to their children . . . [Their dwellings are] much better than the Kodiak's: clean, dry, well kept. . . . Manners are observed. Fat is rendered, meat is cooked" (VanStone 1988:30–31).

The Russian explorers were not the only ones favorably disposed toward the Yup'ik Eskimos they encountered. Their positive evaluations were echoed in the writings of Russian Orthodox priests such as Iakov Netsvetov, who served at Russian Mission from 1845 until 1863. The opinions of Russian explorers and Orthodox priests, however, had no influence on the generalized image of Eskimos building in America and Europe during the nineteenth century. Both Korsakovskiy's journal and the accounts of Vasilev's expeditions remained unpublished in Mother Russia, as the Russian-American Company had no intention of making accessible information that might help its competitors. Zagoskin's report and Netsvetov's voluminous journals were not translated and made generally available to the English-speaking world until 1967 and 1984, respectively (Michael 1967; Black 1984a).

The first major ethnological observations in western Alaska were carried out by Edward W. Nelson. Between 1877 and 1881 Nelson worked for the U.S. Army Signal Service at St. Michael and also collected for the Smithsonian Institution during an extended sledge journey over the Yukon-Kuskokwim Delta region (Nelson 1882, 1897). Results of these expeditions were published by the Bureau of American Ethnology in 1899. True to his time, Nelson's work consists of a meticulous catalogue of the ten thousand objects he collected for the Smithsonian Institution during his years in western Alaska, accompanied by detailed ethnological observations. His *The Eskimo about Bering Strait* remains the single richest source of information on the nineteenth-century Yup'ik Eskimos.

For all its variety and detail, Nelson's collection was born of a particular cultural premise. Like his contemporaries in the Bureau of American Ethnology, Nelson materialized culture and represented it through collections of things. These collections were perceived as an addition to Western science rather than to indigenous understanding. The Smithsonian's Museum of Natural History was founded at the peak of social evolutionism. Its main displays of non-European artifacts were predicated on ideas of people adapting, placing contemporary Eskimo society into a timeless zone drained of historicity. This conception of culture continues as an active element in the representation of Eskimos, Yup'ik and Inuit alike.

Except for the work of Nelson, almost no mention of western Alaska was made in the published record during the nineteenth century. Ivan Petroff (1884) briefly described the region in his U.S. Census report for 1880. William Healy Dall's (1870a, 1870b, 1877, 1884) publications also contain some useful descriptions. Although *Alaska and Its Resources* was a trade book, the rest were published in thick government documents and had no meaningful effect on the general understanding of the Yup'ik way of life.

In 1927 Curtis visited Nunivak Island, followed in the 1930s by Hans Himmelheber. Except in their accounts, Yup'ik Eskimos virtually disappeared from the literature until the publication in 1946 of Margaret Lantis's "The Social Culture of the Nunivak Eskimo." The first full-scale description of any Alaska native group, Lantis's publication was the single most valuable contribution since Nelson's work. It was followed by Oswalt's *Napaskiak* in 1963 and James VanStone's ethnohistory of the Nushagak region in 1967. The two broke ground in Eskimology by giving the first detailed descriptions of Eskimos living in the woods. Aside from the work of these three anthropologists, the region remained sadly neglected into the late 1970s.

Explorers and ethnographers were not the only ones to ignore the Yukon-Kuskokwim Delta and its inhabitants. Commercial interest has also been markedly absent. The region lacked significant amounts of any of the commercially valuable resources that initially attracted non-native entrepreneurs to other parts of the state. The shallow coastline hosted neither the sea otters that drew Russians to the Aleutians in the late eighteenth century nor the bowhead migrations that brought American whalers into arctic waters farther north by the mid-1800s (Fienup-Riordan 1983:8–9). No gold or mineral deposits comparable to those found in either northern Alaska or the upper Yukon were discovered in the region. Though furbearers were present, both the scattered human and animal populations served to undercut the ability of non-natives to exploit them (Oswalt 1990: 115–120). Fish constituted the region's most valuable resource, and canneries were established and had a major impact in Bristol Bay beginning in the early 1900s (VanStone 1967:63–82). Although the effects of the canneries extended to the Yukon and Kuskokwim rivers, small salmon runs and difficult access meant that the impact was less intense.

The relative lack of commercially valuable resources meant that the Yukon-Kuskokwim Delta experienced the direct influences associated with non-native contact later than other regions of Alaska. Although Russian traders and Orthodox priests made their appearance in the 1830s, it was not until the late 1800s that the pace of cultural and economic change in western Alaska accelerated. Increasing missionary efforts, contacts with vessels serving the Seward Peninsula mining boom towns, forays by miners into local river systems, and modest demands for local services (such as the provision of furs, food, and firewood) gradually opened the region to outside influences (Fienup-Riordan 1991).

As a direct result of the lack of commercial resources and late contact, the Yup'ik Eskimos remain as central to retaining, and in some cases reinventing, Eskimo ideology as they were peripheral to the Western comprehension of Eskimos. Yup'ik Eskimos owe both their cultural integrity and relative obscurity to their virtually invisible location and place in Western history. True, non-natives increasingly came to live in the region, beginning around 1900 with the discovery of gold on a Kuskokwim tributary, the Yellow River (Oswalt 1990:94–95, 100); but the miners and traders had little interest in describing the people they encountered to the outside world.

This social separation is reflected in the paucity of references to Eskimos in the books published by traders, white prospectors, and miners. The few in which they are mentioned tend to be condescending. For example, to the fur trader Bernhard Bendel, the Kuskokwim Eskimos appeared "small, dirty fellows, a low race, but seem quite friendly so far" with "a horrible odor" and dwellings that "seem more [like] mudpiles" (Vitt 1987:30, 39). Ironically, perhaps, the non-natives who wrote about their experiences in the northland often depicted themselves using the same idealized, romantic images that nineteenth-century explorers had applied to Eskimos. For instance, the biographer of the prominent early-twentieth-century Kuskokwim physician, Joseph Romig, presented the doctor as the perfectly

FIGURE 1.9. Kuskokwim Eskimos photographed by the Moravian missionary Adolphus Hartmann in 1884 (Courtesy Moravian Archives).

adapted, rugged individualist and his Eskimo patients as filthy and ignorant, no better than wild beasts and in many cases worse (Anderson 1940).

The missionaries who began to establish themselves in western Alaska in the late 1800s more often than not described the Yup'ik people in the Romig tradition. Unlike the miners, they wrote voluminously about the sad condition of the impoverished "heathens" they found on their arrival. Their letters home to mission societies pleaded the cause of these unfortunates, simultaneously depicted as Rousseauian "noble savages" and Hobbesian barbarians.

The first missionaries in the region described the people they encountered as both simple and depraved and in desperate need of being brought into the light. For example, Ferdinand Drebert (1959:16), an early Moravian missionary particularly sensitive to the strong points of his parishioners, nonetheless entitled a photograph of several coastal youngsters taken in the first decade of the 1900s "Heathen Boys, or Poverty and Filth," juxtaposing it and a portrait of their civilized selves taken some years later.

To be fair to early missionaries and traders, their reports were in many respects factually accurate descriptions, although they often failed to understand the rationale for the actions they observed. For example, in the nineteenth century before the advent of plank houses and lumber boardwalks, mud was unavoidable any time the weather was above freezing. Moreover, urine was the primary cleansing agent, and there usually was not enough boys' urine—women's urine was proscribed—to clean a fur parka thoroughly or regularly. Cleanliness was a stated Yup'ik ideal, but oil, blood, soot, and body odor were the facts of life. When the missionaries spoke of "dirty Eskimos," they were describing accurately from their point of view what they were observing. The people of western Alaska presented a very different appearance from the igloo dwellers of the snowbound north, and early descriptions immediately and amply reflected those differences.

At the same time missionaries were forming their opinions concerning the character and habits of the local people, the Yup'ik Eskimos were also forming an impression of the well-intentioned although sometimes troublesome new arrivals. In one particularly memorable response, a Napaskiak shaman labeled the missionaries of the turn of the century "children of thunder. . . . Everything they do and everything they have is accompanied by noise" (John H. Kilbuck, Box 5:7 MA).

The images of Eskimos sent home by missionaries from western Alaska both were a product of and helped to reinforce the extant Eskimo stereotype as alternately noble and base. At the same time, their character as "real people" was immediately apparent. In some cases the distinctive aspects of Yup'ik life were described, as in the ethnographic writings of the Moravian missionary John Kilbuck. But whereas Mrs. Kilbuck's heartfelt descriptions of her simple and benighted charges were published in *The Moravian*, the periodical of the Moravian Church, her husband's detailed ethnographic manuscripts were not.

The Yup'ik Eskimos Today

Yup'ik Eskimos in many parts of western Alaska have been actively engaged in encounter with non-natives for just over a century. Their lives have changed considerably since the arrival of Russian Orthodox priests in the mid-1800s and Protestant and Catholic missionaries in the 1880s. Following a dramatic decline in the population brought on by the epidemics that accompanied the arrival of nonnatives, the present population has grown to surpass its aboriginal number. Today, nearly twenty thousand Yup'ik Eskimos make their homes in western Alaska, scattered among seventy small communities ranging in size from 150 to 600. Each of these modern villages has both an elementary and a secondary school, city government or traditional council, clinic, church or churches, airstrip, electricity, and in a few cases running water and flush toilets. The residential separation of men and women has been abandoned in favor of single-family dwellings. Children spend their time in public school, watching video movies, or playing basketball in the new high school gymnasiums instead of listening to their elders tell stories in the men's house.

As in the past, communities are without exception located along the water, either salt or fresh, and the plank or aluminum boat, outboard motor, and snow machine are as common today as the skin-covered kayak and dogsled were a century ago. Small planes are also an integral part of village life and disgorge everything from postage

FIGURE 1.10. Unloading goods, Toksook Bay (Courtesy James H. Barker).

stamps to Pampers on their daily trips to and from the regional center of Bethel and smaller outlying villages.

These changes are relatively recent, however, dating from the early 1900s along the Yukon and Kuskokwim rivers and the 1930s in the more isolated coastal communities, including Nunivak and Nelson islands. Until then, the majority of the coastal population lived much as they had a hundred years before, in sod-insulated log houses located at scattered seasonal camps. As a result, the Central Yup'ik language continues in use throughout the region. Extended family relations and subsistence harvesting have been retained as major foci of activity, and traditional dances and ritual distributions continue as important aspects of community life (Fienup-Riordan 1983, 1986b).

The paucity of commercial resources and the geographical isolation that reduced contacts with and innovations from the outside world allowed the Yup'ik Eskimos to retain their native language and essential aspects of their way of life. At the same time, this isolation has had disturbing economic and social consequences. At the time of statehood (1959), when Alaska natives in general were seen as an extremely disadvantaged group, non-natives viewed the Yup'ik Eskimos of the Yukon-Kuskokwim Delta as one of the most impoverished groups among them: The availability of modern housing was minimal; educational levels were extremely low; and a tuberculosis epidemic more destructive than the influenza and smallpox epidemics that had preceded it was running rampant (Fienup-Riordan 1982:221–230).

In the 1960s a number of federal War on Poverty programs aimed at rectifying problems in the region were set in motion. These were followed by the passage of the Alaska Native Claims Settlement Act (ANCSA) in 1971, which completely transformed land tenure in the state and is the major determinant of land status in Alaska today. The act extinguished aboriginal land claims (litigation continues), giving in return fee simple title to forty-four million acres of land and nearly one billion dollars (Arnold 1978:146). The act also set up twelve regional for-profit corporations (and one nonresident corporation) as well as individual village corporations to administer the land and money received under ANCSA. The Calista Corporation (from *cali-*, to work, literally "the worker") was established to manage the corporate resources of the Yukon-Kuskokwim Delta.

The "Molly Hootch decision" followed in 1976, mandating the establishment of local high schools in all the smaller communities of the region requesting them—communities that had previously sent their children to boarding school in Bethel, St. Marys Catholic Mission, or outside the region. Both of these pieces of legislation were critical in reforming village organization and economy. These acts and decisions of the 1960s and 1970s jointly are responsible for shaping the modern villages of western Alaska.

Since the 1960s the coastal communities of western Alaska have experienced steady growth, supported in large measure through ANCSA village corporation activity and the state education industry. During this period communities have used employment income and cash transfers of other kinds in part to provide support for local subsistence harvesting activity. Income has not been saved and invested to provide stepping stones out of the village. Instead the villages have grown dramatically in both population and modern facilities (Fienup-Riordan 1986b:215–275).

As churches, schools, and stores began to be established at centrally located sites throughout the region, the traditionally mobile Yup'ik population became more and more settled. And, as the delta's population steadily coalesced at permanent sites, the regional economy was also radically transformed. Along with the continued importance of harvesting activities, the most significant feature of village economy in western Alaska today is its dependence on government. A small portion of the aggregate local income is derived from commercial fishing and trapping, craft sales, and local service industries. The far larger portion of income (as much as 90 percent) flowing through the village economies comes from the public sector. Wages and salaries paid to teachers, administrators, construction workers, and health and social service workers constitute some of this public-sector income, as do transfer payments made directly to households and grant and loan monies for the purchase of heavy equipment, fuel, and miscellaneous supplies for public use. As a consequence, most local service and distribution businesses in the private sector depend on purchases made by persons and organizations that themselves depend on public-sector income and transfers (Fienup-Riordan 1988a:34–38).

Contemporary Yup'ik villagers are integrated into the national economy as clerks, welfare recipients, commercial fishermen, and bureaucrats, but they also maintain themselves in a large part through traditional harvesting practices. Integration is on the periphery, or it is marginal, and domestic activities focus on extraction and consumption rather than investment and production. The overall pattern is still predominantly the combination of the complementary activities of wage employment and the harvest of local resources for both commercial and subsistence use.

The marked dependence on public sources of income is one of a number of social ills that currently plague the region. The region is also beset by high rates of alcoholism, child abuse, sexual assault, suicide, homicide, and mental illness. Although the rate of infant mortality has dramatically declined since 1970, the regional suicide rate has increased from 5.5 to 55.5 per 100,000 during the same period. This suicide rate is five times greater than the national rate, and in nearly all cases alcohol is a contributing factor (Lenz 1986:4,5).

In the delta region, the expression of personal and family problems tends to be inner-directed or directed at close kinspersons. Overt conflict more often occurs in interethnic confrontation. A suicide epidemic in the Yukon Delta village of Alakanuk in which eight persons killed themselves in a sixteen-month period is an example of such inner directed violence. These suicides were committed in a relatively large coastal community by young adult residents (Fienup-Riordan 1988a:44–48). Tragedy of these proportions has not beset the more traditional and tightly integrated communities of the Bering Sea coast or the tundra and Kuskokwim villages that have become politically active in the Yupiit Nation sovereignty movement; however these communities have also experienced a dramatic rise in rates of alcoholism, suicide, and domestic violence.

Although painfully aware of their economically marginal position and its attendant social problems, the Yup'ik people are at present seeking creative solutions that will allow them to continue to live in their traditional homeland. They are also trying to transform the non-native image of the Eskimo as, alternately, heroic yet outdated tradition bearer and skid-row drunken bum. Contrary to non-native expectation, they do not see themselves as merely surviving on the limited resources of an impoverished environment but as living in a highly structured and worthwhile relationship to that environment, a relationship they hope to maintain.

Ironically, the isolation of western Alaska that contributed to both its historical obscurity and economic marginality has recently resulted in a dramatic and unprecedented inquiry into Yup'ik culture, past and present. As the primitive vanishes from the face of the earth, the Western world peers with increasing interest on remnants of that bygone world in "historical/cultural backwaters" such as western Alaska. With their aboriginal language still in use and vestiges of traditional ceremonies still performed in many parts of the region, the

Yup'ik Eskimos have proved particularly attractive to those interested in documenting the "living fossils" of the modern world.

In the decade following the publication of Oswalt's Napaskiak study in 1963, only a handful of research projects was carried out in western Alaska. Beginning in the late 1970s, this neglect was replaced by unprecedented activity. The exponential growth of interest in Alaska following the discovery of oil at Prudhoe Bay in the late 1960s combined with the passage of ANCSA in 1971 to raise interest in Alaska to an all-time high.

For example, during the one-year period from the fall of 1983 through the fall of 1984, Alaska hosted the Nelson collection of traditional artifacts of the Bering Sea Eskimos in the form of the Smithsonian's Inua exhibit (Fitzhugh and Kaplan 1982). It also hosted the performance of *Yup'ik Antigone*, a Yup'ik adaptation of Sophocles' drama. Next came a weekend of performances and demonstrations at the Anchorage Museum of History and Art by, among others, the Yup'ik mask maker Nick Charles and a group of dancers from Nelson Island. That same year KYUK broadcasting station in Bethel completed a video production showing the mask-making workshop and the masked-dance performance held in Bethel in the fall of 1982. *National Geographic* published a photo essay on the village of Toksook Bay and the people of Nelson Island (Richards 1984). Producers of an educational film program funded by Chevron USA also began inquiring as to where they could find a traditional Bladder Festival to film somewhere in western Alaska between March 3 and 11, when their camera man would be in the state. In June 1984 the Bethel traditional dancers, as well as several skilled native artists from the region, were flown to Washington, D.C., to participate in the Smithsonian Festival of American Folklife (Fienup-Riordan 1984b). At the same time the cast of *Yup'ik Antigone* performed in Paris and New York and, the following summer, in Greece.

Not only have the Yup'ik Eskimos been on display both nationally and internationally, but scholarly interest in the region has also dramatically increased (Burch 1984). After a period of relative neglect, anthropologists and linguists are quickly making up for lost time. Here again 1984 saw the publication by the Alaska Native Language Center of the long-awaited *Yup'ik Eskimo Dictionary* (Jacobson 1984) and of Anthony Woodbury and Leo Moses's elegant translation of a dozen traditional tales from Chevak (Woodbury 1984). Elsie Mather (1985) completed a manuscript written in Yup'ik entitled *Cauyarnariuq* [A Time for Drumming], which Phyllis Morrow (1984) abstracted in English, greatly enriching what we know about the traditional Yup'ik ceremonial cycle. Kenneth Pratt (1984), Ann Shinkwin and Mary Pete (1984), and I continued work on unraveling the complexities of traditional Yup'ik social groupings. Robert Shaw (1983) finished a dissertation on the archaeology of a site to the south of Hooper Bay, and Robert Wolfe continued to write about the subsistence economy.

All these efforts add to what we know about the Yup'ik past and the complex historical processes of appropriation, invention, and revival that have characterized the recent Yup'ik encounter with the Western world. Much work remains to be done, however, to counter the popular tendency to pull from the Yup'ik Eskimos pieces of themselves (dance performances, grass baskets, carving demonstrations, traditional tales) that are then neatly designated as cultural artifacts of a noble but primitive past and as a result are never allowed to either threaten or enrich us.

By taking selected pieces of what the Yup'ik Eskimos produce, of what we value within the bounds of our definition and conception of culture, we continue to reinvent them in our own image as opposed to trying to understand them in their own terms. To paraphrase Marshall Sahlins (1981), it is not that the primitive Eskimos are simple, but that our understanding of them is primitive.

Although the following chapters cannot exhaustively describe what it means to be Yup'ik in the modern world, they can introduce the reader to important aspects of Yup'ik ideology and practice, past and present. In the process they can point the way toward a fuller recognition of how Yup'ik Eskimos differ from the popular Western image of the Eskimo, which was born largely without reference to Yup'ik reality. By placing the "facts" of Yup'ik life alongside the circumstances of their collection, interpretation, and in some cases invention, we can extend our understanding of Eskimos in general and Yup'ik Eskimos in particular.

Part One

Yup'ik Cosmology: Ideology in Action

*M*uch of what has been written concerning arctic peoples emphasizes their ability to survive in their environment. Relatively little has been published about the values that make such survival possible and culturally meaningful. In fact, a close look at the value systems of the peoples of the Far North reveals less reliance on environmental determinism than cultural imagination.

The following two chapters attempt to explain the system of symbols and meanings that continues to guide the daily lives and activities of the Yup'ik people of western Alaska. Unlike other peoples of the North Pacific–Beringian region, who have lost most or much of their traditional spiritual culture, coastal Yup'ik Eskimos have retained many of their traditional beliefs. In this discussion both formal oral traditions as well as informal prescriptions for the culturally appropriate living of life will be drawn on to present the Yup'ik point of view. They will also give the reader a sense of the complex ways in which apparently discrete domains of activity, including hunting, domestic life, and the ceremonial cycle, embody the common system of values and meanings that make up a particular culture in the Arctic or elsewhere.

The Ideology
of Subsistence

IN DESCRIPTIONS OF THE COASTAL
Yup'ik Eskimos, as well as of other Es-
kimo groups, their ability to survive in a frigid and inhospitable
environment has often been emphasized to the exclusion of a comprehensive account of the value system that makes such survival meaningful. In fact, by idealizing their survival ability, we emphasize that
aspect of their way of life most comprehensible within our own cultural system. Small wonder the students of Malthus and Darwin are
continually drawn to the contemplation of the life ways of the inhabitants of the Arctic, whose cultural adaptation seems to epitomize
the necessary fit between natural constraints and human response.

Yet a close look at the value system and ritual exchanges that characterize their elegantly efficient, traditional technology reveals less
common-sense environmental determinism than cultural imagination. Certainly the fact that the traditional distributions of seal meat
serve to feed the aged and the needy cannot be denied. In fact, the
periodic random distribution of the products of the chase may well
be ecologically required, something on the order of give now so that
in your turn you may receive and so survive. Yet how this redistribution is accomplished, through an exchange of gifts between male
cousins or between married women who are not related, is culturally
determined and not nearly as preordained as one might suppose.

As the whole of symbolic anthropology is definitely an interpretive
endeavor, and as the bulk of my work as an anthropologist has been
directed toward this interpretation, I would like to relay in narrative
fashion the experiences that taught me the significance of traditional
and contemporary systems of exchange. I say *experiences* instead of
evidence because anthropologists, just like other humans, are notorious for finding what they are looking for. I am under no illusion that
what I "saw" while in the field was not at least partially a product of
what I sought.

Further, and more important, I hope that by speaking through my own experiences I may help introduce the reader to a cultural logic that is difficult to convey through abstractions alone (such as, "the traditional Yup'ik Eskimos respected animals; they believed these animals had souls"). Thus, I take the tack of the seasoned hunter who requires the attention of the uninitiated while I tell a story of what it means to subsist.

In 1974 I was working in Anchorage, without experience of bush Alaska and without wish or desire to seek out such experience. I was studying anthropology and going off to investigate the mainland Chinese, and that was that. Then I was hired by the Nelson Islanders under a grant from the Alaska Humanities Forum to see what I could locate pertaining to the history and archaeology of pottery production in western Alaska. Whatever information I was able to find I was asked to take to Nelson Island in the spring of 1975. At that time I was to make a trip to Toksook Bay, the location of the Nelson Island School of Design, a production pottery that had recently been constructed in the village as a means of encouraging local industry and employment.

When I arrived on Nelson Island, I was initially impressed with how modern and Western the village of Toksook Bay seemed. It had electricity and running water, and most of the people I met during the first few days spoke English. Maybe they had once been exotic, but they certainly were not any more.

While I stayed in the village, I slept in the pottery workshop on an old army cot brought down from the National Guard armory. Every morning at about 7:30, with no knock or courteous inquiry as to whether I was presentable, several older village men would come into the building, turn up the stove, turn on the coffee pot, and take their places on the benches along the wall. From the back room where I had my cot, I could hear them talking slowly, softly. One might begin to mend an *uluaq*,[1] while another continued an ivory carving that he had started a few days before. Later during the morning, and again after the midday meal, younger men would drift into the pottery workshop, stand around, and silently watch what the older men were doing. No one paid any attention to me, although several of the older men were interested in the pictures I had brought of traditional Eskimo pottery from other parts of the Arctic. Also, no one paid any attention to the new pottery wheels and equipment that filled the workshop area.

At first I was bewildered by this apparent apathy in the face of government largesse. Community Enterprise Development Corporation had put up a substantial amount of money for the facility. Why were the old men here? Why was no one making pottery? I soon found that no one was making pottery because they were too busy doing everything else. It was spring, seal hunting was about to begin, and what little pottery production had taken place during the winter was at a standstill. Wages could not lure workers into the pottery. Hunting came first.

That old men gathered in the warmest communal space available (the community hall had no heat) was no surprise. In their youth most of them had lived together in the traditional *qasgiq*, or men's house. What better use to make of this new building, which had quickly proved itself incapable of housing Western industry as a design school. So the old men had taken over. Before I left the village, several snow machines were also moved in for repair, and there was talk by one village elder of using the building to cover the construction of a new boat.

The upshot of finding that my bedroom was in the modern version of the traditional men's house was that I didn't spend much time in it. Rather, I visited the houses and talked to the women. They said that I had come at the best time of the year, that the seal parties were about to begin.

Seal parties? What were they? I'd never read about seal parties. I'd never even heard of them. Well, my new friends told me, seal parties were given when the men and boys of the village brought home the first seals of the season. They were very exciting and lots of fun, as not only was the meat and blubber of every man's first-caught seal given away, but lots of other things as well. I was intrigued and waited eagerly for the parties to commence.

They began the next day—three parties in a row. I was just up and having a cup of tea when a little girl ran in the door and said to come quick. There, right next door, a woman was standing in her porch throwing Pampers and packs of gum into the waiting hands of a large group of women. I joined the fun and followed the group to the next house for a repetition of the event. I noticed that not all the same women attended, but other women joined the group. I asked about this later and was told that when a woman gives her seal party, her relatives could not attend; only her nonrelatives received the gift of meat.

By this time I was extremely excited. Here was a distribution of goods through which social relations were articulated. My interest in

FIGURE 2.1. A seal party in the village of Toksook Bay, 1981 (Courtesy Don Doll, S.J.).

anthropology had originally been in the study of kinship systems. Also, I was convinced that one could not learn much about people's social relations simply by asking them genealogical questions such as "Who is your sister?" or "Who is your cousin?" Rather, to learn anything important about kinship, one must see it in action and witness what it means to be a sister or mother. The seal party provided a wonderful window into how the people of Nelson Island still thought about and acted out their ideas of what it meant to be related.

I found out later that while the explicit rule was that only nonrelatives attend one's seal party, in fact only sisters, mothers, mothers-in-law, and parallel cousins were excluded. More important, the hostess of the seal party normally "gave away" the privilege of throwing the gifts to an older woman, who in her turn singled out one individual in the audience to receive a special gift. These women were usually cross-cousins, the mothers of children who would be, or had already been, married. Also, it was significant that what they gave each other was raw meat, for the gift of raw meat was traditionally the exchange that marked the marriage relationship between a man and a woman. Thus, the seal-party exchange paralleled the marriage exchange. During the event a woman gave away the products of the hunt of her husband and sons, the symbolic proof of their potency, not just to anybody, but to women who could eventually give their daughters to the hosting family as brides.

Much more might be said on the metaphorical marriage between cross-cousins that the seal party represents. What is important is that, as I found later on, the seal party is not an isolated relic of traditional culture but rather is part of an annual cycle of ritual distribution. Pieces of this cycle are no longer practiced, but other parts are still alive and well and still express coastal villagers' attitudes toward their land and their lives.

The immediate counterpart of the seal party on Nelson Island is the men's and women's exchange dance (*Kevgiruaq*), in which men and women are said to fight through the dance. This sequence takes a slightly different form in the lower Yukon villages of Emmonak and Alakanuk, but the message is comparable. On the first night of the exchange dance, all the women in the village pair up as married

FIGURE 2.2. The presentation of gifts during the men's and women's exchange dance (*Kevgiruaq*), Toksook Bay, 1979.

FIGURE 2.3. Mark John playing the part of wife during the men's and women's exchange dance, Toksook Bay, 1979.

couples, one woman taking the part of the husband and the other the part of the wife. Then, together, the women dance a multitude of gifts into the community hall and on the following morning give them out to the men of the village. The men perform for the women on the following evening, and the next morning the women receive gifts in their turn. The entire sequence of dances and gift-giving takes hours and hours, as everyone in the community has a turn on the dance floor. As each mock married couple comes out to dance, they are greeted by much laughing and teasing from the audience. The particular dance that is performed is always the same, but each couple vies with the others to make its rendition particularly hilarious. Young men put mop ends on their heads for hair. Fur parkas are turned inside out to imitate age and senility, and fake muscles are pushed into the dresses of the women who are playing the role of husband.

Even if one knew nothing about Yup'ik cultural configurations, the exchange dance would still be a splendid and exuberant performance to behold. Seen in the light of the seal party, its eloquence becomes apparent. Whereas in the seal party gifts are thrown out the doors of the individual houses, in the exchange dance gifts are danced in the door of the community hall. In the seal party these gifts consist of strips of cloth and bits of string, in fact bits and pieces of every conceivable household commodity. In the exchange dance, whole cloth is given, whole skeins of yarn, and sometimes quilts or bedspreads made from the very bits of cloth given away during the seal party. The length of cloth that a woman receives in the exchange dance she usually tears into strips for her seal party distribution. With the strips of cloth that she has collected from the various seal parties she has attended, she fabricates a quilted cover that she will then give away during the next year's exchange dance. If all that was required was a cover for the bed, the Yup'ik people have certainly taken a circuitous route to ensure its provision. In fact, after all the giving and receiving has been accomplished, no one is much the richer or poorer in material goods. Their world view, their whole cultural mode of being, has, however, been put on stage along with the dancers, acted out, and so reestablished and reaffirmed.

Social relations are also articulated in the dance. When I asked women how their dance partners were related to them, they said to me simply, "They are my relatives." In itself this was certainly an acceptable answer, but these so-called relatives were, in fact, the same persons who had been designated as nonrelatives at the seal parties! Cross-cousins who had stood on opposite sides as host and guest in one event joined together to host the entire community as a "married couple." As with the cycling of goods between the two events, relatives seemed to be cycling as well. Instead of a moral on the order of "never the twain shall meet," the Yup'ik celebrations seemed to imply that always that which is separated (socially, physically, and, as we shall see, metaphysically) will in the end be reunited.

As this ideological program is somewhat abstruse, let me detail a few more experiences to show how this point of view pervades village life today. In the spring of 1978 I made a visit to Nelson Island while I was pregnant with my first child. I was, of course, quite proud of my condition and sure that with the proper food and exercise the pregnancy and birth would go well. My Yup'ik friends, however, were not so blasé and proceeded to teach me an elaborate set of dos and don'ts that still accompanies pregnancy and childbirth in the village. I was to sleep with my head toward the door. As soon as I got up every morning, I was to run outside as fast as I could. Only then might I come in, sit down, and drink tea. In fact, any time during the day that I left the house I was to do it quickly without stopping in the doorway. If I were to pause in my exiting, the baby was sure to get stuck during delivery.

This series of prescriptions draws an obvious parallel between the womb in which the unborn baby lives and the house in which the expectant mother resides. Analogically, the throwing of gifts out of the house through the doorway at the time of the seal party is comparable to their birth. Analogous relationships exist between the progress of the souls of the human dead and the return of gifts into the community hall at the time of the exchange dance. In fact, imagery of birth and rebirth pervaded the system of symbols and meanings that was beginning to become apparent. The finality of death was everywhere averted, in both action and ideal.

Another anecdote will help make the significance of this cultural framework clear. During the time I lived on Nelson Island I had hoped in my heart of hearts that someone would give me a real Yup'ik name. No one ever did. They gave me a nickname that translated loosely as "big piece of fat." But that was as close to a traditional name as I got. Certainly I had asked about naming procedures, just as I had asked about pregnancy taboos, but with little solid response. I was made to feel acutely nosey. And, in fact, part of the message of this story is how little progress one can make in understanding the coastal Yup'ik people if one confines oneself to information acquired through a questionnaire approach. It certainly never worked for me, and in fact my best friends used to lie to me, in a good-natured way, to show me how foolish and misguided my occasional bouts of verbal curiosity were. Watching and listening, however, were different matters. And so it was with my understanding of the significance of naming.

Although I had never been given a name, when I returned to the village with my newborn daughter in the fall of 1978, she was immediately named. The older woman who had been my real teacher while I had lived on the island had had a cousin. That man had drowned not three weeks before. No sooner had my daughter and I come into the village than she came to where we were staying and gave my daughter the name of her dead cousin. Then, in every house in which we visited, people would ask me what my daughter's name was. When I told them, they would laugh and say such things as "Oh, he's come back a *kass'aq* [white person]!" or "He always did want to learn English!" or "To think now he has red hair!"

All this verbal play on the baby's name was a kind way of welcoming my daughter into their midst. But, as important, these endearments were wonderfully explicit expressions of the belief that in the newborn child the soul of the recently dead is born again. In the Yup'ik world, no one ever finally passes away out of existence. Rather, through the naming process, the essence of being human is passed on from one generation to the next.

This cycling of human souls is especially interesting when considered in light of the traditional belief that the souls of the seals must be cared for by the successful hunter in order that they, too; will be born again. Seals as well as other animals and fish are believed to give themselves to men voluntarily. A seal, for instance, is said to sense, and in fact to see, the merits of a hunter. If the hunter is seen to be "awake" to the rules of the proper relationship between humans and animals, and between humans and humans, then the seal will allow the hunter's harpoon or bullet to kill it. When the seal is hit, if the seal is likewise awake, its soul will retract to its bladder. Although its body will die and so provide life to humans, its soul will stay alive and await return to the sea. In fact, traditionally, the coastal Yup'ik Eskimos held a Bladder Festival every winter. At the Bladder Festival the bladders of the seals caught during the year along with the bladders of other animals were inflated, hung at the back of the men's house, and feasted and entertained for five days. Then, on the fifth day, each family took the bladders of the animals they had killed to the sea and pushed them down through a hole in the ice so that the souls of the seals might be born again.

Through these events the circle is completed. Not only do goods cycle, as do the seasons, but human and animal souls likewise are continually in motion. The birth of a baby is the rebirth of a member of its grandparental generation. The death of the seal means life to

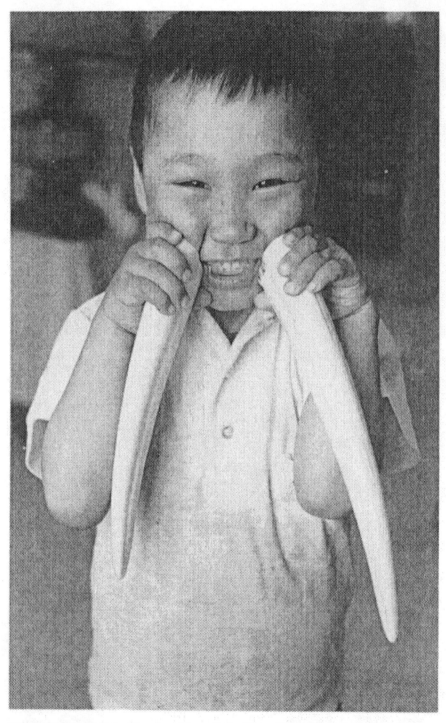

FIGURE 2.4. Fritzie Nevak with walrus ivory, Toksook Bay (Courtesy Don Doll, S.J.).

the village. The same people and the same seals have been on this earth from the beginning, continually cycling and recycling through life and death. Through this generational cycling, a life-celebrating system is put forward. The coastal Yup'ik Eskimos are not simply surviving on the resources of their environment but are living in a highly structured relationship to them. This relationship is important to comprehend, not as an exercise in Eskimo esoterica, but as the key to why they act and feel the way they do.

In light of the current subsistence debate,[2] the focus of present cultural consciousness on the coast and an issue that is not likely to be quickly resolved, one final anecdote is worth relating. In the spring of 1979 I revisited Nelson Island. It had been a good spring, and numerous seals and walrus had been taken. But Alaska Department of Fish and Game officials had unfortunately found several walrus carcasses at Cape Vancouver. Head hunters had taken the valuable ivory and left the rest of the meat to rot. Nelson Islanders accused Nunivak Islanders of the infraction and vice versa. Talking to an old man about the incident, I played devil's advocate and queried, "What difference does it make who killed them? Dead is dead and nothing can bring them back now, can it?" That I should have been so cavalier even now amazes me. The old man never lifted his eyes from the bench. "No," he said, "if they had been properly cared for they would have been able to return. Now they are gone forever."

Can these experiences help you to see the significance, in Yup'ik eyes, of the threat of an oil spill or game mismanagement? Although active shamanism and the celebration of the Bladder Festival are no more, too many embodiments of the traditional cosmology remain to be casually catalogued as superstition or to allow the scientific attitude toward species extinction to hold sway. Even the youngest child is still instructed in a code of etiquette toward natural surroundings that is as important as any code of etiquette toward other human beings (see also Nelson 1977). Given this cultural framework, it is possible but altogether inappropriate to reduce subsistence activities to mere survival techniques and their significance to the conquest of calories. Their pursuit is not simply a means to an end but an end in itself.

In what little literature exists on western Alaska, authors often comment that, even given alternatives, living off the land is still the preferred pattern. This preference is explicable only if being a hunter has intrinsic value. What Richard Nelson says of the Iñupiat is equally true of the coastal Yup'ik Eskimos: "One of the things that continually amazes me when I go back there is that people are still out there hunting, dedicated—sometimes almost passionately dedicated—to continuing this way of life" (quoted in Schiller 1981:16).

Small wonder the words of the Nelson Island elders were echoed by their children and more sophisticated contemporaries during testimony in Bethel in the spring of 1981 on the repeal of the subsistence legislation. Everywhere the emphasis was on the real kinship between the people and their environment. Stewardship, not to mention ownership, of resources is taken with a grain of salt, as the real power is not in people, but in the continuing relationship between humans and the natural world on which they depend.

The Mask: The Eye
of the Dance

3

FOR AT LEAST THE PAST TWO
thousand years, the Yup'ik Eskimos have
made their home in the rich coastal and riverine environment of the
Yukon-Kuskokwim Delta. The natural abundance of the lowland tundra and adjacent coastal waters has for centuries supported relatively stable human settlement patterns. These settlements in turn
set the stage for the development of a complex ceremonial tradition,
central to which were the construction and use of large and elaborate
hooped masks.

The hooped masks of the Yup'ik Eskimos have been the subject of
a largely descriptive body of literature. They are mentioned in the
work of Edward Nelson (1899), Ernest Hawkes (1913), and Margaret
Lantis (1946, 1947). More extensive commentary has been written by
Hans Himmelheber (1953), Dorothy Jean Ray (1967, 1981), and, most
recently, William Fitzhugh and Susan Kaplan (1982). This chapter
attempts to expand the scope of past interpretations by providing
additional information not normally considered in discussions focus-
ing on the mask as ethnological artifact or ceremonial object. Here,
both formal oral traditions and informal prescriptions for the culturally appropriate living of life will be seen as essential to a full understanding of the mask and all that it embodies.

The Loss of Vision and the Rebirth
of Masked Dancing

Less than a hundred years ago, the mask (*kegginaquq*, from *kegginaq*,
face, plus -*quq*, one that is like; hence "thing that is like a face") was
a central element in Yup'ik dance performances. At the same time,
masked dances were a central element in the Yup'ik representation

49

to themselves of their world, both spiritual and material. Over-whelmed by the pagan implications of these traditional representa-tions and the ceremonial cycle of which they were a part, the missionaries who arrived in the Yukon-Kuskokwim Delta at the turn of the century did their best to discourage the performance of masked dances. Recreational dancing survived in the areas missionized by the Catholics, but along the Kuskokwim River, where Moravian influ-ence prevailed, dance performances, masked or otherwise, were com-pletely suppressed. Masks continued to be carved, but as wall decorations and not as face coverings.[1] The eyes of the mask were no longer essential and were rendered as painted marks rather than carved holes. Although masks were still made, they were functionally blind.[2]

In the fall of 1982 a mask-making workshop was organized and held in Bethel specifically to promote the transmission of traditional carving skills. Three Yup'ik carvers, including the Bethel mask maker Nick Charles (originally from Nelson Island), produced masks that were subsequently used in a local performance of masked dances by the Bethel Native Dancers (Figure 3.1).

The mask that Nick Charles carved during the workshop tells of a specific shamanic vision. Nick had seen masks made in the same style during his youth on Nelson Island in the early 1920s. The mask he made represents his interpretation of a well-known event in the oral history of the delta region. The face of the mask, instead of depicting an animal's spirit, represents the spirit of the shaman Issiisaayuq (Figure 3.2). This shaman lived at Aproka, at the mouth of the Eek River, before the first white person came to the region. There he had a vision in which he saw a boat approaching, a boat that would bring the first white men to the area.

> Long ago there was a shaman named Issiisaayuq who directed his people to carve a mask depicting a freight ship. This was unfamiliar to the people, but they followed his instructions even so. On the forehead of the mask was a boat with three masts. The center mast had a platform with a man on it. On the deck of the ship was a caribou. The following summer a ship, exactly like the carving, arrived from the sea. On the sides of the ship were images of half human faces. When it arrived at the mouth of the Kuskokwim River, the people warned each other not to desire or want the goods from the boat because they would come to no good. One day [when] one of the men came to the boat, he noticed that the eyes on the faces were turning toward the sea.

FIGURE 3.1. Participants in the Bethel mask-making workshop, fall 1982. *Left to right:* Kay Hendrikson, Nick Charles, Sr., Moses Chanar (*standing*), student, Joe Friday, John Kusauyuq (Courtesy Suzi Jones).

FIGURE 3.2. Joe Chief, Jr., performing in the Issiisaayuq mask at the Smithsonian Festival of American Folklife, 1984 (Courtesy Smithsonian Institution).

The ship sailed away and all the trade goods the people acquired disappeared. Issiisaayuq's daughter cried for a necklace that she saw on the boat. Since she would not stop crying for the necklace, Issiisaayuq instructed his wife to spread a skin outside. When she did so, it began to hail. The hail that landed on the ground melted but the hail that landed on the skin did not. They brought these [hailstones] into the *qasgiq* [men's house] and made a necklace for the daughter. The ornament did not last for long and the following summer a real freight ship arrived as prophesized by Issiisaayuq. (Ali and Active 1982)

This story is behind the tattooed figure that Nick carved. It is perhaps significant that this mask, which represents how the first contact between Yup'ik and Western culture was foretold, should be worn at the first masked dance performed for both Yup'ik and non-Yup'ik people since the missionaries suppressed Yup'ik ceremonial dancing.

For the performance, Nick represented the human face and large-eyed half faces that had appeared on the sides of the visionary freight ship in abstract form on the sides of the model perched on Issiisaayuq's head. During the performance, as in the shaman's vision, the eyes moved from side to side, encompassing all in their powerful gaze. As Nick said, "This mask is the eye of the dance." It is the vision of this vision that Nick set out to capture in wood.

The Eyes of Awareness

The eyes of the mask, however, are more than a metaphor for sight. The circle-and-dot motif, so common in Yup'ik iconography, is specifically designated *ellam iinga* (literally, "the eye of awareness") in Central Yup'ik. As in the name for the wooden hoop surrounding the mask (*ellanguaq*), the term is derived from *ella-* (translated variously as outdoors, weather, world, universe, awareness) plus *-m* (singular possessive) plus *ii* (eye). Comparable to Sila in the Canadian Arctic, however, *ella* appears to be personified and was seen as a being in contexts other than that of a human or animal face.[3]

In the anthropological literature the nucleated circle has sometimes been designated as a joint mark and thus part of a skeletal motif. Alternately, it has been labeled a stylized woman's breast, which might then be substituted for a woman's face (Himmelheber 1953:62; Ray 1981:25). The sexual and skeletal motifs may well have been part of its significance; however, it was not merely that the nucleated circle marked joints, but rather that joints were marked with circular eyes in various ritual contexts. According to Phyllis Morrow (personal communication):

> The circle-and-dot motif is often seen on the "joints" of carved supernatural beasts. This placement is suggestive of a number of customs that involve marking, cutting, or binding joints, all of which relate to boundaries or a change of state or passage from one "plane" to another. At puberty, for example, a young woman's wrists were tattooed with dots. Red string around an infant's wrists protected it from harm. Strings were also tied around joints to prevent diseases from progressing past these points.[4] E. W. Nelson describes how a hunter sometimes cut the joints of an animal to prevent its spirit from reanimating the body. In one case I have heard, the same thing was done to the body of an evil shaman.[5]
>
> The connection of these customs with shamanism may be clearer when you recall that dismemberment and skeletal rearticulation was an essential part of a shaman's initiation, one that was repeated each time he journeyed to the other world(s) (see . . . Eliade 1964 . . .). Circles and dots placed at the joints thus recall the ability to pass from one world to another, perhaps representing the holes through which the passage was effected. The ability to see into other worlds was also characteristic of the shaman. Thus, it is particularly appropriate that the circle and dot, both an eye and a hole, equates physical and spiritual movement between worlds.

Although historical connections are beyond the scope of this discussion, in fact joint markings are not a unique feature of Yup'ik Eskimo iconography. As early as 1897 Franz Boas recognized the special function of the eye as a joint mark in the art of the Northwest Coast. In Carl Schuster's (1951:17) article on joint marks, Boas is quoted as saying, "An examination . . . will show that in most cases [the eye] is used to indicate a joint. Shoulder, elbow, hand, hips, knees, feet, the points of attachment of fins, tails, and so forth, are always indicated by eyes."[6]

Examples connecting the circle-and-dot motif with spiritual vision and transformation abound in the Yup'ik ethnographic data, once the

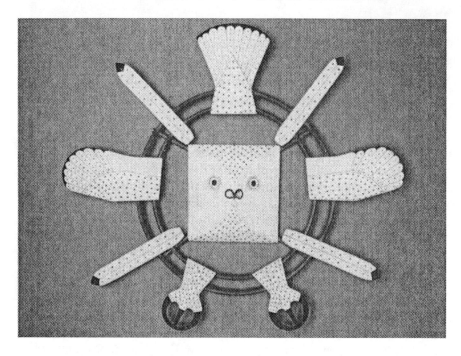

FIGURE 3.3. Owl mask by Nick Charles (Courtesy University of Alaska Museum).

significance of the motif becomes apparent. Not only did eyes mark joints, but joints were, on occasion, explicitly given as the home of spirits with eyes. Here, an observation by William Thalbitzer, although not specifically referring to the Yup'ik conceptual system, has special significance: "According to Eskimo notions, in every part of the human body (particularly in every joint, as for instance, in every finger joint) there resides a little soul" (quoted in Weyer 1932:291).[7] Nick Charles's owl mask (Figure 3.3) represents a Yup'ik incarnation of this theme. The mask depicts a shaman's watcher or guardian bird, a snowy owl. According to Nelson Island oral tradition, this bird was originally endowed with supernatural sight and protective powers by being covered with feathers, each of which was marked with a circular eye belonging to one of the shaman's spiritual protectors (John 1977).[8]

Ritual dismemberment and shamanistic marking are also perhaps comparable to the circular tattoos that were sometimes applied to young men's wrists and elbows at the time they first killed certain animal species.⁹ In both the shaman's eyed joints and the puberty tattoo, the circle-and-dot design connotes enhanced vision effected through spiritual and social transformation. In fact, transformed characters in the oral tradition are signaled by, among other things, black circles around their eyes.¹⁰ One Chefornak hunter recalled his mother circling his eyes with soot when, at age nine, he returned to the village after killing his first bearded seal. Pubescent girls on the Yukon Delta are still advised to encircle a single salmonberry blossom with a hair of their head, which they then tie to a nearby grass plant so the blossom will not blow away. Ultimately this action ensures not only that year's salmonberry harvest but the young woman's own future social and biological productivity as well.

In some contexts the encircling ring has been interpreted as signifying completeness and imparting spiritual wholeness (Fitzhugh and Kaplan 1982:202). The implication is that the completed circle stabilizes and establishes the spiritual integrity of the artifact to which it is attached. More accurately for the Yup'ik Eskimos, as can be seen from this discussion, the circle and dot is a concrete metaphor for and means to achieve a dynamic movement between worlds, be it spiritual cycling, supernatural vision, or social transformation.

In dance fans that Nick Charles carved for his wife, Elena, the vision imagery of this motif has been retained (Figure 3.4). With her own eyes cast down during the performance, Elena even now speaks of the fan's eye as seeing for her while she dances. Her lowered eyes and restricted sight are marks of respect typical of all Yup'ik dancers. They are comparable to the lowered eyes of a novice or a young host or hostess and, traditionally, to the covered head of a young woman during puberty restrictions. As Elena gives the dance blindly, however, the audience receives it with a full gaze.

In all social as well as ritual situations, in fact, direct eye contact was traditionally, and continues to be, considered rude for young people, whereas downcast eyes signify humility and respect. Sight is the prerogative of age, of knowledge, and of power. For example, the powerful man in the moon has a bright face, and people fear to look at him and must look downward (Nelson 1899:430). Conversely, the warrior-hero Apanuugpak was said to have been able to see his enemies from afar, while to them he was invisible (Fienup-Riordan 1983:242–243). Powerful images and hunting fetishes, some marked with the circle and dot motif, were supposed to watch for game and, by clairvoyant powers, sight it at a great distance (Nelson 1899:436).

FIGURE 3.4. Dance fans carved by Nick Charles for his wife, Elena, with circle-and-dot motif (Courtesy James H. Barker).

In addition, the powerful shades of the dead were traditionally said to hear and see nothing at first; however, by the time they reached the grave they had attained clairvoyance (Nelson 1899:425).

A particularly eloquent and explicit example of the relationship between socially restricted sight and powerful supernatural vision is contained in the Nelson Island traditional tale of the boy who lived and traveled with the seals for one year to gain extraordinary hunting knowledge and power:

> And his host [the bearded seal] said to him,
> "Watch him [the good hunter], watch his eyes, see what good
>   vision he has.
> When his eyes see us, see how strong his vision is.
> When he sights us, our whole being will quake,
> and this is from his powerful gaze.
> When you go back to your village, the women,
> some will see them, not looking sideways, but looking directly
>   at their eyes.
> The ones who live like that, looking like that,

looking at the eyes of women,
their vision will become less strong.
When you look at women your vision will lose its power.
Your sight gets weakened.
But the ones that don't look at people,
at the center of the face,
the ones who use their sight sparingly,
as when you have little food, and use it little by little.
So, too, your vision, you must be stingy with your vision,
using it little by little, conserving it always.
These, then, when they start to go hunting,
and use their eyes only for looking at their quarry,
their eyes truly then are strong." (John 1977)

Nick remembers well the admonishment given him in his youth never to look into the eyes of women. As we have seen, this was more than a matter of etiquette circumscribing his manner of vision within the human world. Instead, restricted human sight was profoundly significant: it framed a man's future relationship with the seals and other animals on whose good opinion, as a hunter, he would depend.

Note here the comprehensive symbolic significance of the admonition that a novice attend to a teacher or an elder with downcast eyes as a sign of respect. This simple action confused and confounded innumerable bush educators and convinced them that their Yup'ik students were bashful or stupid or both. In fact, downcast eyes are an eloquent expression of the relationship between socially restricted sight and powerful supernatural vision, all of which teachers unwittingly undercut when they "help" Yup'ik children in school to overcome their apparent shyness.

Just as sight in the proper context is coincident with power, lack of sight is equivalent to the ultimate biological, social, or spiritual infirmity. For example, in the famous dart incident, a village virtually destroyed itself and a war began as the result of the accidental blinding of a young boy by his playmate (see Chapter 7). Paul John of Nelson Island told of a cruel hunter who, upon finally recognizing his defeat, covered his eyes with his hands and was subsequently killed by an arrow from his opponent's bow. John Henry of Scammon Bay recalled the story of the stingy hunter who saw game but refused to tell his fellow villagers. Suspecting his treachery, they followed him, and seeing his eye peeking over a rock, they pulled him forth and killed him. Afterward, the site became known as *Iillkiavik* (literally "place of the eye"). Another traditional tale, related by Jack Williams of Mekoryak, recalls the fate of a group of infamous hunters from St. Lawrence Island who traveled to Nunivak Island and cruelly corralled and blinded a caribou herd, then decimated it. In retribution, the irate Nunivakers confined the intruders in the men's house, blocked the entrances and exits, and left their captives to starve to death.

In these examples, lack of sight is directly related to starvation and death. Conversely, the supernatural vision of a young girl was said to have alleviated a period of severe famine in the coastal area. Journeying out from her village in search of food, the girl sighted a woven pack basket full of blackfish. She immediately raised her arm and made a circular motion in the air to "liken the fish to the sky" (possibly referring to the circular concept of the different levels of the universe) so that the fish would remain visible, and edible, for her starving family. Similarly, during a time of famine, a shaman from the Yukon area advised his son to circle their trash heap at dawn and to tell him what he saw. The son reported sighting animal tracks, which the family then successfully followed in search of food (Fienup-Riordan 1986b:366–367). Likewise, in a tale recorded by Nelson (1899:497–499), a mythical doll (in fact the inventor/originator of masks) came to life, completely circled the edge of the world and then the village of his new human parents. Only then did he enter the village and make himself visible to its inhabitants.

Finally, the direction as well as the act of encircling was significant, in certain contexts producing visibility and in others invisibility. For example, a ghost could be banished if a person ran out of the doorway and circled the house in the direction of the sun's course. In the event of a human death, a ritual "erasing" was traditionally performed. The bereaved circled the outside of the house in the direction of the sun's circuit, at the same time rubbing its walls all around with a whetstone to close the entrances and make them invisible and therefore impenetrable to the spirits of the dead (John 1977). Likewise, on the fifth day after a human death on Nelson Island, the mourners circled the grave in the direction of the sun's course to send away the spirit of the deceased. Similarly, on the third or fifth day after the birth of a child, the new mother traditionally emerged from her confinement, marking her return to social visibility by circling the house, again in the direction of the sun's course. When a man hunted sea mammals at certain times, he had to circle his kill in the direction of the sun's course before retrieval. The boat itself was ritually circled before launching in the spring, in both Alaska and Siberia (Bogoras

1904:404; Moore 1923:369; Usugan 1982). All these ritual acts recall the magic circle of the Netsilik region reported by Rasmussen (1927:129, 1931:60); people walked in a circle around strangers who approached their camp so that their footprints would contain any evil spirits that might have accompanied the new arrivals.[11]

The Ringed Center

The image of Issiisaayuq is, in a way, a reflective statement on the significance of all hooped masks as eyes into a world or worlds beyond the mundane. Traditionally, the face was the visual means of representing and embodying an other-world reality for human audiences. At the same time it was the means of seeing into the human world for that other reality. The mask is literally and figuratively a ringed center. As such, it is a condensed image of the traditional Yup'ik universe as well as the cosmological system that defined it. The ringed center is an often-repeated image obvious in many contexts once the concept of vision and spiritual transformation that it embodies is revealed. Without such a framework, however, its significance remains invisible, as it has in previous discussions of traditional masks and masked dancing.

The mask itself is structurally a ringed center. In Nick's work (Figure 3.5), as in that of other contemporary and traditional carvers from Nunivak Island and along the Kuskokwim River, the face of the mask is often framed in multiple wooden rings called *ellanguat* (literally "pretend or model cosmos"). These concentric rings represent the different levels of the universe, which was traditionally said to contain five upper worlds and the earth (Ray 1967:66). This same heavenly symbolism was repeated in ceremonial activity in which the masked dancer was a key participant. For example, multiple rings, also called *ellanguat* and decorated with bits of down and feathers, were lowered and raised from the inside of the men's-house roof during the traditional Doll Festival; they were said to represent the retreat and approach of the heavens, complete with snow and stars (Charles 1983; Nelson 1899:496; Ray 1967:67).

The men's house (*qasgiq*) in which the dance was performed in Nick's youth was also an image of the universe. Not only did the ceiling represent the celestial canopy during the Doll Festival, but in various rituals the central skylight was believed to provide exit from

FIGURE 3.5 Nick Charles's double-headed hawk mask with encircling rings and appendages (Courtesy University of Alaska Museum).

this world to another level of reality. For instance, during the closing performances of the traditional Bladder Festival, the shaman climbed out through the skylight to enter the sea, visit the seal spirits in their underwater home, and request their return. These spirits, in turn, could view the behavior of the would-be hunters by watching the condition of the central smoke hole in their underwater abode. If hunters were giving them proper thought and care, the smoke hole would appear clear. If not, the hole would be covered with snow and nothing would be visible, in which case the seals would not emerge from their underwater world or allow themselves to be hunted. As a young man Nick sought to maintain this vision as he carefully cleared snow from skylights and ice holes alike.

In addition to permitting movement and communication between the worlds of the hunter and the hunted, the central *qasgiq* smoke hole was also a passageway between the worlds of the living and the dead. For example, in the event of a human death, the body of the deceased was pulled through the smoke hole after first being placed in each of its four corners. By this action the deceased, on the way from the world of the living to that of the dead, gradually exchanged the mortal sight that it lost at death for the supernatural clairvoyance of the spirit world (Nelson 1899:425). Although both smoke holes and ice holes were rectangular rather than round, their shape does not undercut their significance as spiritual eyes. One variant of the circle-and-dot motif was a rectangle with four small projections, one at each corner, within which was carved a dot surrounded by concentric circles.

The numbers four and five figure prominently in Central Yup'ik ritual, representing among other things the number of steps leading to the underworld land of the dead. The Bladder Festival rituals use four corners and four sets of hunting and boating gear. At one stage in its performance on Nelson Island the bladders were presented with model spears, miniature pack baskets, and other tiny tools in sets of four to enable them to capture the food that they were given. Painted bentwood bowls and incised ivories have spurs that occur in units of four. The square or rectangular holes and the quadrangle functioning like a circle and dot may form a logical symbolic complex with this added sacred dimension.

The image of the ringed center recurs again and again in Nick's work, always with the connotation of vision, if not movement, between worlds. In fact, the *qasgiq* in which Nick grew to manhood was itself the spiritual and social window of the community, surrounded by individual sod houses (*enet*). In these *enet* his mother and sisters prepared food and clothing and cared for the younger children. The reproductive capacity of the women's house was explicit. In certain contexts, its interior was likened to the womb from which children would be produced and, concurrently, from which the spirits of the dead would be reborn in human form as they reentered the world of the living. Elena remembers the pregnancy taboos that required her to exit quickly and repeatedly through the doorway so that her unborn child would emerge in a similar manner from her body. One story of an unborn child depicts it as it first becomes aware of itself in a room inhabited only by a toothless old woman. The baby ultimately finds the door and exits.[12] Also, Nick recalled that his sisters were not allowed to take their dolls (*irniaruat*, literally "pretend children") out of the house until after the first crane had nested in the spring. At puberty they were themselves confined to the house, their social invisibility approximating a fetus's hidden state.

Physical birth, female productivity, and seasonal rebirth, as symbolized by exit from the traditional woman's house, were the counterpart of the spiritual rebirth and vision of an other-worldly reality accomplished in the *qasgiq*. Just as most masks were carved in the *qasgiq*, most masked dances and communal events were performed there.[13] Visions of the supernatural usually were realized in material and dramatic form in the *qasgiq*. Nick's sisters might have carved in the earth a transitory representation of daily events with their ivory story knives.[14] Yet the elegantly carved knife itself (Figure 3.6) as well as the symbolic designs on it were made in the men's house by their father, grandfather, or one of their uncles.

The social interpretation of human sexual differences was not framed as an opposition, but as a circle, both encompassed and encompassing. The cyclical nature of Central Yup'ik cosmology has been detailed elsewhere (Fienup-Riordan 1983) and is summarized in Chapter 2—images of birth resolving into rebirth, torn parts sewn into whole cloth, spring dying into winter and out of winter spring

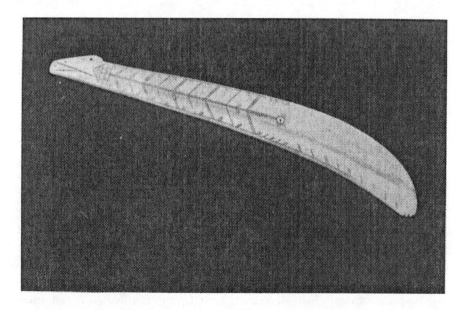

FIGURE 3.6 Ivory story knife with circle-and-dot motif (Courtesy University of Alaska Museum).

being born again. This fundamental belief of the Central Yup'ik Eskimos concerning the spiritual constancy underlying temporal flux is embodied in a multitude of forms, including naming patterns, marriage patterns, and ceremonial observances such as sending the souls of seals back under the ice during the traditional Bladder Festival. A minute but telling example of this point of view is the practice among Nelson Island women of removing a tassel from the back of their fancy dress parka after the death of a close friend or relative. The tassel is then sewn back in place on the occasion of the birth of a child who is thought of as the deceased's replacement.

Traditional village structure involved this same endless circle. For example, although the sexual distinction was pronounced in the division of social space into separate men's and women's houses in the larger winter villages, many of the camps that Nick knew in his early years consisted of a single dwelling in which men and women lived and slept side by side. In various ritual contexts also the complementary relationship between the sexes was explicitly played on. For example, there was gender ambiguity when Nick's aunt dressed as a man in a formal serving ritual. Likewise, there was gender fusion when the shaman in touch with the spirits of the animals was confined in the *qasgiq* like a woman in childbirth or in menstrual seclusion. Note also in this context the mixed sexual imagery on the mask of Issiisaayuq, which includes both male labrets and a female chin tattoo. In each case, images of biological production—confinement, food presentation—might be seen to accomplish social and cosmological reproduction. In a fundamental sense, through marriage a generational cycle was completed. Children would be born, and through them their grandparents, and ultimately their parents, would be born again.

The social interpretation of human sexual differences is also visible in the separation of men and women on the dance floor during a contemporary masked performance (Figure 3.7). Kneeling on the floor facing the drummers and singers, a male dancer begins to play out the stylized motions that tell the story behind Nick's mask. His quick staccato motions are accompanied by the graceful movements of the women dancers standing in a semicircle behind him. Together, dancers and drummers form a circle reminiscent of the rings (*ellanguat*) encircling the mask. This image is, according to several Nelson Island women, taken further by the decorative belts worn around the waists of the women as well as the beaded wolverine crowns encircling the

FIGURE 3.7 St. Marys Dance Festival: *Yupiit Yuraryarait* (from *Tundra Drums*, Bethel, Alaska, Sept. 30, 1982, p. 15).

dancers' heads and covering the studiously downcast eyes of the performers.

The image of the encircling ring can also be seen in the rounded dance fans, fringed in fur and feathers, held in the hands of the performers, both men and women. These fans are reminiscent of the mask worn by the central dancer. In fact, traditional and some contemporary dance fans often have faces (Nelson 1899:412–415). Women's dance fans made and used on the Yukon Delta today by carvers such as Emmonak's William Trader still display faces, both animal and human. Nick also explicitly compared the open-work design of the fans held by the men on Nelson Island to the pierced hand found as an appendage on many traditional masks. The hole in the hand's center, like the opening in the dance fan is by Nick's account a symbolic passage through which the spirits of fish and game come to view their treatment by men and, if they find it acceptable, to repopulate the world. Thus both male and female dancers, holding dance fans and with their arms extended in the motions of the dance, are like gigantic transformation masks, complete with animal-spirit faces to which the wooden pierced hands are appended.

Given this perspective, one may reasonably contrast the efficacy of the mask's supernatural sight to the lowered gaze of the human performers who dance so that they may truly "see" and that the spirits may see through them. According to Nick, the traditional application of a white clay base and colored finger spots to the bladders inflated for a Bladder Festival was likewise an attempt to promote spiritual vision on the part of the souls of the seals. The painting of the wooden masks as well as the painting of the body of the dancer had a similar effect, allowing the dancer to become visible to the spirit world and in fact to embody the spirit at the same time that his personal identity was hidden from the human world.

Compare the expert dancer, performing inside the *qasgiq*, with the disguised participants in *Qaariitaaq*, a traditional ceremony held outside the *qasgiq* just before the Bladder Festival in late November, during which the participants went door to door around the village. Through the mask the dancer was simultaneously endowed with supernatural sight and made visible to the spirit world in acceptable form. In *Qaariitaaq*, however, the disguises were possibly used as a protection against the spirit world (Morrow 1984:122), an attempt to maintain the separation between the human and nonhuman domains. Covering the face, painting the face and body, and shutting the eyes were in certain contexts effective means of maintaining the boundary between the worlds of the living and the dead (Morrow 1984:122). For example, a child's face might be painted with red ocher or blackened with soot to protect the child from disease (Usugan 1982). Rather than being a contradiction, this practice suggests a continued tension between restricted sight and disguise as protection for the novice and full sight as a prerogative of the spiritually knowledgeable and, in fact, a necessity for spiritual knowledge and transformation. Morrow (1984:123) recognizes this same tension when she notes the discrepancy between disguised participants in *Qaariitaaq* activities and the social, and presumably spiritual, visibility entailed in the presentation of marked bowls and other goods in specific individuals' names in the succeeding Bladder Festival.

The image of the ringed center, implying both vision and movement between worlds, is mapped not only in village structure and in the structure of the dance performance, mask, and fans, but also on the structure of the world at large. When Nick was a boy, he was taught that the earth was an island space (or hole) surrounded by water. The coast was the rim of the world as it was known. Venturing from it was a hunter's task, and while Nick was gone in search of specific species, his wife, Elena, had to remain relatively motionless inside the house lest her actions scare away the animals that her husband pursued. At fall camp, when she heard her husband returning, Elena would quickly exit, climb to the roof of the sod house, and dance, humming her own accompaniment.

Not only does action in the female domain affect the hunter's world, but it is equivalent to that world under certain circumstances. For instance, if a man happened to meet a female ghost, he was admonished to touch her between the legs. One man who had done this was said to have disappeared. When he awoke his arm was deep in the ice. He pulled it out and the ice closed after him. In this case the world (specifically the sea or watery world) is equivalent to a female body, a sexually potent one, and one that does not hesitate to contain its opposite.

Human biological processes—birthing, seeing, dying—were literally built into the structure of the house, the world in which the house existed, and the mask that represented this cosmological design. The processes of both animal and human spiritual transformation were likewise encoded into village space. The significance of entry and exit from a human habitation is especially clear in the case of the walrus-tusked entryway of the men's house. During the dance performances that Nick watched when he was young, dancers often emerged from behind a screen or through a tunnel that several Nelson Islanders specifically likened to an animal's mouth as it opened into the men's house. Here, the vision of the spirit world came, literally and figuratively, out of the animal's body. The cyclical relationship between humans and animals, spiritual and material, was realized in the tunnel entrance to the *qasgiq*, where the passageway was simultaneously a metaphor for human reproduction and spiritual consumption. As the masked hosts came forth to entertain and feed their guests, the spirits of the animals symbolically consumed those who were fed and who, in turn, would exit to pursue them for future consumption.[15] Thus, there is ambiguity in the cultural regulation of natural vitality. The dramatic transformation of hunter into hunted effected during the masked performance enabled the hunter ultimately to participate in the spiritual world on which he depended.

Conclusion

The Yup'ik Eskimo universe, both social and metaphysical, was traditionally depicted as subject to constant alteration yet ultimate unity in the repetition of reproductive and productive cycles. The hooped mask and the performance of masked dances ultimately embody both the alterations and the unity. Traditionally, each mask was unique and the product of an individual vision and experience. Each was crafted as part of a performance and then discarded, as new visions and new masks would replace it in succeeding years.[16] Continuity in the use of the hooped mask today provides a vivid image for the system of cosmological reproduction through which the Yup'ik people traditionally viewed and to some extent continue to view the universe. The same image of supernatural sight that dominates Nick's masks can also be seen in the rounded lamp and the ringed bowl, the hole in the kayak float board, the decorative geometry of traditional ivory earrings, the central gut skylight opening from the men's house, and the decorative celestial rings suspended from its ceiling for a dance performance. The world was bound, the circle closed. Yet within it was the passageway leading from the human to the spirit world. Rimmed by the *ellanguat* and transformed by paint and feathers, the eyes of the mask, themselves often ringed, look beyond this world into another.

Part Two

Negotiated Meaning:
The Yup'ik Encounter
with Christianity

*I*n the preceding chapters, I have described key aspects of Yup'ik cosmology as it continues to be played out in the twentieth century. Although a distinctive Yup'ik view of the world can be recognized in western Alaska today, this view has been subject to profound transformations over the last hundred years. Beginning in the nineteenth century the Judeo-Christian world-view was introduced by missionaries of several faiths. Although the animism of the past was far from eradicated, the ways and means by which it was expressed would never be the same.

Analysts of and participants in the native-missionary encounter in the Arctic have tended to depict conversion as an all-or-nothing process in which the native culture either is left intact or is totally transformed. The missionary encounter is presented not as a dialogue, but in terms of relative failure or success (Martin 1978; Tanner 1979). For example, Oswalt (1963a) attributes the easy acceptance of Moravian ideology along the Kuskokwim to an inherent weakness in the traditional nineteenth-century Yup'ik value system. Many descendants of that encounter, however, modern natives and non-native clergy alike, maintain that Christianity simply gave new form to old beliefs, that in effect there has been no change (Aloysius 1986).

As a result of the view that the native-missionary encounter was either pure oppression or enlightenment, missionaries alternately have been criticized for imposing themselves on native peoples and have been reified as the saintly bearers of "good news." Following Kan (1987a:3), the history of native-missionary interaction can rather be seen as an encounter between different systems of meaning.

In western Alaska this encounter has resulted in neither total commitment to nor total rejection of one by the other. Instead, a subtle internalization of selected cultural categories has taken place (see, for example, Comaroff and Comaroff 1986:15). The people involved made conscious choices based on perceived congruities, and in some cases incongruities, between Yup'ik and Christian systems of meaning. This "negotiation," sometimes intentional and deliberate and sometimes not, characterized the relationship between natives and Christian missionaries. As Lechat (1976:7) shrewdly points out for the Canadian Arctic, from the moment of contact, this relationship was not a continual series of cultural "rapes" but rather a series of legitimate, fruitful "consenting unions." The next two chapters provide examples of such unions.

The Real People and the Children of Thunder

Yup'ik from *yuk* human being, plus
+*pik* genuine, real; literally "a genuine person"; plural *Yupiit* real people.
(Jacobson 1984:416)

There was an old shaman at Napas-
kiak, who strongly preached against adopting the white man's
teaching. His strong point was that the white people were the
children of thunder—therefore were not really human. He
said—"Everything they do and everything they have is accompanied with noise." (John H. Kilbuck, Box 5:7 MA)

BETWEEN 1885 AND 1900 MISSIONARIES WERE THE PRIMARY
force of change in western Alaska, and the Moravian couple John and
Edith Kilbuck were among the most effective. Christianity as presented by the Kilbucks interacted with traditional Yup'ik ideology
and action. A careful reading of the Kilbucks' story challenges the
unidirectional and "modernization" views of history built on the assumption of the eventual success of salvationist Christian orthodoxy
over traditional native belief. Ideological change is, rather, a creative
process and, for the Yup'ik Eskimos of the Kuskokwim drainage, has
led to the development of their own particular mix of Christian and
native belief. In a number of ways Christianity, itself internally fractured and changing, may be rejected, marginalized, absorbed, or
transformed by the people it encounters. This chapter suggests the
dynamics of that encounter for the Yup'ik Eskimos of the Kuskokwim
drainage.

The Real People

In 1885, when the Kilbucks came to work in western Alaska, they
found a people possessing a highly developed sense of themselves and
their place in their world. Yup'ik values and notions of history, society, and eternity were grounded in a view of the world fundamentally
different from that of the Kilbucks. The uniqueness of the Yup'ik view

of the world is particularly visible in the notion of personhood. Each society possesses a definition of what a "real" person ought to be. A careful look at the attributes ascribed to a person provides insights about how people think of themselves and their relationship to others.

On the most basic level the Yup'ik people at the turn of the century viewed society as primary. The life of the individual took on meaning only in the context of a complex web of relationships between humans and animals, both the living and the dead. This idea contrasts sharply with the Hobbesian view of Western society, in which every person is seen to confront every other as an owner. According to Hobbes, social relations result from the actions of a multitude of individuals seeking to serve their own needs, and a person is a bound, unique center of awareness. Although this Hobbesian perspective was but one part of the cultural baggage the Kilbucks brought with them to western Alaska, its impact on the Christian/Yup'ik encounter was considerable.

For the Yup'ik Eskimos, society included both human and nonhuman members. They extended personhood beyond the human domain and attributed it to animals as well. They did not believe that only humans possessed immortal souls in contrast to and dominant over mute beasts that served them. On the contrary, the Yup'ik Eskimos viewed the relationship between humans and animals as collaborative reciprocity; the animals gave themselves to the hunter in response to his respectful treatment of them as persons (albeit nonhuman) in their own right.

According to the world view of the Yup'ik Eskimos, human and nonhuman persons shared a number of fundamental characteristics. First and foremost, the perishable flesh of both humans and animals was belied by the immortality of their souls. All living things participated in an endless cycle of birth and rebirth; the souls of both animals and people were a part of this cycle, contingent on right thought and action by others as well as self.

For game animals, the rebirth that followed their mortal demise was accomplished in part through the ritual consumption of their bodies by the men and women to whom they had given themselves in the chase. During the midwinter Bladder Festival (*Nakaciuq*) as well as the masked dances performed during *Kelek*, the spirits of the game were hosted and feasted as honored guests at the same time that as victims they were totally consumed. Given the missionaries' relatively circumscribed concept of personhood, it is no wonder that they had difficulty in comprehending the double meaning of the endless winter feasting that characterized traditional Yup'ik ceremonial activity. They interpreted as profligate and irrational squandering of scarce and limited resources an active attempt by the Yup'ik people to become worthy subjects of a reciprocal generosity on the part of the spirits of the game to whom, in the capacity of guests, they had given everything (Sahlins 1986:12; Brightman 1983:446–450).

Along with the belief in an essential spiritual continuity that bridged the gap between the past and the future, the Yup'ik people held that men and animals alike possessed "awareness." According to Joe Friday (1985) of Chevak, "We felt that all things were like us people, to the small animals like the mouse and the things like wood we liken to people as having a sense of awareness. The wood it is glad to the person who is using it and the person using it is grateful to the wood for being there to be used." The existence of such awareness was simultaneously indexed by and allowed an individual a sense of control over his destiny. This awareness was felt to be the product of experience. People lacked a sense of self at birth. Gradually, however, they became aware of their surroundings.

As they matured, both human and nonhuman persons received a multitude of prescriptions and proscriptions for the culturally appropriate living of life. Three related ideas underlie the elaborate detail of these rules: the power of a person's thought; the importance of thoughtful action in order not to injure another's mind; and, conversely, the danger inherent in "following one's own mind."

First, regarding the power of a person's thought, the message was that attitude was as significant as action. Thus, young men were admonished to "keep the thought of the seals" foremost in their minds as they performed daily duties. In all these acts, by the power of the mind, they "made a way for the seals" they would some day hunt. Animals were also subject to this stricture. For example, young seals were said to be admonished by their elders to "stay awake" to the rules, both literally and figuratively, so that their immortal souls could survive the hunter's blow. If they were asleep when they were hit, they would "die dead, forever" (Fienup-Riordan 1983:179).

In all tasks undertaken the appropriate attitude was considered as important as the action. Conversely, both humans and animals gave help to individual elders and avoided their displeasure because of the "power of the mind of the elders" to affect their future.

Second, as proper thought effected success in the domain of human and animal interaction, so careful thought had to reign over thoughtless action in order not to injure the mind of another.[1] Just as a person's mind was powerful, it was also believed to be vulnerable. A reticence to hasty verbalization as well as the value placed on a person's ability to retain equilibrium in a tense situation derived from this belief. Ideally, smoothness and acquiescence were the appropriate masks for a person's emotions.[2] The value placed on the appearance of agreement partly explains the verbal assent missionaries sometimes received to their proposed reforms, followed by no real change in a person's behavior. The Yupiit probably deeply resented (though they did not say so) the rude intervention of the missionaries, which ran counter to their own highly refined system of indirect, yet nonetheless effective, interaction.[3] From the Yup'ik point of view, people were supposed to admonish a recalcitrant person without injuring the offender's mind in the process.

Third, and corollary to the belief in the power of human thought and the importance of thoughtful action, Yup'ik ideology maintained that one should refrain from following one's own mind when one's ideas conflict with the collective wisdom of the spiritually powerful elders. Individuality, as we understand it, was not a valued attribute. On the contrary, the pursuit of individual ends was often seen as conflicting with the good of the whole and was considered reprehensible.

A metaphor for what it meant to be a real person, according to the Yup'ik conception of reality, can be found in the opposition between sleeping and waking. Those who possessed powerful minds were said to be aware of or awake to their surroundings. Conversely, those who paid no attention to the rules and led thoughtless lives were considered to be unaware or asleep. The opposition between sleeping and waking is a frequent theme in Yup'ik moral discourse and signifies a spiritual as well as a physical condition. For example, a young boy who paid attention to what he was told was said to be awakened by the words of the elders. Elders encouraged young people to live on little sleep and to rise early and quickly. To be a lazy person or a sleepyhead was not approved on moral grounds, as inordinate sleep was considered the outward sign of inner flaccidity and weakness.[4]

This same opposition between sleeping and waking also characterized animal society. For example, if a seal killed by a hunter's harpoon was awake when hit, its soul was said to retract to its bladder, where it would lie dormant until, well cared for by the successful hunter, it was returned to the sea to be reborn the following year. In the same way, when a person was dying, relatives would watch over the person, never going to sleep. Directly following a death the mourners set up a loud wailing to wake up the spirit for the journey ahead. Were the spirit allowed to sleep, like the seal it would be barred from rebirth in the future. Ironically, the Kilbucks deplored these funeral lamentations, taking them as signs of heathen grief that they would alleviate with their message of eternal life. In fact, a perpetual cycling between birth and rebirth characterized Yup'ik ideology; nothing ever finally passed away unless, through mental slumber or thoughtless action, one allowed oneself to "die dead, forever."

As can be seen, a number of specific attributes went into the Yup'ik definition of a real person and how a person might act in relation to others. These attributes differ significantly from the definitions of personhood and society that the Kilbucks held. The Western view of society, Christian and otherwise, can be characterized as a gathering of separate parts, which we know as individuals, each with distinct needs and desires and each seeking to augment its own ends. Consequently, individual freedom is generally considered a virtue and society a constraint. Within a Hobbesian framework, society evolves when individual self-interest is tempered by fear of other people. Reason dictates that people get together because they cannot satisfy their individual needs unless they do.

These two different views of personhood and of society entail two different views of history as well. In the Western view, society originates in the unification of natural diversity. Although the Moravians stressed the community of believers, they saw this unity as forged from an original diversity. Western history depicts society as resolving, or at least as increasing control over, individual needs and desires. The Kilbucks manifested this view in their belief that people were born in sin, and life was spent controlling ever-present tendencies toward evil manifested in the frailties of the flesh. This belief, in turn, ties back to the Western definition of culture, both individual and societal, as one's increasing control and refinement of oneself (Wagner 1975:21). In its specifically Christian form, this epistemology guided the Kilbucks. Their work among the Yupiit paralleled their contemporaries' work in the marketplace to the extent that they abstracted Yup'ik culture as a thing that people did and had and could lose. On the contrary, for the Yup'ik Eskimos culture was a means of knowing, not something to be known, and as such was much more abiding than the Moravians allowed.

The view of society as the unification of an original diversity stands in direct contrast to the Yup'ik view of the origin of society and of history. By the Yup'ik view, as given in their oral tradition, society begins in peace and unity and coactivity. Traditional tales (*qulirat*) explain how this original reciprocity among humans and between humans and animals, was in specific instances broken. These stories usually tell of a person who, in pursuit of individual gratification, loses sight of the rules and, as a result, either figuratively or literally loses his humanity. Conversely, in the Western view, the pursuit of individual ends is taken for granted as a condition of being human and (to the Kilbucks) was evidence of man's original sinful state. To the Yup'ik Eskimos it was not. To them, people were social beings first and individuals only if they forgot themselves, in which case their downfall was assured.

For example, by one account, warfare among the Yup'ik people originated in an incident that occurred in a coastal community; it was sparked by the antisocial behavior of a man from the Yukon Delta who had married into another group. This particular hunter, eager to succeed but lacking the requisite skills, killed his hunting companions to steal their catch. His crime ultimately brought about armed conflict between the coastal and Yukon villages. This account is also given as the reason for the emergence of distinct social groupings out of an original unity, as Yukon and coastal Yup'ik Eskimos subsequently constituted two separable endogamous groups. Conversely, the conflict was laid to rest during a period of famine when a man from the Yukon and a man from the coast shared in the catch of a seal and saved each other's lives (Fienup-Riordan 1984a:76).

Together, these two tales provide a cyclical view of history and an ultimately unified view of society. Whereas the original conflict divided a group united by marriage, the resolution brought about the rapprochement of two originally distinct groups. Though beginning in theft and the refusal to cooperate, the conflict ended in a return to food-sharing and trading. And though it began with the in-group murder of several successful hunters, it ended with the revival of an outsider who was close to death. Finally, the breach centered around the food quest and the relationship between humans and animals as well as between men. Again, proper social relations were seen not as isolatable but as dependent on the correct relationship between hunter and hunted.

Although the Yupiit possessed a view of humanity fundamentally different from that of the men and women who came to "enlighten" them, in the interchange apparent similarities often masked the differences. In a number of important respects the Yup'ik code for right living is comparable to the Moravian "brotherly agreement," with its emphasis on a Godly life lived with "due economy," industry, and rigorous training. Edith's careful needlework drew moral as well as practical approbation from native women, who connected the quality of their stitchery with the quantity of their husbands' catch. Both camps deplored waste, though defining it differently. Also the Yup'ik definition of laziness bears a marked resemblance to John's own standards (J. Kilbuck, Apr. 16, 1918, MA).

When the Kilbucks preached industry, they reached open ears, as the Yupiit were already committed to thoughtful action as an expression of one's proper spiritual state. The missionaries' emphasis on individual thrift, however, often cut against the elaborate social reciprocity through which the Yupiit expressed a multitude of relationships, both social and spiritual.

To a certain extent both the Yupiit and the Moravians conceived a person's resources as finite, as opposed to the infinite resources of the universe (*Ella*) and God, respectively. Just as the Yupiit taught their young men and women not to squander their sight or breath, nineteenth-century Moravian parents advised their children not to read too much in order not to hurt their eyes and not to masturbate as it would waste their seed. Use of the spoken word was carefully circumscribed by both the Yupiit and the Moravians because it was considered powerful and potentially hurtful (J. Kilbuck, May 9, 1918, MA).[5] Just as the Yupiit believed themselves dependent on the impersonal but all-powerful spirit of the universe (*Ellam yua*), so the Moravians saw themselves as unable to succeed without God's aid. A fundamental but independent similarity might also be suggested between the Yup'ik idea of the conscious and willing sacrifice of the animals for the sake of the human hunter and the Christian belief in the sacrifice of the lamb of God to redeem mankind. These congruences subtly aided and abetted the conversion process.

The Kilbucks also played on a significant isomorphism when they spoke of "waking up" the heathen, with its connotation of increased awareness. In 1889 John wrote: "The school children are quite awakened this winter. . . . Another young man came into our sitting-room . . . and said: '. . . While I sat listening to your words, it seemed to me that I was just waking up from a long sleep. I am indeed thankful, for now my eyes are open'" (Fienup-Riordan 1988d:255). A fundamental tenet of Moravian doctrine is that death is a transition rather than a final state. Old Moravian church registers headed the column for the date of death "Fell Asleep" (Hamilton and Hamilton 1967:45). Thus when the Kilbucks taught that to know God was life eternal, they hit a responsive chord, playing as they could on the Yup'ik belief in ever-cycling and, in this sense, everlasting life. These congruences, though historically accidental, were highly significant. They originated in different views of the world but provided a framework for mutual comprehension.

Although the Kilbucks were the harbingers of Western civilization in significant respects, their devout Christianity set them apart from their fellow *kass'at* (white men). Along with the nineteenth-century Yupiit, they shared the belief that a person's material state manifested that person's spiritual condition. Visionaries within their own society, they deplored the de facto Western separation of the sacred and profane. Also, they shared a belief in personal responsibility. For both the Yupiit and the Moravians, the connection between thought and deed, action and ideal, was fundamental. Thus, the Moravian admonition that belief in Christ must be supported by daily acts on his behalf found a comprehending audience among a people for whom right thought and efficacious action were inseparable.

For both the Yupiit and the Moravians, harmony was the expressed ideal. Likewise, both admonished against vaunting good deeds in public. A contemporary Yup'ik account of traditional rules for living provides a striking parallel to (or perhaps culturally appropriate translation of) the advice given in Matthew (6:1–6) that a person not pray and perform charitable acts standing on street corners to be seen by others but rather in secret to be rewarded by God:

> Only at night he clears the paths.
> If he does it during the day,
> letting the people see him
> already then,
> through the people he has his reward.

> But if he does that with no one watching him
> and nobody is aware of him,
> only the one watching him,
> the ocean or the land, . . .
> the *Ellam yua* [person or spirit of the universe] will give him
> his reward.
> (Fienup-Riordan 1977–1987:Tape 57)

In the same way both the Yupiit and the Moravians placed a high value on personal encounter with an unseen power through prayer. John's contention that the prayer of a sinner would find direct heavenly response was interpreted in the light of traditional sympathetic hunting magic. Familiar with the use of ritual performance to ensure the success of future action, John's Yup'ik audience was already primed for what amounted to his creative reformation of that accustomed form.

Moreover, from the beginning, rather than suppressing traditional rhetorical forms, the conversion process employed the elders' practice of perpetually speaking out to advise the young people of their responsibilities. Just as discourse in the men's house figured as a central element in the traditional Yup'ik socialization process, the Moravians preached that continual public restatement was necessary for the Word of God to be received. Also, although both the Moravians and Yupiit possessed religious specialists—the church leadership and the shamans—both laid primary emphasis on the person as the one responsible for his or her own actions and fate and on the congregation as the embodiment of power and authority.

Another point of congruence can be found in the great importance Yup'ik tradition placed on the power of the human mind. The Yup'ik people used this fundamental ideological tenet to make sense of, restate, and understand the Moravian message of Christ's love. Many years later, in a sermon John delivered on gift-giving, his emphasis on intention approximated Yup'ik admonitions concerning the relation of thought and deed. He wrote, "My sermon was on the Widow's mite, as recorded by Mark. . . . In giving with the heart in it, we give a double portion" (Apr. 14, 1918, MA). In another sermon, John's advice concerning the hardness of the human heart rang true to Yup'ik listeners, who brought to the sermon a belief in the power and the fragility of the human mind (June 2, 1918, MA).

In the same way, though the concept of original sin was foreign, the Christian emphasis on salvation and life eternal fit with the traditional belief in rebirth made possible by proper action in life. The conquest of death is one of the ultimate goals of Christianity and an important element in Moravian theology. This victory is achieved when sinners are "born again" in this life and the spirit of God is instilled in them. For the Moravians this spiritual rebirth cancels out the original sin that is part and parcel of human physical birth. On the contrary, in the Yup'ik view of the world, rebirth is physical birth writ large.

In part, the people of the Kuskokwim resolved contradictions between Christian theology and the collective aspects of nineteenth-century Yup'ik daily life by practicing Christianity so as to give less attention to individual salvation than to harnessing divine help in improving the well-being of the community of believers. Although the differences between the Yup'ik and Western views of the world were profound, the Kilbucks' Christian ideology proved to be a powerful intermediary in the process of religious conversion, which was also a process of cultural translation. A century later, the extent of their success was voiced on the occasion of the ordination of a native deacon, Bob Aloysius, in Bethel. According to Aloysius (1986), "It had to take the Son of God to teach people to live like the Yup'iks. The main command of the Yup'ik people is to love one another and never put yourself above other people, and to look after your fellow man. What is the difference between true Christianity and the Yup'iks? I don't see any myself." Although Aloysius did not speak the whole truth, he spoke a portion of it worth keeping in mind.

The Children of Thunder

> Civilization is one immense interrogation point standing up before them. Is it not to any one? (E. Kilbuck, journal to her father, Dec. 5, 1888, MA)

Although the resemblances between Yup'ik and Moravian ideology and action may have aided the initial presentation of Christianity, they also masked profound differences in expectation. To the Kilbucks, action in this world was preparatory to life in the next. For the Yupiit, the meaning of existence was already given in the here-and-now, and the purpose of following the rules was to maintain the proper social and spiritual relationship between the human and spirit worlds. Whereas Yup'ik ceremonies sought to re-create essential relations already in place, the Moravians sought to participate in God's intended transformation.

On their arrival the Kilbucks viewed the Yup'ik mind as a blank slate as far as religion was concerned, ready to receive their message of eternal life. The self-imposed task of civilizing and bringing to Christianity the indigenous "heathen" consumed their energy and imagination. During the early years, when the differences between the aboriginal and "civilized" worlds stood out in sharpest contrast, the Kilbucks wrote their harshest judgments, condemning the "barbarism" and immorality they found:

> They as a rule are very kind to each other. . . . One crime they do commit which none of them recognize as such, and that is, to kill off unwelcome infants, especially girls; and they also kill old and helpless persons. . . .
> They sometimes club to death and burn with oil a "shaman" or "witch" who is suspected of killing too many innocent people. Such dreadful deeds are shocking to us. (E. Kilbuck 1889:533)[6]

Infanticide, ritual execution (for that is probably what the killing of the accused witch signified), and abandonment were, in fact, part of a cultural complex and survival strategy both foreign and abhorrent to the Kilbucks.

Traditional Yup'ik sexuality also drew sharp criticism. Edith wrote:

> I fully believe that some of these women have ten to twelve husbands before they settle down and even when they have children and are old enough to be steady they think nothing of leaving their husband and taking some one else. . . . My heart aches for the girls of our part of Alaska. They are made perfect prostitutes by their parents from the time they are nine or ten years old. (letter, Mar. 20, 1888, MA)

Like the improvidence associated with the midwinter ceremonial cycle, the apparently fickle and overindulgent character of Yup'ik sexual activity drew harsh condemnation. Culturally committed to monogamy and the ideal of repressed sexuality characteristic of late nineteenth-century Western society, Edith especially could never view Yup'ik sexuality as regulated according to a view of society whereby social needs actually overshadowed individual desires. To her, Yup'ik sexuality retained the appearance of unregulated desire rather than desire regulated according to a cultural logic different from her own.

True to the late nineteenth-century evolutionary view of human history, the Kilbucks assumed that the Eskimos were at a lower "stage of spiritual development." They judged their beliefs to be superstitions, which could not be based on the "higher impulses" such as love or morality: "The affection that has developed could hardly

be termed love—in the usual acceptation of that term. . . . The kashigi [men's house] has robbed the family of homelife—for the father
and son virtually live in the kashigi—not even being regular boarders
at what should be their home" (J. Kilbuck in Fienup-Riordan
1988d:19). In their contradictory evaluation of the Eskimos, although
individual Yupiit might merit respect, their way of life did not.

More distressing than the specific acts that their sense of right and
wrong condemned was what the Kilbucks took to be a lack of recognition by the Yupiit of the inherent evil of their actions. Edith wrote,
"The people are not vicious or dangerous in any way, but they continually practice so many of the evils found among uncivilized people
that it is shocking at times how little they think of the wrong there is
in it all. This is one more of our hard tasks, to get the people to *suffi-
ciently understand the vileness of sin* to leave off from doing it" (letter,
Mar. 20, 1888, MA).

Initially, the Yup'ik response to this condemnation was totally frustrating to the missionaries, striking them as duplicitous: "They may
say 'yes' and agree that it is all wrong, yet they will not give it up,
but only try to hide it from your view; and with this they are satisfied" (E. Kilbuck, letter, Mar. 20, 1888, MA). For the Yupiit, however,
verbal assent acknowledged respect for the speaker or recognition of
the speaker's power, not necessarily agreement. Behavior interpreted
as duplicitous was in some cases no more than a limited attempt to
be civil.

The Kilbucks were also grieved that initially they could not elicit
condemnation of their fellows from those who verbally expressed
agreement with them. Edith wrote, "Even those who have never done
such a deed and say it is wrong, think no less of those that do, and
treat them the same as other persons. . . . They think little or nothing
of the cruel deed itself, not even giving it a second thought" (letter,
Mar. 20, 1888, MA). This supposed indifference was more likely the
manifestation of the Yup'ik people's highly developed sense of personal responsibility and, the other side of the coin, of the inappropri-
ateness of direct interference with the actions of others.

Just as presumed indifference on the part of the Yupiit irritated the
Kilbucks, their own directness was incompatible with Yup'ik etiquette. John and Edith were blithely unaware that their own blunt
talk might appear "barbarous" to the Yupiit, and they did not hesitate to catch questioners in contradictions or to ridicule traditional
taboos by word and deed. While the Kilbucks' emphasis on personal
responsibility and lived faith was perceived as appropriate, their in-

terference, which the Kilbucks saw as saving the people from themselves, was not.

Another aspect of the "thunderous" nature of the Kilbucks that never lessened was their poor opinion of those who lacked their sense of the inherent value of work. They were extremely critical of what they took to be Yup'ik lethargy and lack of motivation. Edith's criticism of one of the schoolboys is an early example of this evaluative absolute: "Johnny has all the good intentions in the world but very little ambition to carry them out. He never does anything exactly bad, but will scarcely exert himself to do anything beyond what is daily required of him. To tell the truth, he is decidedly lazy" (letter Mar. 20, 1888, MA). Rather than being a reflection of natural passivity, the child's reserve may have been a culturally appropriate reaction to the decisive and opinionated character of the missionaries. In the beginning, especially, the Yupiit responded to the Kilbucks' thunder by watching and withholding active judgment. The Kilbucks in turn interpreted this reserve as "natural ignorance" and stupidity.[7]

Along with their perception of the barbarity, immorality, duplicity, and indifference of Yup'ik attitude and action, the Kilbucks also believed that the Yup'ik people were inordinately superstitious. This behavior was particularly frustrating as they saw no reason for it. To them, ritual acts of cleansing and purification, such as holding one's breath or averting one's gaze in particular contexts, were nonsense, and they taught strongly against them. In so doing they undercut the system of ideas of which the acts were but the visible manifestation.

The haircuts given to the children who came to the mission school provide a good example of such a battle. The Yupiit traditionally refrained from cutting a child's hair to provide protection from sickness, and they resisted the Kilbucks' insistence that young boys cut their hair before entering the mission school on the grounds that if they did so the boys would sicken and die:[8] "We have one boy . . . whom we had a task to get. . . . His mother would not agree because we would cut his long hair. . . . Whenever I came out she would shake her fist at me and say *don't you cut his hair; not one bit of it. I don't want him to die*" (E. Kilbuck, letter to her father, Aug. 14, 1888, MA).

The Kilbucks unremittingly condemned what they viewed as a groundless superstition connecting the cutting of hair with illness. Ironically, Edith voiced a reverse cultural logic, also couched in natural terms, to justify her own actions: "We have cut off [our daughter] Katie's hair. . . . She got rush of blood to the head and we thought best to have it short. . . . It was too long and heavy for a growing child to support. She did look sweet with it though" (letter to her father, May 12, 1889, MA).

Another example of a misunderstanding was the Kilbucks' response to the insistent request of Yup'ik traders from the coast that John drop what he was doing to trade with them immediately on their arrival. Although he usually complied, Edith deemed these requests uncalled-for impositions. In fact, Yup'ik etiquette required that a young man or woman (Edith and John were twenty-three and twenty-seven at the time) respond to the demands of their elders, regardless of how inconvenient from their point of view. What the Kilbucks perceived as unreasonable was probably no more than what common courtesy required.

The character of their enterprise limited the degree to which the Kilbucks could accurately interpret, let alone empathize with, the Yupiit as they found them. They are perhaps more impressive in the extent to which they described an increasing sympathy for, if not positive understanding of, the Yupiit. The whole of John's descriptive manuscript "Something about the Innuit" is characterized by this sympathy, which is a primary reason it remains valuable. For example, his comprehension of the traditional custom of wife-lending is remarkable for a member of the nineteenth-century American middle class, especially a missionary: "This is not promiscuously done—but two men may agree to do so—and thereafter hail each other by the title—Kathoon [*qatngun*, half sibling]" (Fienup-Riordan 1988d:18; see also Nelson 1899:292).[9]

Another example is John's description of the situation underlying the annual food shortage that plagued life along the Kuskokwim. Although not devoid of a certain patronizing tone, John's explanation is less biased than that of a number of his contemporaries who uncritically condemned all traditional ceremonial distributions because they were felt to provide the opportunity for "wasteful and wanton distribution" (Fienup-Riordan 1983:28).

There are, in the journals, passages that make particular Yup'ik people appear foolish, as when Edith described a woman holding a picture magazine upside down and then loudly blaming the senseless illustrations on the *kass'aq* author rather than the turn of her hands. However, both Edith and John wrote their observations in the same tone that they used to describe human failings in general. As deeply religious as they were, humanism increasingly transcended the evangelism of their early letters. Years later, their daughter Ruth recalled that the only time her father ever spanked her was as punishment for slapping a Yup'ik playmate (personal communication). Although the Yup'ik and the Kilbuck definitions of humanness remained disparate, that did not prevent a mutual respect.

The Response

As John and Edith's letters and journals reveal their feelings about the Yup'ik people, they also reveal the Yup'ik response to their presence. On their arrival, John noted an initial confusion: "The first work has been, to make them understand the object of our coming: that we have not come to trade with them, but to teach them. . . . The majority still believe that we are traders, and this in spite of our protestations to the contrary, and our absolutely refusing to buy their furs" (1886:473).

The separation between the spiritual and the material was much more than an issue of classification. Though their goal was to raise the standard of living of the people, the Kilbucks did not do so by giving goods directly as the traders might but by teaching a new attitude toward life in the present as well as in the hereafter. This issue was long standing. As late as 1895 the newly converted native helpers successfully played on the distinction between the traders' load of costly goods, which are soon gone, and the priests' spiritual load, which "never is lost, will not wear out" (J. Kilbuck, Box 5:13 MA).

Four years after their arrival, in the journal he wrote to Edith on his trip to Nushagak, John described how far from a trader he had come in Yup'ik eyes: "I now have learned why the natives believe that I belong to their country. Their supposition is that some one of their number was carried off on the ice, as it frequently happens, and that this man was rescued or landed among the white people and that I am his off-spring" (1890:57). Probably no higher compliment could have been paid John than the supposition of common descent. Yet it is not surprising. John Kilbuck was a full-blooded Delaware Indian raised on a Moravian mission in Kansas, and his dark complexion gave him a Yup'ik appearance. Also, his command of the Yup'ik language set him apart from white traders and explorers with whom the Yup'ik people had contact.

Nor did he stay at home during the winter but instead preferred to travel and visit. Traveling on his own and with a good knowledge of

FIGURE 4.1 John Kilbuck, 1897 (Courtesy Moravian Archives).

the language, John was able to see and hear things that helped him understand the significance of Yup'ik ideology and action in ways that a monolingual, stay-at-home missionary never could. Moreover, when he arrived in any village he was ready and willing to accept Yup'ik hospitality, bed and board included. In the same paragraph in which he described the Yup'ik claim of common descent John described his first taste of seal meat: "It was killed in the morning, so it was quite fresh. It was fine" (1890:57).

Edith attracted her share of notoriety. She was appalled when she learned of a rumor that described her as no less than common property of all the men on the Kuskokwim. The natives as well as the traders on the Yukon River circulated the rumor, and she expressed some, perhaps justified, concern that it would spread to San Francisco. Known as Suchdullera (*Sugtulria*, literally "one who is tall") because of her stately figure, she increasingly presided over the social life of Bethel, where visitors brought her small gifts of berries and fish and continually sought her out for aid and conversation.

In gifting, especially, the Yupiit tried to engage the young missionaries in their world and not without success. Even before they had seen their first change of season on the Kuskokwim, they were receiving tokens of hospitality: "An old man just came with a nice fish for a present. We get 'Pinchtamkins' (presents) nearly every day" (E. Kilbuck, journal to her father, Oct. 1, 1885, MA). When the children were born, the people asked gifts in their name. Joe Kilbuck, especially, served to pull his parents into the distribution process: "Little Joe snared his first ptarmigan today, and the natives clamour for a treat. . . . Ice cream and fish were dealt out and games were played" (E. Kilbuck, journal to her father, Feb. 1–2, 1895, MA).

Yup'ik parents also gave Edith gifts for her work on behalf of the schoolchildren. For instance, she received a wooden bowl in the winter of 1888 in thanks for making clothes for the schoolboys (journal to her father, Feb. 8, 1888, MA). Another time a woman made her a calico cap and said she must wear it because she was a married woman too: "They were much pleased when I wore it all day" (journal to her father, Dec. 1889, MA).

The degree to which the Kilbucks were pulled into traditional social exchanges is another way in which they distinguished themselves among their missionary cohorts. During their first years in Bethel, John, along with William Weinland, visited nearby villages especially to witness major ceremonial events. However, their early participation in and comprehension of these events were, by their

FIGURE 4.2 Edith Kilbuck and her daughter Katie, 1893 (Courtesy Moravian Archives).

own admission, minimal. At the end of the first year John (1886:473) wrote, "We have learned something about their religious belief, something about their customs, and their plays or eckeruschkas;[10] but as we are not quite satisfied with the information and desire to examine these subjects more carefully, we have decided not to write anything about them at present."

In the years that followed, as the missionaries began increasingly to understand the meaning of the ceremonies, they became openly critical. The missionaries rigorously suppressed overtly "pagan" ceremonies, including the Great Feast for the Dead (*Elriq*), the annual Bladder Festival (*Nakaciuq*), and the "Masquerade" (*Kelek*), as soon as they begn to awaken to their full implications.

At the same time that a handful of ceremonies came under heavy attack, other, less offensive, exchanges were spared. Both Edith and John wrote lively accounts of their participation in traditional exchanges during their early years in Bethel. John, especially, seemed

FIGURE 4.3 The Real People dancing in the late 1920s (from a film made by John Snow between Akiak and the mouth of the Kuskokwim River).

able to enter into the spirit of what he witnessed. At the end of a detailed description of the dramatic reception of guests at what was probably a Messenger Feast (*Kevgiq*), he wrote, "Somewhere in me, there must be some of the old Injun left, for I was strangely stirred, and I could not but help thinking of my forefathers, who not so many generations back, were such proud boasters. I think it is on this account, that I feel so drawn to these people, and helps me enter into their feelings" (journal to Edith, Aug. 30, 1897, MA).

Even in his declaration of personal identity with the natives, John's description was that of an observer. Edith's rendition of a *Petugtaq* exchange, however, is typically down to earth and describes in detail her family's part in the festivities:

> The present excitement is the friendship Ekrushica being held between our place and the Post. . . . Two nights ago Mr. Lind and the two men came over to present their gifts. . . . They placed everything in the kitchen then Wasca came in to me with a *large* grass mat, then went out and brought in a grass basket. Next time a large wooden dish, then four nicely dressed rabbits in another dish and last of all several lbs. of dried venison. Then came Kiackshack with grass mat, *very large* and fine, wooden dish, grass basket, another dish with four large whitefish in, (something rare for so late in the Fall) and dried venison. Mr. Lind gave me a pair of new deerskin boots. Katie two pr. of boots, a panful of cookies and a large piece of corned beef. Procopi gave me two small lap boards of use in fur sewing, a grass basket and a sealion skin and fresh fish. He bought the skin of Mr. Lind purposely for me. It is used for bootsoles, has a market value of $1.25. . . . Today I returned the giving. (journal to her father, Feb. 1889, MA)

John and Edith's descriptions testify to their family's early integration into community life, at least as far as the post and mission were concerned. When they understood the sexual exchanges associated with the exchange of gifts during *Petugtaq*, this event also came under attack. This revelation did not occur until 1896, however, by which time the Kilbucks had, to some extent, internalized the structure of Yup'ik gifting.[11]

John and Edith were most successful in their ability not to think but to act in Yup'ik ways. They took part in a number of vital cultural exchanges including speaking, eating, traveling, visiting, and gifting. Ironically perhaps, although the Kilbucks assumed that it was the

Christian character of these acts that won converts, it was their Yup'ik quality that gave them their efficacy. Insofar as they acted in a Yup'ik manner, their parishioners assumed that they were thinking in a Yup'ik manner as well and that their appropriate acts were the product of "appropriate" Yup'ik motivation. It would be many years before Christian charity and sacrifice in God's name would be understood as such. In the beginning, however, the Kilbucks' participation in Yup'ik meals, plays, and gift exchanges was likely the chief means by which they won both converts and respect.

Although they certainly never became Yup'ik, no more than the Yup'ik people became *kass'aq* under their tutelage, the cultural exchange the Kilbucks engaged in was impressive. John especially was able to participate in this exchange because of the ambiguity of his own background, which served over and over again as a bridge in the conversion process. In the winter of 1890 Edith was able to use John's background to translate her message concerning the value of education into comprehensible, if not acceptable, form:

> I explained to a houseful of them that John was taken away from his home and relatives in order to be educated, just as we wished to do with their children. White people did not kill or harm him and today he was thankful to them for what they did for him. This was news to most of them. They think he is *blood of their blood;* and love him accordingly but they had never thought anything about this past life. Some of them immediately said that it was foolish to be afraid of white people and object to send their children to school. I hope it *will* soften the parents hearts towards us a little. (journal to her father, July 1890, MA)

Over the years, both John and Edith became personally connected to the people among whom they worked. John acquired trading partners and regular hosts in a number of distant villages. As he continued to travel, he was increasingly grounded through gifts and formal social obligations: "At Crow village I met, what the natives call 'Ahla-nax-lux' [from *allaneq*, stranger] i.e. a stranger literally, but it really means, a stranger with whom you make a permanent friendship. Those holding this relationship always treat each other extra well, the best they can. I have three such relationships" (journal to Edith, Jan. 16, 1892, MA). Although Edith rarely traveled, she received a

FIGURE 4.4 Lily, the Yup'ik child the Kilbucks adopted, playing with her doll, Akiak, early 1900s (Courtesy Kilbuck Family).

constant flow of visitors, whom she increasingly valued until, in the summer of 1893, she could write:

> Nearly all the old neighbors have come to visit me. Women are here from eighty miles up the river. They help me out with sewing and I spend as much time with them as I can. The newer members of our party must often wonder why I leave the work that seems endless and sit and talk first in one tent and then in another. O, if they could only understand our conversations, if they loved these people and could talk, they would do just as I do, I am sure. (journal to her father, Aug. 29, 1893, MA)

In the spring of 1890, in response to a child's plea that she not leave on the annual trip to meet the supply ship at the mouth of the Kuskokwim, Edith voiced her commitment to remain among the "real people": "You can hardly realize how bound we feel to our work and how thoroughly one we are with our people. It is no light thing that will cause either one of us to leave" (letter to her father, Mar. 1890, MA).

As the Kilbucks became increasingly tied to their work along the Kuskokwim, their influence and stature among the Yup'ik people grew until their name became synonymous with that of the mission itself. In the fall of 1890 two white men traveled from the Yukon, where they had taken the census. At Bethel they told the missionaries that "the natives farther up the river had talked so much about the 'Kilbuchamuks' that they expected to meet another tribe, not known as yet. As the natives were only referring to those living about the mission station, they were disappointed" (Weber 1890:787). Not only had John and Edith received Yup'ik names, but their own surname was used to designate the small missionary band in the manner of a unique subgroup of "real people."

Selaviq: A Yup'ik Transformation of a Russian Orthodox Tradition

I don't see what the big deal is. They do the same thing at every house. They even eat the same food. (visitor to Kasigluk, 1989)

At each house, also, the children were given bags of candy. For three days, no one under the age of fourteen in the village ate anything else. . . . It was by far the most awesome, revolting, and chilling orgy of sugar consumption I'd ever seen. (Joe McGinniss, *Going to Extremes*, 115)

ANYONE WHO HAS LIVED IN WESTERN ALASKA HAS LIKELY heard about and sometimes been lucky enough to participate in *Selaviq*—the cross-cultural, ethnically diverse, and regionally unique celebration of Russian Orthodox Christmas. Most visitors to the festival probably are unprepared for the depth and richness of cultural elaboration that begins on January 7 and continues in full swing for the next ten days. Those unfamiliar with *Selaviq* are often perplexed by its repetitive form and sugar-laden content. Indeed, *Selaviq* makes no sense within the Protestant ethic, which values individuality and moderation over repetition and abundance. *Selaviq* is viewed alternately as a squandering of scarce and limited resources or as an unnecessarily tedious series of similar meals, and the cultural bounty and creativity that it embodies are often lost in translation.

The name *Selaviq* derives from the Russian *slava/slavit*, meaning praise or glory, and is at base a celebration of the birth of Christ through prayer and song. The event is also often referred to as "Starring" because of the large fabricated stars carried door-to-door in ceremonial procession. This Starring tradition originated in the Carpathian Mountains of the Ukraine in the sixteenth century as a grassroots response by Orthodox laity to the forced Latinization of the Russian Orthodox Church. The Starring songs and customs of the "Little Russians" were unknown in other parts of Russia and helped maintain a separate Orthodox identity in regions of western Russia occupied by Poland into the mid-twentieth century (Oleksa 1987:104). Ironically, *Selaviq* has placed aspects of this Slavonic tradition within a framework of Yup'ik interpretation and style to produce an event as central to the maintenance and expression of local identity as was its original.

Selaviq in Kasigluk

> Thy Nativity, O Christ Our God, hath arisen on the world as the light of knowledge, for at it those that served the stars were taught by a Star to worship Thee, the Sun of Righteousness. (Troparion (hymn) of the Nativity)

> The Magi journey with the Star; for our sakes he is born a little child. (Kontakion from the Orthodox Christmas liturgy)

Selaviq is celebrated in many Russian Orthodox communities throughout Alaska, including those in the Yukon-Kuskokwim Delta. Russian Orthodoxy is practiced in close to half the communities in the delta region (Figure 5.1). In the half dozen predominantly Orthodox villages, *Selaviq* marks the biggest ceremonial event of the entire year, a ritual distribution, community celebration, and religious holiday all rolled into one.

Russian Orthodox communities in western Alaska and elsewhere vary a great deal in how they celebrate *Selaviq*. Yet the basic form is the same. The celebration always begins on January 7, Christmas Day according to the Julian calendar.[1] On that day the faithful attend church. Following the service, they emerge from the church and begin a house-to-house processional following a large wooden star. At each house a song service is held, followed by a distribution of candy, food, and other gifts. Within this loose format, the variation is tremendous within as well as between Orthodox congregations.

One community in which *Selaviq* is celebrated is Kasigluk, a village of just over four hundred people located approximately thirty miles west of Bethel in the tundra region of western Alaska. Together with the people of nearby Nunapitchuk and Atmauthluak, the people of Kasigluk constitute the *Akulmiut* (from *akula*, land between two

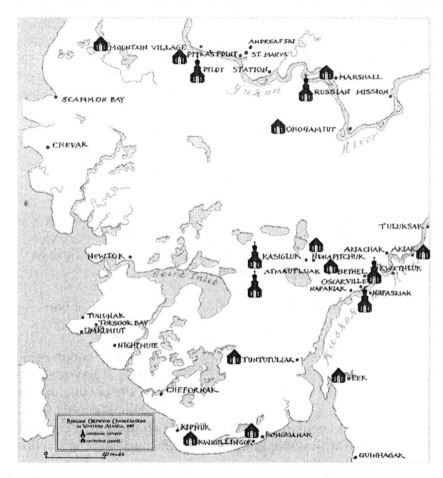

FIGURE 5.1 Russian Orthodox congregations in western Alaska, 1989.

topographical features), referring to their residence in the alluvial flats lying between the Kuskokwim and Yukon rivers.

The *Akulmiut* were visited sporadically by Orthodox priests from the mid-1800s, when Aleut-born Father Iakov Netsvetov served as the single ordained priest for the entire Yukon-Kuskokwim delta region (Black 1984a). Although a number of *Akulmiut* were baptized Orthodox prior to 1900, their geographical isolation meant that a priest visited them only infrequently. The Moravian missionaries who arrived in Bethel in 1885 judged the *Akulmiut* no more than "baptized heathens" and set to work to win their souls. Moravian efforts, however, were hampered by both the traditional shamans, who remained active in the area, as well as by the baptized Orthodox, who resented the Moravian efforts at social as well as spiritual transformation. Although the Moravians eventually won converts in the area, many *Akulmiut* clung to Orthodoxy as a "traditional" (meaning original and therefore "authentic") form of Christianity more compatible than Moravian theology with Yup'ik cosmology.

Selaviq has been celebrated in Kasigluk since the people moved from the old village of Nunacuarmiut in the early 1930s and built a Russian Orthodox church at the site.[2] Older villagers remember the introduction of *Selaviq* by Father Nicolai Epchook and Father Zakhary Guest,[3] who brought it down from Russian Mission, where it had been introduced by Father Zaharii Bel'kov in 1878 and reinforced by Father Iakov Korchinsky in the late 1800s.[4] Both these Orthodox priests were familiar with the *kolyadi*, or Ukrainian folk carols, composed in Eastern Europe hundreds of years ago and sung to celebrate Christmas.

Father Korchinsky was Ukrainian and as a boy had probably participated in the elaborate folk celebration of Christmas in his native land. In the Ukraine, a procession of carolers went from house to house carrying a long pole topped by a small star. In the center of the star was an icon of the Nativity illuminated by a candle. This Starring tradition continues to be practiced in some parts of the Ukraine to this day, including the area around Lvov, where the Stalinist suppression of church processionals did not occur.

Like its Alaska counterparts, Starring in the Ukraine varies considerably. In some areas, it is preceded by the Holy Supper on Christmas Eve. This meatless meal marks the end of the fasting before Christmas. Soft hay is laid down in the houses and the meal is served by candlelight in remembrance of the stable where Christ was born. An extra place is set at the table for the souls of the dead or should a stranger come to the door. As soon as the host sees the first star in the sky, he carries a bowl of boiled wheat around the house three times, reciting prayers. After returning to the house, he stands in the doorway and calls out to the souls of the ancestors to join the family at supper. When the meal is done, candies are strewn in the hay under the table for the children to find. The family then sings *kolyadi* in the home, after which they all go to church. The next morning the three-day, house-to-house caroling begins, during which only *kolyadi* are sung without church songs (Vaughn 1983:6–8).

In western Alaska, the Ukrainian celebration of the Holy Supper

did not take root. The Slavonic Starring and caroling traditions, however, were joined to Yup'ik hosting practices embodied in the traditional ceremonial cycle. The traditional Yup'ik ceremonies were
discouraged by the Russian priests in their pure form. Villagers recall, however, that from the 1930s the priests actively encouraged the
elaboration of *Selaviq*. In so doing, they prepared the way for its incorporation of Yup'ik ends and means.

When the *Akulmiut* first celebrated *Selaviq* after they settled at Kasigluk, it consisted of services at the new church followed by house-
to-house visiting for each of the three days of Russian Christmas
(January 7, 8, and 9). Every night the full congregation—men,
women, and children—entered each of the dozen village households
and sang Russian Orthodox hymns as well as Ukrainian Christmas
carols in both Yup'ik and Slavonic. According to Irvin Brink, Sr., the
hostess might sometimes give out pieces of dry fish, soup, and *akutaq*,
a traditional feast food consisting of berries, sugar, seal oil, and short-
ening. The families who had recently lost a close relative tended to
provide the most elaborate feasts.

Gradually, more and more families hosted the *Selaviq* singers with
food and drink. Occasionally, children were given small presents
such as a pair of grass socks, mittens, or a wooden bowl. When available, treats also included an apple or orange or a piece of bubblegum.
The villagers moved from house to house, alternately singing and eating, singing and eating. Over the years, the feasts involved more and
more food. Participants insisted, however, that no matter how much
they ate there was always room for more.

In the village of Kasigluk in January 1989, *Selaviq* began with
Christmas Eve services on the evening of the 6th and continued all
through the next week and into the following weekend. During that
time, all but a handful of village households were visited once and
two-thirds of the houses a second time. Each visit took up to three
hours, beginning with a song service after which candy and gifts were
passed out and 50 to 250 guests feasted. Out of consideration for village tradition, as well as to avoid students' sleeping through the day
on their desks, school closed for the entire week, and most non-native
teachers flew out of the village for a belated Christmas vacation.

The people of Kasigluk had been preparing for *Selaviq* since the
summer when they had netted and dried salmon and gathered berries to make *akutaq* for their guests. If a hunter took a moose in the
fall, he was careful to put by some of the meat for the *Selaviq* feast.

In early December, the church choir began regular practice for *Selaviq*. Choir members made handwritten copies of the numerous hymns and carols. Only a handful of the congregation, including the priest and the readers, knew the full meaning of the Slavonic songs. Yet they were faithfully transcribed and memorized by the dozen men and half dozen women who made up the church choir.

At the end of the month the congregation prepared the church for *Selaviq*. The church at Kasigluk is a simple, rectangular building divided into three parts:[5] the vestibule, which represents the world; the nave, in which the priests serve and the worshippers stand in attendance; and a smaller sanctuary, the holy of holies, separated from the body of the church by the iconostas ("image stand"), a partition screen adorned with icons (Figure 5.3).[6] As in other Orthodox communities, the sanctuary of the Kasigluk church faces east as a reminder that the Christian worshippers enter from the darkness of impiety into the light of truth. According to Orthodox theology, the true faith came from the east[7] as did the star announcing Christ's birth, and the rising of the sun symbolizes the coming of Christ.[8] Furthermore, the icons on the iconostas are arranged in a definite

FIGURE 5.2 Holy Trinity Russian Orthodox Church, Kasigluk (Courtesy Andris Slapinsh).

FIGURE 5.3 Father Alexie standing before the iconostas in the Kasigluk Russian Orthodox Church (Courtesy Andris Slapinsh).

pattern as a visual proclamation of the creed. In its entirety, the church building is itself an icon of the Kingdom (Oleksa 1987 : 76–77; Sokolof 1899 : 8–9).

To prepare the church for *Selaviq*, parishioners came together to clean the building and decorate it with tinsel, foil stars, and a Christmas tree with electric lights. They also unpacked and decorated the two large, wooden, five-pointed stars that would be the focal point of the house-to-house visiting to come. These stars, representing the Star of Bethlehem, were carefully placed in the sanctuary in the front of the church to await the celebration of *Selaviq*.[9]

Finally, the individual households got ready. Women brought dried fish in from their storehouses to be sorted and cut for the coming guests. By the first of January the ordinarily well-stocked shelves of the village corporation store were all but empty. Families purchased tremendous quantities of rice, tea, sugar, and flour, along with sides of reindeer meat, to feed their guests. They also took home small presents by the caseload for distribution, including gloves, socks, needles, pens, combs, and bars of soap. No less than thirty thousand dollars worth of candy had been purchased wholesale for the occasion, and each family spent as much as three thousand dollars in preparation for its part of the feasting. Thanks to the arrival of Alaska Permanent Fund dividend checks in December, even those families without steady cash income were able to host elaborate distributions in their homes.[10]

Selaviq at Kasigluk opened with a two-and-one-half-hour Christmas Eve service held at the church on the evening of January 6 and attended by some fifty men, women, and children. This elaborate service was punctuated by hymns and closed with a short sermon delivered in Yup'ik by the Eskimo priest, Father Phillip Alexie.[11] During the service, the choir stood at the right of the entrance with the men standing behind them, while the women stood on the left. The congregation remained on their feet throughout the entire service, except for a short time during the sermon when most sat on the floor.[12] Songs and chants were delivered alternately in Yup'ik, English, and Slavonic. At the end of the service families dispersed to their homes.[13]

As they left the church, the congregation filed past the adjoining graveyard, in which the Orthodox crosses marking the graves had been decorated with colored Christmas lights. These lights would be left on throughout *Selaviq* as would the lights of the church. In the not too distant past the graves had been lighted with candles and later with kerosene lanterns. Into the 1950s graveside prayers had marked both the beginning and end of *Selaviq*. This tradition has been replaced in Kasigluk by a single song service at the cemetery when the *Selaviq* ceremonial circuit has been completed.

The next day at 9 A.M., well before sunrise, more than one hundred people gathered for an elaborate three-hour Christmas morning communion service and divine liturgy. Married women came to church wearing brightly colored wool scarves,[14] sarafans (long dresses), and belts trailing colorful ribbons reminiscent of those traditionally worn in Russia. Young girls wore their hair in braids down their backs decorated with elaborate hair ribbons. Men were equally clean and neat, and one young boy wore a three-piece suit.

Worship during the service is designed to replicate worship in heaven, with hymns sung in the present tense. More than reenacting the glory of Christ's birth, the worshipers reexperience it. The Orthodox emphasis, both experiential as well as intellectual, is on the church as community, particularly among laity, where saints and sinners are interrelated. The dead buried in the adjoining churchyard are also included in this community: "Even in death the Christian remains a member of the living and resurrected Body of Christ, into which he has been incorporated through Baptism and the Eucharist" (Meyendorff 1979:199). During the Christmas service Christ and the saints are made present through the icons, and together the human and heavenly communities celebrate the glory of Christ's birth. Thus, for the congregation the Christmas service is not merely dry repetition of ritual but an encounter in which the ritual sacraments are dimensions of experience—opportunities for and places of engagement.

At the end of the service—during which songs and sermons alternated with chanted prayers—four young men brought the two stars and two icon banners from the sanctuary through the doors of the iconostas into the body of the church and presented them to the congregation. Each star represented the Star of Bethlehem. The lighted candles of the icon banners, each embroidered with an Orthodox cross, were to guide the procession announcing the birth of Christ. Just as the three kings followed the Star of Bethlehem to the place of Jesus' birth, so the *Selaviq* procession followed the ceremonial star during the celebration of Russian Christmas. Some people said that the star entering the houses was a symbol of Christ entering the homes of the people and being reborn in their souls.

Each star was two-and-a-half feet across and was hung from a thick strap worn round a young man's neck. At the star's center was a painted Nativity scene. Electric Christmas lights had been used to frame the Nativity, requiring the bearer to plug himself in at every house. During the song service in the church as well as in the individual houses, the bearer stood facing the congregation with downcast eyes. Throughout the service he kept the star spinning in a counter-clockwise direction to the right by regularly pushing a half dozen heavy metal balls weighting the star at its back. At the end of the service, during the singing of "Many Years,"[15] the motion of the star alternated between clockwise and counterclockwise. In the Dillingham area this alternation was said to signify pushing the old year away and bringing in the new year (Agibinik 1973:91).

As the stars and banners were held facing the congregation, the choir led the people in a series of songs and formal blessings that would be repeated in every household throughout the village. The song service opened with Russian Orthodox hymns sung in both Slavonic and Yup'ik. The hymns included the Gospel of St. Luke (2:1–20) and the Nativity Troparion and Kontakion, which together told the Christmas story. These were usually followed by the first, third, and ninth odes of the church canon and the Hymn of Light (Exapostelarion) from matins, which the choir normally sang in Yup'ik. Along with the hymns, Ukrainian *kolyadi*, or folk carols, were sung alternately in Ukrainian and in English; they included up to ten verses each (Oleksa 1987:355). The villagers consider the *kolyadi* and the Orthodox hymns equally "traditional"—that is, having to do with the unique oral history of the Yup'ik people. As is the case with their traditional tales (*qulirait*) and historical accounts (*qanemciit*), church members have passed them down orally by rote memorization "from their ancestors." Their "traditional" character notwithstanding, new *kolyadi* have recently been added to the village repertoire from commercial recordings of Ukrainian church music.

The song service closed with "Many Years" sung in Yup'ik, after which everyone said "Merry Christmas" in English. The star- and icon-bearers then led the congregation out of the church to the home of the village priest. There the company entered and repeated the song service. Again the star- and icon-bearers stood facing the congregation, directly in front of the icon corner of the house,[16] which the priest had illuminated with electric lights for the occasion.[17] Just as the world at large stands at the door of heaven in the entryway of the church, so the sacred icon corner places the "holy doors" of the iconostas within the home. As the church is a mirror of heaven, so the house is a mirror of the church.

At the end of the song service, Father Alexie delivered a short sermon, in which he gave thanks for Jesus' birth and welcomed his guests to his home. Similar sermons were given by either the host or one of the church readers following each individual household song service. These talks could last up to thirty minutes but were also sometimes quite short. Along with their twofold object of welcoming the guests to the feast and celebrating the birth of Christ, the sermons often contained references to the importance of following both the traditional Yup'ik moral code and the lessons Christ taught, speakers often playing on the overlap between the two.

Following the sermon the guests took seats anywhere they could. The narrow hallways were filled with company. When all who could be were seated, the host family began a careful and lengthy distribution of candy. The priest, his wife and daughters, and several of the altar boys each took a carton of candy and circulated through the rooms, giving the treats directly into the hands of the guests. In a large house full of a hundred people, this passing could take up to forty-five minutes, with each guest receiving a dozen different treats. Other households gave less, but all included a handful of Christmas hard candies that were, like the Ukrainian carols, considered a "traditional" ingredient of the event.

FIGURE 5.4 The *Selaviq* feast inside Father Alexie's home (Courtesy Andris Slapinsh).

After the candies had been passed, cakes with candles were presented to two of the members of the congregation with birthdays on Christmas Day, and the choir sang "Happy Birthday." The priest then blessed the feast with holy water and with the help of his wife and children began to pass out pieces of dried fish, bowls of moose and reindeer soup, and plates of *akutaq*. The older men and church readers seated themselves at the table and were served first, followed by the younger men. When all the men had been served, the women took their turn. The serving continued until both young and old were fed.

The people eating together in the house often included an even mix of villagers and out-of-town guests. Friends and relatives attending *Selaviq* at Kasigluk included people from near-by Nunapitchuk, Atmauthluak, Napaskiak, and Bethel. Guests also arrived by plane and snow machine from upriver and down the coast, including people from Akiachak, Lower Kalskag, Quinhagak, Eek, and Newtok. Many of those who came to visit for *Selaviq* were from Kasigluk originally but had since moved away. *Selaviq* was a time when they could visit

with old friends and family while participating in the Christmas celebration of their childhood.

Not only were out-of-towners welcome, but non-Orthodox guests
were also in abundance. Approximately 80 percent of Kasigluk's four
hundred residents are Russian Orthodox, yet almost the entire village participated in *Selaviq*. Not only did the non-Orthodox members
of the community attend *Selaviq* as guests, but they also hosted and
feasted the *Selaviq* procession in their own homes. Father Alexie emphasized that before the arrival of the Moravians all the *Akulmiut* had
been Russian Orthodox and that for this reason all were encouraged
to participate in the "traditional Yup'ik Christmas celebration."

Finally, as the last of the women finished their tea, one of the
church leaders put his head into the room to let them know it was
time to move the stars on to the next house. The star-bearers and
their companions carefully carried the stars and icon banners out of
the back bedroom where they had hung during the meal. Women and
children rose to follow the star out the door, where they were joined
by the men and boys who had gathered outside.

FIGURE 5.5 Following the *Selaviq* star at Kasigluk (Courtesy James H.
Barker).

After the initial three-hour feast at the priest's house, the congregation divided into two groups. The first group walked across the river and continued visiting the houses in the old village. The second group loaded its star into a station wagon and took it one mile downriver to Akula Heights, the site of the new village housing project. There they entered the home of the first reader of the church and began the service all over again.

As the *Selaviq* procession moved from house to house, the participants enjoyed variations on the initial feast. The song service might be shorter or longer, depending on which choir members were leading the singing and who was following. Although the order of the songs did not vary, the number included and the language in which they were sung did.

As a general rule, the procession was at its largest early in the afternoon and evening, and smaller late at night. The first night of *Selaviq* in Kasigluk in 1989 was a Saturday night, and the houses at both the old and new villages were packed to overflowing with as many as two hundred people each, including many guests from out of town. On Sunday night, however, the crowds thinned as weekend guests returned home. Later in the week, with the beginning of the second round, the crowds exceeded even the first night.

As *Selaviq* progressed, the feasting and gift-giving became increasingly sumptuous and elaborate. After the candy had been passed during the second round, the distribution of gifts, small and large, took place. Some households confined their giving to useful notions such as washcloths, gloves, or spools of thread, while others treated their guests, especially the children, to luxury goods, including toys and expensive clothing. On the last night, all the villagers and both the stars again met in a single house in the new village for the grande finale, in which the gift-giving outdid that on all the previous nights.

These elaborate gift distributions functioned as a system of wealth distribution, and a family's prestige and status were enhanced by its generous performance. Households vied with each other to see who could entertain the most guests. Villages also prided themselves on the number of days they required to complete their *Selaviq* circuit. Moreover, to host the final *Selaviq* feast was considered a great honor, as by custom the last house distributed the most gifts. Household income varies dramatically in western Alaska communities, depending on how many family members, if any, have full-time jobs or commercial fishing permits. The contemporary *Selaviq* distribution provides one of the few remaining opportunities for the equalization of these differences beyond the extended family throughout the community at large.

The foods served during the *Selaviq* feasts were as plentiful as the company. Together, the dried fish, boiled meat, and *akutaq* constituted a full-scale traditional Yup'ik feast, and the ingredients included the most prestigious as well as the most expensive and labor-intensive elements of the harvest. Some households gave out only candy, and for less well-to-do families this was acceptable. For a rich household, even a Moravian one, to do so was not, and the majority served the full feast. In the past the hosts fed their guests' dog teams as well. *Selaviq* is undeniably an occasion that feeds the body as well as the soul.

Ten days and over a hundred feasts later, the congregation returned to the cemetery, where they repeated the song service one last time. After the service, they returned the stars to the church, to be stored until the following year. The Christmas season closed several days later with the celebration of Epiphany on January 19. On that day the congregation ordinarily follows the priest in a procession to the river for the Great Blessing of the Water.[18] There the priest submerges the cross three times in the river through a cross-shaped hole cut in the ice. Then the people draw water from the hole, which becomes holy water with healing powers and is subsequently used to bless their homes, cure their sick, and preserve them from harm. In 1989 this final ceremony was not performed because of the extremely cold weather.

Since its introduction in Kasigluk more than fifty years ago, *Selaviq* has undergone many changes and will likely undergo many more in the years ahead. In the 1930s, when the population of Kasigluk was less than one hundred, the congregation traveled from house to house as a single group. When there were only a dozen houses, each could be visited by the entire congregation on each of the three nights of Russian Christmas. The village circuit would be completed by five or six o'clock in the morning, at which point the star would be returned to the church to await the next round. Children who fell asleep in one house were left behind as the procession moved on, to catch up later when they woke up.

As the village began to grow, so did the magnitude of *Selaviq*. By the early 1960s the number of houses and people in Kasigluk had doubled, as had the time it took to complete the *Selaviq* visitations. As a result, the people divided into two groups following two stars. The first group consisted of the children, who started at one end of the village and were given candy at each house. The second group included the adults, who ate a full feast in each home. By dividing the village, the people still managed to visit each house three times in three days.

By the 1970s the increasing number of houses made it difficult for participants to complete the full *Selaviq* cycle. One choir member remembered those as difficult years. With so many houses, and so much food, it was harder and harder to breathe and sing at the same time.

Although the magnitude of *Selaviq* became increasingly unmanageable, the conservative older generation resisted changing the way it was celebrated. In 1983, however, thirty-seven houses were built at the new downriver village site. With the number of houses doubled, it became impossible for all the people to visit each house three times in under a week. As a result the number of visits began to decrease. In 1989 fifty-nine of the village's sixty-seven households were visited once, forty-five of them a second time, and the third visit was eliminated altogether. Also the amount of time needed to complete the visitations dramatically increased. What had originally been a three-day celebration became a ten-day marathon of singing, feasting, and gift-giving.

As a result of the huge amount of time and resources necessary to host such a large number of people, local church leaders are presently considering cutting back *Selaviq* to a single visitation per house. Sentiment is divided however, as the second and third rounds customarily involve the most elaborate gifting and feasting. Though cognizant of the apparent impracticality of the full-fledged celebration and the degree to which it has grown out of its original form, villagers are equally proud of their capacity to host such a spectacular distribution. *Selaviq* is testimony to their ability to celebrate Christ's birth and their deep commitment to Christianity at the same time that they host their friends and relatives with an intensity reminiscent of that experienced in the elaborate ritual distributions of their ancestors. Both Christian and Yup'ik traditions are joined in this single, extraordinary celebration, the full enactment of which will be relinquished only reluctantly.

In the end the people of Kasigluk are open to changing *Selaviq* but only enough to allow it to remain essentially the same. This attitude is apparent in another current debate concerning the future of *Selaviq*. At present, there is some talk of changing church holidays to the

Gregorian calendar, in which case the celebration of Russian Christmas would be moved back to December 25 and Epiphany to January 6. Yup'ik Orthodox church members view this as a potentially positive alteration if and only if the *Selaviq* feasting still takes place during the first week in January. As they see it, if the lengthy Christmas services are moved into December, the *Selaviq* season will be even more open to elaboration than it now is. If the feasting were also moved back, however, ecumenical participation would be greatly hampered, as Protestant friends and relatives would be too busy with their own Christmas services to attend *Selaviq* as guests. Although the attendance of these guests is not essential to the Orthodox meaning of the event, the people of Kasigluk see total community participation as an indispensable ingredient to their "traditional Yup'ik Christmas celebration."

Nineteenth-Century Yup'ik Cosmology

The people of Kasigluk explicitly identify *Selaviq* with their past, both Yup'ik and Orthodox. Yet in practice it is a dynamic, new tradition, unlike any of its predecessors (Yup'ik, Russian, Ukrainian, or American) and more than the sum of its parts. Modified from decade to decade since its introduction fifty years ago, it remains a strong expression of the value placed on "the teachings of our ancestors" at the same time that it creatively reestablishes and reaffirms the integrity of the contemporary Yup'ik community.

Russian Orthodox ideas concerning the importance of the Nativity and Ukrainian ritual reenacting the original adoration have contributed essential parts to the celebration of *Selaviq* in western Alaska. Nineteenth-century Yup'ik ideas about how the world works are also embedded in the specific ways in which this particular Christian rite has been elaborated. Only after a careful look at Yup'ik cosmology can we begin to understand why *Selaviq*, and not Halloween or the Fourth of July, has become the focus of so much attention in western Alaska.

As we have seen in preceding chapters, the nineteenth-century Yup'ik Eskimos possessed specific ideas about how the human and animal worlds were constituted. They inscribed these ideas on the physical world, which they viewed as the concrete manifestation of their cosmology. Differences between men and women framed activities in everyday life and concepts about the sexually specific nature of the space in which these activities occurred. A major component of their annual ceremonial cycle was to transform these relations effectively so as to remake their world and their relationship to it.

For the nineteenth-century Yup'ik Eskimos, the men's house was the spiritual window of the community, surrounded by individual sod dwellings occupied primarily by women and children (Figure 5.6a). As the men's house dominated the center of the community, the younger members of both sexes regularly traveled the space between public center and private productive periphery. Young women and girls brought cooked food to their male relatives in the men's house, while young men swept porches and gathered water for their mothers and sisters. This normal social separation, however, was radically reversed during the winter ceremonials.

As indicated in Figure 5.6b, the winter village was only seasonally occupied. As soon as the ice began to break in the spring, residents of the large winter villages dispersed to the mountains and the coast, then to the river mouths for summer fishing, and later in the fall to the tundra sloughs and streams for trapping and freshwater fishing. With the approach of freeze-up, families returned to the winter village, bringing with them the stores that they had successfully harvested from the tundra and the sea. As in the daily cycle of movement between the men's and women's houses, the annual cycle of movement between the permanent winter village and small, dispersed seasonal camps was a loosely bounded movement between public ceremonial center and private production-oriented periphery.

The motif of successive levels of encompassment (a circle within a circle) apparent in the structure of daily life and movement in the world at large is also apparent in the Yup'ik conception of the universe. Figure 5.6c depicts traditional Yup'ik cosmology in cross section. The world was believed to have originally been thin and permeable and to have hardened since its creation by Raven (Nelson 1899:426). A person journeying far enough in any direction would eventually arrive at a point where the earth folded back up into the skyland, the home of the spirits of the game (Nelson 1899: 497–98). Not only was the earth encompassed by a canopy from above, but below its thin surface resided the spirits of the dead, both animal and human, each in separate villages. Four or five "steps" separated these two distinct but related domains. In cross section the human world can be seen to be encompassed by the spirit world, and the ceremo-

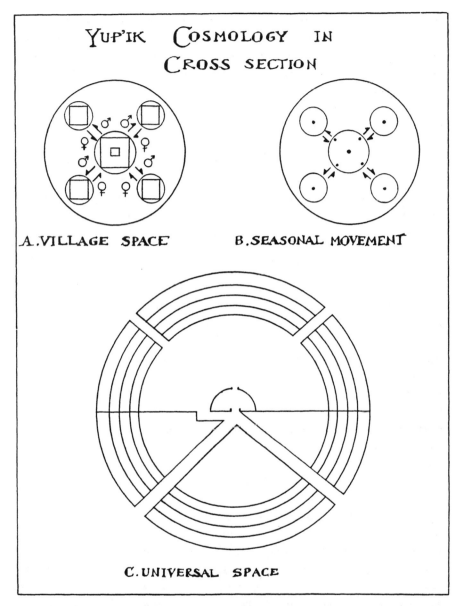

FIGURE 5.6 Yup'ik cosmology in cross section.

nial cycle was annually enacted to travel the distance between domains. If successful, such ritual activity had the power to re-create
the world anew.

In daily life, human action was controlled by the knowledge that
the eye of *Ella* (the universe) was watching and that human activity

was visible to the spirit world (see Chapter 3). For the Yup'ik people, comparable visibility of game (its appearance, disappearance, and hoped-for reappearance) was a central problem and one that their ritual activity directly addressed. In the ceremonies, ritualized movement reversed the rules and the rigorous separation between domains that daily life required. In so doing, the ceremonies powerfully re-created the passages between worlds as well as the power to see into and in some measure control them.

After freeze-up in November the people gathered in their winter villages to enjoy a "round of pleasure," which marked winter as the ceremonial season. Six major ceremonies were performed during this period, three of which focused on the creative reformation of the relationship between the human community and the spirit world. In these three ceremonies (the Bladder Festival, the Feast for the Dead, and the masked dances known as *Kelek*) members of the spirit world, including the human dead, were invited into the community. There men and women formally hosted them with huge feasts and gift distributions and finally sent them back out of the human domain. This ritual movement effectively re-created the relationship between the human and spirit worlds and placed each in the proper position to begin the year again.

Selaviq and the Nineteenth-Century Yup'ik Ceremonial Cycle

The nineteenth-century ceremonial cycle of the Yup'ik Eskimos was elaborate and complex, as was the view of the world that it embodied. The form and meaning of *Selaviq* as it is celebrated in western Alaska today are no less elaborate and complex. Orthodox priests also introduced *Selaviq* to Tlingit, Koniag, and Aleut converts, and it is widely practiced throughout Alaska to this day. Western Alaska, however, is unique in the degree to which *Selaviq* has been elaborated. What was it about the original *Selaviq* tradition that appealed to the Yup'ik sense of appropriate ritual form? The answer may in part relate to common themes present in Orthodox ritual, Ukrainian custom, and the nineteenth-century Yup'ik view of the world.

The history of *Selaviq* in western Alaska is at present only generally understood. We can, however, see striking points of articulation between the celebration of *Selaviq* in western Alaska today and the nineteenth-century Yup'ik ceremonial cycle. Understanding the ways in which this Christian ritual is performed in a decidedly Yup'ik manner can help us understand how and why *Selaviq* has acquired its present regal stature in the contemporary Yup'ik ceremonial cycle.

On the most general level, the feasting associated with *Selaviq* requires the same seasonal preparations that were such an important part of the traditional annual round—fishing, hunting, berry-gathering. Although the intensity of harvesting effort has diminished and the technology employed has been transformed, life in Kasigluk today continues to alternate between seasonal dispersal for harvesting activities and a winter pulling together at a central village site.

Just as *Selaviq* requires continuity in the annual seasonal cycle, it also reflects traditional social distinctions. In the past village space was divided between a central men's house and the individual women's houses that surrounded it. A woman's activity was directly tied to a man's ability to succeed as a hunter, and thus contact with women was carefully circumscribed. For example, women were secluded during their first menses and forbidden from participating in the major ceremonies while they were menstruating.

In Kasigluk, aspects of this division found confirmation in Orthodoxy as originally presented. For example, Russian Orthodoxy required married women to cover their heads in church, and men and women to occupy opposite sides of the church. Both these restrictions made sense in terms of the traditional Yup'ik sexual division and are followed to this day during the celebration of *Selaviq*. The separation of men from women and children in the individual houses during the *Selaviq* feast also replicates the separation of the sexes in the men's house during nineteenth-century ceremonial events.

Moreover, Russian Orthodoxy as practiced in western Alaska today prohibits women from attending church while they are menstruating and during the forty days after giving birth. These restrictions derive from the Old Testament requirement that no blood be shed in the temple where the "bloodless sacrifice" was offered (Oleksa 1987:367). This was a relatively minor point in Orthodox church doctrine and is not followed in most contemporary Orthodox congregations. What was insignificant in the Orthodox canon, however, remains a cardinal tenet of the faith in western Alaska. Despite assurances from Orthodox clergy that the prohibition against menstruating women has no doctrinal basis, Kasigluk matrons refuse to go beyond the church vestibule while they are menstruating. This spacial/sexual separation corresponds to the traditional Yup'ik belief that socially restricted contact with women is necessary to produce powerful supernatural vision and protection from the debilitating effects of unclean air. Conservative Yup'ik elders still ascribe to this proscription and view Orthodoxy as the preferable form of Christianity because of its accommodation of this facet of nineteenth-century Yup'ik cosmology.

Also, within the contemporary village a division continues to exist between the public male-dominated spiritual center and the private female-dominated secular periphery. According to one contemporary Orthodox priest, "If clergy and male readers have tended to dominate the public life of the church, matushki [priest's wives] and mothers have traditionally played the central role within the parish and nuclear family" (Oleksa 1987:367). Much has changed since the nineteenth century, when the central men's house was the focus of community life. Today the functions performed there are spread among the church, school, and community hall. Yet men still dominate in the church, just as women remain central in the home. Moreover, in the ritual circuit performed during *Selaviq*, the movement out of the church around the community and back dramatically reenacts the traditional ceremonial movement between public spiritual center and private productive periphery.[19]

In fact, a striking synchronism exists between Orthodox and traditional Yup'ik ritual activity in the importance given to the act of circling and the movement from center to periphery. Moving in a circle is an important part of a number of Russian Orthodox rituals. As part of an Orthodox wedding ceremony, for example, the couple walk in a circle around the inside of the church. The Yup'ik term for marry (*kassuute-*) derives from the base *kassug-* (to go around, to encompass), referring to the Russian rite. This circling is always to the right, signifying the sun's rising and Christ's coming.[20]

Formal ceremonial circuits were also an important part of traditional Yup'ik ritual activity and were often tied to spiritual power and the visibility of the spirit world (Chapter 3). For example, the Bladder Festival was in many areas preceded by a ceremony known as *Qaariitaaq*, during which the village boys had their bodies painted and were led for three to five successive nights from house to house, where the women gave them food. Through this ritual circuit, the children (perhaps representing spirits themselves) may have been figuratively "opening" the community to the spirit world.

Aaniq was held directly after *Qaariitaaq* and consisted of two older men—referred to as "mothers"—leading a group of boys around the village. The men collected newly made bowls filled with *akutaq* from the women, a dramatic reversal of the usual pattern of women bringing cooked meat to their men in the men's house. They were also sometimes given tea to drink in the houses, where the male "mothers" might sing a long song (Morrow 1984:118–123).

During *Selaviq* today, two young men lead villagers on a house-to-house circuit of the village, during which the members of the procession sing songs and are feasted on *akutaq* in individual homes. Although invested with a new, Christian meaning, this house-to-house feasting forms a striking parallel to the nineteenth-century ceremonial circuit. Although the contemporary division between church and home differs in important respects from that between the traditional men's and women's houses, in *Selaviq*, as in the traditional ceremonies, the profane, day-to-day gap is bridged by a sacred ceremonial circuit. As the traditional ritual circuit opened the Bladder Festival proper and perhaps marked the entry into the human community of members of the spirit world, so the *Selaviq* procession is said to open people's hearts to the spirit of Christ at the same time it announces his birth.

For the Yupiit as well as the Orthodox, the direction as well as the act of encircling is significant. Just as Orthodox ritual requires processional circuits of the altar and church, a number of nineteenth-century Yup'ik ceremonies involved the performance of a ritual circuit in the direction of the sun's course. For example, during the Bladder Festival young men ran around the village in the direction of the sun's course before entering the men's house bearing bunches of wild celery needed to purify the seals' bladders and to "let them see" the gifts of the people.

The spinning of the star during *Selaviq* is likely tied to these traditional ceremonial acts, both Yup'ik and Orthodox. In Eastern Europe, the star was held stationary; it is only in Alaska that the star is kept in motion. The ritual movement of the star around the village to mark the birth of Christ as well as the star's perpetual movement during its ritual circuit recall the efficacy of the traditional ritual act of encircling. It hardly seems accidental that when the star is put in motion in western Alaska, it is in the direction of the sun's course.[21]

In the celebration of *Selaviq*, we see change as well as continuity in the form and meaning of the traditional ritual process. As in the Bladder Festival, a ceremonial circuit ritually "opens" the human community and connects it to a larger spiritual reality. Both *Selaviq* and the Bladder Festival are opportunities for encounter through which the spirit world is made manifest. Although the movement of human participants in the ceremonies preceding the Bladder Festival and during *Selaviq* is comparable, the movement of spiritual participants is reversed. The traditional ritual circuits were initiated when the spirits were drawn into the community and were closed by sending them back out of the human world. In contrast, the sacred *Selaviq* star, housed in the church during the year, is moved in ceremonial procession from spiritual center out into the world at large and back to spiritual center. The traditional spirit world surrounded and was external to the human world. Christianity figuratively "tamed" that external reality and housed it in the church, in the center of the human community. Although the extraordinary power of the divine was not eliminated, it was, in essential ways, domesticated.

This spiritual domestication is also reflected in the treatment of the human dead. Whereas the nineteenth-century Yup'ik Eskimos buried their dead at the edge of the village, at the boundary of the world of the living, the Orthodox cemetery surrounds the church, signifying that the dead who have been true to the church in life are sheltered by her in death. The human dead are no longer viewed as dangerous to the human community but inhabit its very center.

Differences between the meaning of the traditional Bladder Festival and the meaning of *Selaviq* follow from the transformation of spirituality from an external to an internal reality. Whereas the drumming and singing performed in the *qasgiq* during the Bladder Festival worked to "draw" the animal spirits, the *Selaviq* caroling glorifies God and his son and extends this praise outside the church into each home. The Christian pantheon is felt to possess a spiritual perfection that humans can seek yet never attain. Thus *Selaviq* is performed for the glory of an almighty God. In contrast, the traditional Bladder Festival strove to influence the animal spirits and to elicit good hunting during the following year.

Nineteenth-century Yup'ik ceremonies were "sexy" events, both in the sense of being essential for the generation of future life and in the imagery of birth and rebirth that the ceremonial process embodied. Christian iconography, with its emphasis on the immaculate conception and the virgin birth, does not share this generative focus. God is viewed as eternal life, all powerful and all encompassing. In this sense he is unlike the human and nonhuman spirits who were traditionally conceived as interacting with living men and women to produce life. Yet in *Selaviq*, Yup'ik participants employ traditional generative acts, including a ritual circuit involving elaborate feasting and gifting, to celebrate the Christian miracle of Christ's birth. In this way, they have in part transformed what was introduced to transform them.

Along with continuity in the annual movement between ceremonial center and productive periphery as a means of spiritually "opening" the human community, a number of other formal parallels exist between the nineteenth-century Bladder Festival and the contemporary celebration of *Selaviq*. Just as the Bladder Festival opened the traditional winter ceremonial season, so *Selaviq* is the first major Orthodox ritual, followed by the celebration of Russian New Year, the Epiphany, and finally Paskha, or Easter. Also, like the Bladder Festival, *Selaviq* is an enjoyable, festive celebration, during which food replaces famine and light replaces dark. Even the electric Christmas lights kept burning in the church and on the graves outside during *Selaviq* are reminiscent of the lights kept burning night and day in the men's house during the traditional Bladder Festival.

During the Bladder Festival, the men's house and its residents were ritually purified by repeated sweat baths as well as by the smoke from wild celery. The people set routine activities aside and devoted their days to athletic competitions and instruction in the men's house as well as to the presentation of special feast foods. During *Selaviq* participants still regularly employ sweat baths to cleanse and relax their bodies, while the priest purifies worshipers with incense during church services. Likewise they give over the days of *Selaviq* to extraordinary activities, including long sermons both in the church and in the individual houses. Finally, just as men and women circumscribed their activity in the presence of the bladders of dead seals during the Bladder Festival, today they forgo smoking and drinking in the presence of the star.

On the last night of the Bladder Festival, the entire village as well as invited guests from nearby villages gathered in the men's house. Parents gave gifts to celebrate their children's accomplishments, and a huge villagewide distribution took place in which large amounts of frozen and dried fish were given away. The gifts and food distributed during the final days of *Selaviq* today in some measure keep this tradition alive.

The Bladder Festival ended with a ceremony at the ice hole where the bladders containing the souls of seals killed during the previous year were returned to be reborn in the year to come. This ceremonial conclusion of the Bladder Festival has a formal parallel in the gathering of the Orthodox congregation around the ice hole at the close of the Christmas season to celebrate the Epiphany on January 19. Instead of placing bladders under the ice, the priest blesses the water with the cross by dipping it into the water and then blesses the people with the newly consecrated water. Although the meaning of the closing ceremony has been altered from the regeneration of the hunted to the reentry into the worshipers of the spirit of Christ, a striking formal similarity remains. We may never know precisely how the nineteenth-century Yupiit reacted to the Epiphany ritual when they first observed it. It is likely, however, that their comprehension of the act of immersion as spiritually powerful helped them to translate what they saw.

The Bladder Festival is not the only nineteenth-century Yup'ik ceremony that has given meaning to the contemporary celebration of *Selaviq*. *Selaviq* also relates to the traditional Yup'ik Feast for the Dead (*Merr'aq* from *meq*, water, *mer-*, to drink). This annual event was the public occasion on which the spirits of the human dead were invited into the community to receive the fresh water, food, and clothing they required. Men initiated the event by placing stakes at the graveside, effectively "opening" the village and inviting the spirits to enter as in the ceremonies prior to the Bladder Festival. As in the Bladder Festival, the village was ritually cleansed in preparation for the arrival of the spirits. Moreover, the people took great care during the ceremonial period to limit any human activity (such as sewing or chopping wood) that might injure or "cut" the souls during their journey to and from the center of the human world. They also carefully covered open bowls to prevent the spirits from entering and getting lost.

The contemporary celebration of *Selaviq* likewise involves ritual acts performed to appease the spirits of the ancestors who participants believe are present during the event. For example, many Russian Orthodox households in Kasigluk today neither sew nor chop wood during *Selaviq*. Just as people covered bowls in the past, today they drape television sets with cloth. For many younger villagers, the detailed beliefs surrounding these activities have faded, and the prohibitions remain in effect for the sake of "tradition," because that is the way it has always been. For older villagers, however, *Selaviq* observations are meaningful acts tied to still-vital pre-Christian views of the relationship between the living and the dead.

During *Merr'aq*, as well as the Great Feast for the Dead (*Elriq*) held at five- to ten-year intervals, participants held that the feeding and clothing of the namesakes of the deceased fed and clothed the dead as well. *Selaviq* continues this tradition of honoring children, in whom the ancestors are in some essential way believed to live again. Today in western Alaska, parents continue to name children for those who have recently passed away. During the distributions attending *Selaviq*, adults often address children according to the speakers' relationship to the deceased for whom the children have been named and give them special gifts in honor of their namesakes. Some spiritual essence continues to be passed on with the name and in an important way the dead are believed to live again through their namesakes.

The Yup'ik belief in spiritual rebirth ties into a special aspect of *Selaviq*—the capacity of guests to repeatedly feast yet never get full. According to Yup'ik tradition, the dead suffer from tremendous hunger and thirst. Even people who no longer hold this belief may still cite it to explain the custom of feasting during *Selaviq*. Today when asked why they never get full during the *Selaviq* feasts, elder villagers say that it is because when they eat they are feeding the insatiable spirits of the dead. Moreover, just as the Ukrainians set a place at the table for the ancestors and a candle in the window to light their way, the windows of Yup'ik homes are typically left uncovered during *Selaviq* to admit the spirits of the departed to the feast.[22] Many modern Christian Yup'ik men and women retain in some measure their belief in the cycling of souls that characterized nineteenth-century Yup'ik cosmology. Russian Orthodox ritual symbolism and eschatology (for example, the belief that the dead are forever present among the community of the living) allowed their Yup'ik converts to become Christians at the same time that they continued to view the world from a pre-Christian point of view.

Along with the capacity to consume huge amounts of food, the contemporary practice of distributing thousands of dollars worth of candy and gifts also relates directly to nineteenth-century Yup'ik ceremonial activity. Traditional ceremonies involved the distribution of tremendous quantities of goods, and the most valuable gifts were often given to the youngest children who were, by name, their ancestors incarnate.

The early missionaries, both Moravian and Russian Orthodox, who worked along the Kuskokwim were appalled by the amount of goods distributed during traditional ceremonies and the resulting impoverishment of the host village. Like the Western observers of *Selaviq* quoted at the opening of this chapter, they found this lack of economy more reprehensible than the ideology that motivated it. For the Yup'ik people the elaborate distribution and display of the bounty of the harvest during the Bladder Festival, the Feast for the Dead, and other traditional ceremonies provided a clear statement to the spirits of dead humans and animals alike that right had been done by them and that the human world was ready to receive them anew. The close relationship between the living and the dead was a central feature of traditional Yup'ik cosmology and has left its mark on the Yup'ik comprehension of contemporary Christian ritual.

Instead of using money and store goods in a conservative Western way—for example, by accumulating capital and investing profits— the Yup'ik people annually continue to disperse large quantities of hard-earned goods. Like the seal parties hosted by Nelson Island women (Chapter 2), the outstanding feature of *Selaviq* is its transformation of Western "stuff" and material wealth into a statement of community. Such stupendous generosity is almost incomprehensible to Westerner observers. To them, *Selaviq* appears to do little more than provide everybody with a multitude of free meals and countless sacks of candy. At the most it may be viewed as a parochial expression of social stratification insofar as houses differ in how much they give.

In sum, both contemporary *Selaviq* and nineteenth-century Yup'ik ceremonies focus on annual spiritual renewal and rebirth. Both are built around the ritualized dramatization of inherent conflicts or oppositions, including feast-famine, light-dark, birth-rebirth, and center-periphery. The referent has changed, from the renewal of game and seasonal rebirth to the birth of Christ and the salvation of mankind. Yet the feasting and gift-giving that attend *Selaviq* do not affirm the dominance of the mission system and its attendant moral and social order over the traditional Yup'ik view of the world—they signify instead their consenting union. *Selaviq* demonstrates a predominant renewal motif that is based on subthematic oppositions like those found in both the Russian Orthodox and nineteenth-century Yup'ik ceremonial cycles. Far from reflecting the primacy of the Christian mission, *Selaviq*, in its historical roots, is as much Yup'ik as Orthodox.

During *Selaviq* native parishioners have the opportunity to host their community, both the living and the dead, in a decidedly Yup'ik manner. As among the Tlingit (Kan 1987b:50), the openness of Orthodoxy to pre-Christian interpretation may have provided the original attraction to the more conservative natives for whom traditional prestige and status through elaborate ritual distributions remained important. Moreover the parallels between the nineteenth-century Yup'ik and Russian Orthodox cosmologies may in part explain the special appeal of Orthodoxy to the more conservative members of the Yup'ik community today. In fact, the Orthodox church in western Alaska has been able to retain considerable loyalty despite meager financial resources and active competition from both Catholic and Protestant missionaries beginning in the late 1800s.

Yup'ik participants in *Selaviq* today differ in the extent to which they interpret Orthodox ritual acts in traditional Yup'ik terms. Whereas elderly villagers may view the endless feasting that attends *Selaviq* as actually feeding their ancestors incarnate in the youngest guests, younger villagers view the celebration more as a remembrance. These younger villagers often do not recognize the Yup'ik origin of many of the features of *Selaviq*, but they refer to it as a "native" event. They have made the Orthodox Starring tradition indigenous and from it created a celebration that enacts what it means, in their eyes, to be Yup'ik.

In the celebration of *Selaviq* in Kasigluk today, multiple pasts collide, coexist, and interact in the present. Russian Orthodox, Ukrainian, American, and indigenous systems of knowledge and practice all contribute to the event that the Yup'ik people of western Alaska have constructed and continue to modify as a new Yup'ik "tradition." Unlike the Nelson Islanders described in Chapter 2, who have retained highly charged nineteenth-century Yup'ik ritual distributions outside the Christian denomination (Catholicism) they have embraced, the Yup'ik Orthodox have Christianized traditional distributions to create a new vehicle for old meanings.

Many non-natives consider *Selaviq* to be primarily a Russian Orthodox tradition because of its focus on Christmas and its reliance on Orthodox liturgical and Ukrainian folk traditions. Today in Kasigluk, however, Yup'ik Eskimos understand *Selaviq* as an important part of their own history, which includes but is by no means controlled by their interaction with Russian Orthodox clergy. In fact, many people in Kasigluk view their church as the repository of traditional Yup'ik values. The songs they sing, whether in Slavonic or Yup'ik, have been passed down "from their ancestors." Moreover the intra- and inter-village feasting involving both native and non-native people from all over the region is recognized as an essentially Yup'ik celebration. In this sense, *Selaviq* is a cultural celebration in which everybody participates—Russian Orthodox, Protestant, native, and white. Far from being the corruption of a Russian tradition or the manifestation of a secularized or compromised Yup'ik tradition, *Selaviq* retains communion and feasting in a sacred ritual context. For the nineteenth-century Yupiit, communal feasting was a spiritually significant act, and in the form of *Selaviq* it continues so to this day.

Part Three

The Eskimo Image

*P*art of my effort over the last decade has been to increase my understanding of Yup'ik history and cosmology. Every time I explored an issue, I found discrepancies between what Yup'ik people said about themselves, what had been written about them, and what non-native people in Alaska believed to be true. This dangerous disjunction between what non-natives say about Eskimos and what Yup'ik Eskimos say about themselves is the focus of the final five chapters.

The "problem" of the following pages is the discrepancy between the popular image of Eskimos and "real" Yup'ik people—not only as they are today, but as they were in the past. Why have Euro-Americans pictured Eskimos in the way they have? And what are they really like? These questions cannot be answered naively. Early written reports on the Yup'ik Eskimos are sketchy at best and often tell us more about the men and women who authored them than about the people whom they purport to describe. Current testimony by the Yupiit themselves on their history is also often biased—an ideal view framing their past in an effort to affect the present.

Although there is no easy way to answer these questions, evidence can be presented to cast doubt on the simplistic image that has been created of "the Eskimo." Some of the reasons for the creation of that special image can also be found. In this sense these chapters are self-examining—they reveal not only something about Eskimos but also something about "us" and "our interest" in Eskimos. The anthropology of indigenous peoples rarely fails to tell us something about ourselves, and these pages are no exception.

There is a chronology to our ideas about Eskimos (Chapter 1). There is also a perpetual opposition at any one point in time—Eskimos simultaneously viewed as noble and base. Conflict causes the contradictions in our images of Eskimos to surface. For example, Eskimo tradition is seen as noble and pure when dramatically carved masks are hung on the walls of a museum exhibition hall. When confronted in courts or in meeting rooms during testimony on the rights of sport hunters versus those of subsistence users, the modern Eskimo is viewed less as the "noble savage" and more as an impoverished white man. Claims to a special relationship to the land are perceived as a threat, both to the rights of individual non-natives and to the notions of democracy and equality enshrined in the American way.

It is especially important to reconsider our ideas about Eskimos because of the immense impact these ideas have on the indigenous peoples of Alaska today. Our ideas about Eskimos help create the framework they are forced to reside in. To the extent that non-natives continue to have an ideal image of Eskimos, however complimentary, real comprehension of essential differences between the Western and Yup'ik views of the world cannot take place.

Robert Redford, Apanuugpak, and the Invention of Tradition

A PROJECT IS CURRENTLY UNDER way to produce a full-length feature film in the western Alaska village of Toksook Bay on Nelson Island. The screenplay, appropriately enough, focuses on a traditional hero—Apanuugpak—and epic tales of bow-and-arrow warfare that are still very much a part of the oral tradition of the Yup'ik Eskimos who make Nelson Island their home. There are, however, discrepancies between Yup'ik history as it can be read from oral tradition and as both the scriptwriter and the people of Toksook Bay choose to present it in the film. These discrepancies relate to both the making and the marketing of tradition, on Nelson Island and beyond.

The current rethinking of ethnographic inquiry has focused on the need for anthropological writing to reflect the dialogic character of ethnographic interaction. It follows that the dialogic character of other native/non-native encounters also merits scrutiny. Far from reducing the ethnographic enterprise to fiction, the current reevaluation of the role of the ethnographer lends support to the development of a more critical view of situations of cross-cultural exchange already under way.

My acquaintance with the Apanuugpak film project began in the summer of 1985, when I was living at Toksook Bay working on an oral history project sponsored by the Toksook Bay City Council, a project intended to help villagers record their history.[1] While sharing tea and conversation with friends, I was told that Robert Redford was coming to Toksook to play the part of the famous warrior Apanuugpak in a film that was to be made on Nelson Island in the near future. People proudly announced that this film would soon air on one of the fourteen cable channels that had recently been made available in the community. A standing joke soon developed. Every time we heard a plane pass over (which was often), friends teased that I should hurry and put on lipstick, dress up, and run over to the airport. There I

125

would be the first to greet Mr. Redford, take the part of Mrs. Apanuugpak, and what a fine film that would be!

The apparently farfetched juxtaposition of Robert Redford and Apanuugpak that provided the material for so many jokes that summer had a factual basis and already a very interesting history. The idea for a film based on the Apanuugpak stories was the brainchild of Dave Hunsaker, a Juneau playwright who first came to Nelson Island in 1984 seeking support for a play he had written entitled *Inuit Antigone*. This play was an English adaptation of Sophocles' Greek drama into an Eskimolike genre. Hunsaker was searching for native actors for the production. He met with the Toksook Bay City Council and received their approval of his project with two conditions. The first was that the title of the production be changed from *Inuit* to *Yup'ik Antigone*. The second was that the play be performed in the Yup'ik language.

Yup'ik Antigone was well received from Bethel to New York City and eventually all the way to Greece. The farther the troop traveled from home, the more exotic they appeared. The critical acclaim given to the play was simultaneously refreshing and revealing. The most impressive feature of *Yup'ik Antigone* was not the success of its international debut but the local enthusiasm it engendered. Applause was loudest closest to home. Nelson Islanders clearly enjoyed their introduction to Sophocles. The local production in the village high school was the first masked performance on the island since the missionaries' suppression of indigenous ceremony forty years before. Village elders both approved of and admired the dramatic staging, which shared elements with their traditional performance style.

Although the local enthusiasm *Yup'ik Antigone* elicited is commendable, it was not a factor in the response of the non-native audience. In the final analysis, the rave reviews the play received are telling examples of our Western objectification of culture and the fact that we are for the most part willing to take the other only on our terms—that is, translated through the Greeks. The play was constructed on the flawed assumption of a fundamental similarity between the Yup'ik Eskimos and the ancient Greeks. The face-to-face parent/child confrontations central to Sophocles' *Antigone* illustrate how different these two views of the world are. The Yup'ik pattern of conflict resolution prescribes both diffusion and extreme care in order not to injure the "mind" of the offender (Fienup-Riordan 1986a). One actor later commented on how embarrassed he was by so much "scolding" in the production. Another observer pointed out that a Yup'ik translation of an Italian sex comedy, with all its banter and innuendo, would have been culturally more appropriate than this translation of a Greek tragedy. While bestowing their applause, most of the audience persisted in using the Yup'ik people to define themselves and then concluded that they had witnessed a cultural universal.

Although supportive of *Yup'ik Antigone* and the sympathy it generated for Eskimo people, Nelson Islanders criticized its conflation of Yup'ik and Greek tradition. Villagers maintained that if Hunsaker wanted to produce a really fine play, he should forsake Greek drama and look to Yup'ik oral tradition. Hunsaker was receptive, and soon after *Yup'ik Antigone* completed its foreign tour, he visited Nelson Island to start work on a new production.

The stories that emerged as best suited for such a transformation were those concerning Apanuugpak, the famous warrior-hero of Nelson Island. Dealing as they do with the period of bow-and-arrow warfare in Yup'ik oral tradition, they are full of action and adventure and seemed ideally suited to the production Hunsaker and his Yup'ik co-workers had in mind. In Yup'ik narrative tradition, the Apanuugpak stories form but one set within a larger group of stories concerning the period of bow-and-arrow warfare in western Alaska during the seventeenth and eighteenth centuries. These stories can be divided roughly into four major sets, each pertaining to a different group of regional confrontations. They include the longstanding dispute between the people of Pastolik, at the mouth of the Yukon Delta, and the coastal people around Hooper Bay; the hostility separating the inhabitants of the lower coast and those of modern Quinhagak; confrontations between the lower Kuskokwim Eskimos (*Aglurmiut*) and the people of the middle Kuskokwim living near modern Kalskag; and, finally, the historic animosity between the people of the Kuskokwim drainage and the residents of Nunivak Island.

Aside from scattered references (Michael 1967:281; Nelson 1899: 327–330), nineteenth-century explorers and ethnographers largely ignored evidence of Eskimo warfare, content to foster the stereotype of Eskimos as never hostile, not to mention warlike. Not until recently have the details of their bloody feuds and battles come into focus for outside investigators (Burch 1974; Burch and Correll 1972; Fienup-Riordan 1984a; VanStone 1967; VanStone and Goddard 1981). For the local population these dramatic orations have been a staple of narrative tradition for at least 150 years and probably much longer. The turn-of-the-century Moravian missionary John Kilbuck was among the first to record accounts of all the major confrontations (Fienup-Riordan 1988d:32–34, 43–50, 390–392). Moreover, contemporary oral accounts still exist concerning specific battles won and lost in all four of these major "wars" (for example, Fienup-Riordan 1986b:359–365).

Within this elaborate oral tradition stories of the exploits of the warrior-hero Apanuugpak, defender of Nelson Island, are told up and down the coast of western Alaska from Dillingham in the south all the way to Nelson Island and beyond. Depending on where the stories are recorded, Apanuugpak is depicted as a villain or a hero. In the Togiak area he is said to have been so powerful that no warrior could stand up to him. To protect themselves the Togiak people employed a powerful shaman to put a curse on Apanuugpak. As a result, on his return from a raid in the Togiak area, it is said that he was turned into a rock, which can still be seen when sailing along the coast.

For the people of Nelson Island, however, Apanuugpak is the embodiment of all that is powerful and cunning in a warrior. From his infancy, he is said to have been trained by his grandfather to be tough and strong. Stories recount the strict regimen of his youth, the storyteller often opposing this upbringing to the easy time young people have today. According to oral accounts, his grandfather would wake him up early every morning and have·him run to the top of Nelson Island. On his return he would be given only one drop of water from the tip of the feather of a snowy owl to quench his thirst. Similarly, he was taken down to the beach every day and told to roll naked over mussel shells to toughen both his body and his mind.

Along with numerous stories concerning the rigors of Apanuugpak's training, other tales recount his exploits. In all these Apanuugpak emerges victorious by virtue of superior strength, courage, and ingenuity. The hallmark of his cunning is the mussel-shell armor that he wore under his parka, which rendered useless the arrows of his enemies. This "secret weapon" so annoyed his antagonists that, in one account, an opponent is said to have cried out in frustration, "Where in tarnation can we hit this Apanuugpak so that the arrow head can find its deadly mark?" To this, Apanuugpak answered, "Your arrows do not hit my body. Rather they land on the beaches at Engel'umiut!", referring enigmatically to the mussel shells that protected him (Billy Lincoln, Jan. 26, 1987, NI).

Significantly, the Yup'ik Eskimos categorize the Apanuugpak stories as historical narratives (qanemcit) rather than mythical tales (qulirat). Whereas the narratives are grounded in the experience of a particular person, whether that person is living or dead, the tales are part of the experience of ancient ancestors and never involve particular individuals definitely believed to have existed. In the 1980s the Yup'ik people became more interested in recording and transcribing, although not necessarily translating, both literary genres.

This interest is part of a growing general self-consciousness in western Alaska brought on by intense efforts at cultural conversion, including new and often commercial interests in their traditional dances, carving, and storytelling. During the last decade Nelson Island has been the focus of a great deal of attention from outside writers, photographers, filmmakers, ornithologists, fish biologists, archaeologists, bureaucrats, and cultural anthropologists. Public hearings, held on an almost weekly basis, regularly confront villagers with the responsibility of reacting to proposed developments and changes in the regulatory systems that increasingly constrain their lives. In the face of this massive and unprecedented inquiry, some Nelson Islanders may view their past as inadequate to vindicate present positions. As a result, many are in the process of inventing a new past to meet the situation. At least some view Hunsaker's project as a vehicle for such re-creation. For both natives and non-natives, the dramatization of history becomes a viable mechanism for distancing oneself from the distress of the current political situation, albeit in different ways.

As the project gained momentum during the winter of 1985, Hunsaker spent several weeks on Nelson Island listening to English glosses on a multitude of different versions of the Apanuugpak stories. To reduce confusion the village council advised him to work with only one village elder (Billy Lincoln) and to develop his script primarily from Lincoln's version of the narratives in Yup'ik. A translator accompanied him, and through him Hunsaker heard the tales. Hunsaker was also able to ask Billy Lincoln questions about what he had heard, and he made notes. No detailed transcriptions or translations were made of the interviews. Although the film was to be based on the oral traditions, it was not intended to be a precise enactment of them.

Notes in hand, Hunsaker returned to Juneau, where he wrote a screenplay entitled *Winter Warrior*. He created a storyboard for the film, scene by scene. Several months later, Hunsaker took this picture sequence back to Nelson Island for review. Again he visited Billy Lincoln, to whom he showed the drawings. Through an interpreter Lincoln approved the script. The process was one of negotiation, not simple acceptance, as exemplified by one proposed scene that

Hunsaker agreed to strike early in the going. Significantly, the scene depicted Apanuugpak's opponent confronting him with a gun. Here Hunsaker was attempting a commentary on the devastation and imbalance of power wrought by Alaska natives' acquisition of elements of Western technology. However, given the fact that oral tradition places Apanuugpak before the arrival of the first *kass'aq*, or white man, in western Alaska, Lincoln found the gun unacceptable.

The screenplay takes on a new dimension from the point of view of what the scriptwriter omitted and what Nelson Islanders chose to represent tradition. Just as Lincoln required the deletion of the gun scene because of its misleading reference to the period of historic contact, Hunsaker balked at including evidence of cold-blooded murder on the part of his hero. Rather, Apanuugpak's escalating lust for blood needed to appear consistently motivated by his obsession with revenge. For example, in traditional accounts of Apanuugpak's confrontation with an unarmed Bristol Bay native, Apanuugpak routinely dispatches the man for no reason more obvious than the fact of the encounter. In order not to jeopardize audience sympathy for the warrior-hero by the appearance of unmotivated violence, Hunsaker changed the story and let the man live. Responding differently than he did to the scene with the gun, Lincoln accepted this explanation and approved the change. Clearly, history was viewed as neither totally sacred nor wholly profane but in specific instances open to alteration.

Given the current reflexive mood in anthropology, Hunsaker's dismissal of the perils of translation seems somewhat suspect. Admittedly his intent to collaborate, to make himself the vehicle for a Yup'ik story, is in line with the noblest recent attempts to do away with the power relationship inherent in traditional ethnographic/native relations. Moreover, the ability of film in general and Hunsaker's film in particular to employ traditional dramatic forms, including dance scenes and shamanic performances, has intriguing advantages over discursive ethnography.

The creation of film, like the creations of the written word, can empower a community by manipulating knowledge, but it can also be impoverishing. We cannot dismiss the irony that the film is based on stories no longer familiar to young people on Nelson Island, in part because they are so fully engaged by the movie channel on local cable television. Like ethnography, film might document oral tradition while contributing to its demise, as it is part of a cultural context in which oral literature rarely survives. Like the ethnographers criticized by Clifford (1983) and Rosaldo (1986), the filmmaker has confined to private conversation discussion of the circumstances that shaped his knowledge. In public-relations descriptions of the project, he depicted the story he created out of his encounters with Lincoln as a mirror image of the memory of the tradition bearer himself, thereby validating his creation as authentic and historically accurate. The first page of the screenplay precisely dates the historical drama as occurring in 1650. In the venerable tradition of anthropological realism, Hunsaker asks his audience to view his creation as a "true outline" (Rosaldo 1986:93).

Just as the ethnographer might adopt the trappings of ethnographic authority and proceed under the assumption that one can apprehend native life in unmediated fashion, the filmmaker strikes a collaborative pose that creates the illusion of the direct apprehension of historically and culturally distant acts and meanings. One possible response to this ploy by the anthropologist well versed in Yup'ik oral tradition is to dismiss the film as a variety of Western humanism artfully dressed in traditional Yup'ik fur clothing—a film that tells us more about the meaning people seek to see in their own history than about Yup'ik history itself. Even more interesting than the disjunction between "authentic" oral tradition and "inauthentic" cinematic representation, however, is the creative interchange enacted between filmmaker and Nelson Islanders, each re-creating themselves in terms of the history of the other.[2]

After undergoing the review process on Nelson Island, Hunsaker's next step was to submit his script to the Script Development/Film Laboratory Workshop of the Sundance Institute. Robert Redford founded the institute in 1980 to support and encourage films by independent filmmakers that reflect the richness and diversity of American life. Hunsaker's script was one of nine chosen for detailed review from among more than six hundred entries. At Sundance, a number of nationally known directors and scriptwriters gave the script a thorough critique and helped Hunsaker bring the Yup'ik narrative in line with Western dramatic concepts. At Sundance Hunsaker also had the opportunity to test special effects in filming scenes involving shamanic activity. During this period, Hunsaker remarked that he was especially impressed by the techniques employed by the Japanese cinematographer Akira Kurosawa and hoped to achieve the visual look of Kurosawa's films in his own finished product.

FIGURE 6.1 Apanuugpak's village: the film set constructed in 1985 on Nelson Island.

During the summer before Hunsaker approached Robert Redford's Sundance organization, I was living at Toksook, working on their oral history project and waiting to become Mrs. Apanuugpak. Along with enjoying the joking and storytelling that were a part of that period, I was both surprised and delighted when, at the end of July and the close of the summer fishing season, the people of Toksook began building the set for the Apanuugpak film. Two dozen men and boys were employed in the construction of four sod houses, located on a point of land half a mile down the coast from the modern village. Pits were dug and driftwood hauled to the site. Within a week, the wooden skeletons of three of the houses had been completed and were ready to receive the grass insulating mats that women had been busy weaving back in the village. I visited the site every day and was impressed with how much people were enjoying the work. Older men boasted that they had seen nothing like this since their youth, and, clearly, for everyone under forty years of age this was a new and exhilarating experience.

Lincoln acted as foreman in the work. As the sod houses neared completion, he began directing work on the large *qasgiq*, or communal men's house, which formed the center of the new "old" community. This *qasgiq*, I was told, would never be left to rot as in times past. Instead, after the completion of the film, it would be preserved as a "permanent replica" and used as a shelter for the valuable gut parkas, wooden masks, and other artifacts that would also be produced for and used in *Winter Warrior*. This "living museum" would then function for western Alaska as a tourist attraction comparable to colonial Williamsburg.[3] Here Nelson Islanders' enjoyment in recreating their past is somewhat reminiscent of the pleasurable sentiments expressed by Kwakiutl natives involved in Edward Curtis's famous fictive reconstruction *In the Land of the War Canoes* (1914).

As much as I felt the immediate excitement engendered by the building project, I was particularly interested in rumors that were circulating concerning a celebration villagers planned to hold when they completed the *qasgiq*. I was told that traditionally the building or refurbishing of a men's house in late summer or early fall was marked by an *Ingulaq*, later referred to by the missionaries as a berry festival. This celebration was characterized by slow ceremonial dancing, also known as *ingulaq*, as well as the presentation of and feasting upon bowls of *akutaq*, a festive mixture of berries, oil, and snow.

FIGURE 6.2 The unfinished *qasgiq*, Toksook Bay in the background.

Islanders had not held such a performance for more than forty years and greatly anticipated the impending celebration.

Suddenly, two weeks later, both the construction of the old village and the plans for the *Ingulaq* were called to a halt. Apparently there had been a misunderstanding about the film's funding. Although the filmmaker had promised to pay workers if and when the film was funded, as yet no backers had been found and villagers had begun construction on the site without the filmmaker's knowledge. When the anticipated paychecks did not arrive, disgruntled workers refused to continue what they had begun spontaneously with such goodwill.

I was disappointed, as were many other people in the village. The turn of events was not without its irony. Here were men and women working to re-create a model of a bygone age, which they firmly maintained was more valuable to them than anything money could buy and representative of a way of life they held superior to modern cash-driven society. Nevertheless, without the promised paychecks, they would stop work rather than continue it for its own sake. They had come to place a price on their priceless heritage, which their actions, if not their words, treated as a commodity.

After my summer in Toksook, I continued to monitor the progress of the film project. Not until the fall of 1986 did I have the opportunity to read a draft of the script. What I read was far removed from Apanuugpak narratives I had heard on Nelson Island. I was reminded that the script was an adaptation for a commercial film, not an attempt at documentary, and that Hunsaker had based his work on the Apanuugpak stories with no intention of merely restating them.

In brief, the screenplay that I read in the fall of 1986 developed as follows. A young man (Apanuugpak) is being educated in the rules for right action by his grandfather. Although talented, he is presented as naive and immature. A neighboring group soon visits his village and seeks its support in a territorial struggle. Apanuugpak is troubled by this overture, having asserted in an earlier confrontation, "The waters don't belong to anybody" (Hunsaker 1986b:11). Moreover, in a fight he accidentally causes the death of the headstrong brother of the chief of the visiting group. To atone for this sin, Apanuugpak leaves the village to seek spiritual renewal. However, during his quest he is captured by a witch-woman who keeps him a prisoner and through daily copulation gradually saps his strength. Fortunately, Apanuugpak is rescued from this predicament by a young woman he subsequently marries. The couple lives happily for a brief time. Yet trouble is already brewing. The feud that began with the accidental killing of the chief's brother escalates into warfare between the two groups, and in the course of the next four dozen scenes, forty-one additional individuals are dispatched on screen and reference is made to numerous others killed off screen. As the killing escalates, so does Apanuugpak's obsession with revenge. Finally, returning to his village to find all its inhabitants, including his grandfather, burned alive in the *qasgiq* (this disaster constitutes the previous scene), Apanuugpak realizes that war is wrong. He then confronts his enemies and declares that weapons are for killing animals, not human beings. Presumably he then rejoins his wife, through whom he begins to rebuild his shattered world.

The cinematographic "present," like its ethnographic counterpart, is given as one step removed from the contemporary world. In the film's closing scene, a young Yup'ik woman views with concern the photograph of her boyfriend, who has the face of Apanuugpak and is dressed in a National Guard uniform. The scene is set in a village on Nelson Island in the 1940s, a period during which the rights and duties of citizenship were introduced in quick succession in the coastal communities of western Alaska. This scene brings the film full circle. The film opened with a scene in which the villagers were gathered in a wood-frame community hall. There the voice and person of Lincoln were introduced, and in turn introduced the life and times of Apanuugpak. Thus, the entire film is framed as a narration concerning the distant past told in the immediate past. In this story within a story the other is represented not altogether accurately but as a trope for a cultural possibility other than our own. The filmmaker's decision to remove his message is new neither to ethnographic nor to cinematic representation. However, it is significant that Hunsaker's predecessors, including both Curtis and Robert Flaherty (*Nanook of the North*) used no such framing scenes. True to the period in which they worked, they were more content with the fiction of realism and less self-conscious in their use of material.

It is noteworthy that another recent attempt at indigenous dramatic representation in western Alaska was framed in a similar way. The play, produced by the village of Chevak (located less than one hundred miles up the coast from Nelson Island), was performed statewide. The main body of the play was a re-creation of the traditional Bladder Festival; five days of feasts were collapsed into an intense three-hour performance that included audience participation.

As in *Winter Warrior*, an element of tradition was taken as the focus, in this case a ceremonial enactment of the belief in an endless cycle of birth and rebirth of human and animal souls. Also like *Winter Warrior*, the play was framed in the present, once removed. In the opening scene a "Brooks Brothers" native moves forward to the sound of disco music and takes a long pull from a flask of whiskey drawn out of a leather briefcase.

From the beginning, the Chevak players neatly juxtaposed the material success of this native Everyman to his spiritual decline; however, the spirits of his past engage him in the Bladder Festival, through which he is reborn along with the souls of the animals. It is perhaps appropriate that the ceremony that traditionally had the power to re-create the past in the future was chosen to represent tradition itself in the present. The Chevak production, just like Hunsaker's, looks to the past to supply the concrete symbolic forms that Western social symbolism has failed to provide. Apparently ethnography is not alone in its propensity to turn to "other times, other customs" (Sahlins 1985:32) to more clearly understand its own.

To return to *Winter Warrior*, the script as summarized here is both carefully developed and dramatically successful by Western standards. Fast paced, it clearly works as an adventure story. To achieve the dramatic force that is its strong point, however, the screenplay has moved far from the Nelson Island oral traditions and Yup'ik dramatic style on which it was based.

This shift is telling. First of all, in oral accounts Apanuugpak was born into warfare and from his earliest youth was trained as a virtual "killing machine." Although the filmmaker heard stories about Apanuugpak's early years, at least in reference, he did not use them because they were not part of Lincoln's account. This omission highlights the problems associated with using Lincoln as sole tradition bearer. Lincoln was born and raised north of Nelson Island, not on Nelson Island proper. Although he knew the stories of Apanuugpak's childhood, they may not have been part of his personal repertoire and consequently part of what he felt he had a right to communicate.

Second, in his screenplay Hunsaker adds substantially to the traditional stories of Apanuugpak's adult years. In Nelson Island oral tradition these narratives all revolve around the battles Apanuugpak fought and won and the tricks he played on his enemies. There are no stories of whom or how he married. However, at the end of his life, he is seen surrounded by his grandsons telling stories in the *qasgiq*.

Thus the witch-woman scenes, as well as the subplot of Apanuugpak's twofold "salvation" by the woman who becomes his wife, are dramatic inventions. A more troublesome alteration concerns Apanuugpak's social role. As a warrior (*anguyaq*), Apanuugpak occupied a social position distinct from that of either a great hunter (*nukalpiaq*) or a shaman (*angalkuq*). In Yup'ik oral tradition, warriors are viewed as men apart, hunters of men rather than men who are hunters in either the animal or spirit worlds. In the screenplay these categories are collapsed, and Apanuugpak is presented as the quintessential embodiment of all three.

Third, in the screenplay Apanuugpak is depicted as the unwitting cause of the onset of warfare. He is also presented as the sadder but wiser restorer of the peace through his ultimate recognition of the evils inherent in warfare. This message is, in fact, a critical part of the meaning of the film and is epitomized in Apanuugpak's dramatic concluding statement: "Weapons are meant for killing animals, not humans." Here Hunsaker is using Yup'ik oral tradition to state what he considers a universal truth: War is wrong and through war a man risks losing his soul. Whatever the merits of this statement, it is ironic that Yup'ik stories celebrating the preeminent war hero of their past should be used as its vehicle.

In the final analysis, Hunsaker's most significant revision is the invention of the beginning and end of warfare and the placement of these accomplishments in the hands of a single human being, however famous. Yup'ik oral tradition does, in fact, have an explanation for the beginning and the end of warfare in general, as well as specific wars. For example, in perhaps the best-known account of the beginning and end of the Yukon Delta/coastal conflict, an unskilled hunter from Pastolik who had married into the village of Hooper Bay killed his hunting companions one after the other and claimed their catch as his own. When the people of Hooper Bay discovered his crime, he fled north to Pastolik. There he sowed the seeds of distrust among the Yukon Eskimos, who subsequently took the offensive against their coastal neighbors. Many battles took place during the ensuing years. However, during a period of extreme food shortage, a man from the Yukon and a man from Hooper Bay formed an unlikely partnership out on the ice while stalking a seal. They shared their catch and consequently saved each other's lives. From that time on the hostilities between the Yukon and coastal areas began to subside (Fienup-Riordan 1986b:38, 359–365).

This complete rendition of the beginning and end of the famous Yukon Delta/coastal conflict is revealing in several respects. It begins in theft and the refusal to cooperate; it ends in food-sharing and trading. Whereas the original conflict divides a group united by marriage, the resolution brings about the rapprochement of two originally distinct regional groups. In addition, the breach pivots around the food quest and a conflict over resources in one region. Although it does not originate as a boundary dispute, in the intervening war episodes men are depicted as defending a range or a site or a kill (Fienup-Riordan 1984a:76–77).

Nelson Islanders have their own account concerning the end of wars (Fienup-Riordan 1983:247). In brief, two survivors approached their enemies seeking revenge after their own village had been destroyed. As they drew closer in their kayaks, they broke the spears they had intended to kill with and instead used them to beat the sides of their kayaks like drums. Then the women of the opposing village walked down to the shore to meet them and, standing in front of their men, began to dance. So it is said, from that time forward, Yup'ik people have never fought with bows and arrows but rather through the dance. Anyone who has seen Yup'ik dancing will know that this is indeed still the case!

Although Hunsaker had viewed Yup'ik dance, he had neither asked for nor received this origin story. He was likewise unaware of the cycle of narratives recounting the beginning and ending of warfare. His invention of such a sequence was thus not based on a considered rejection of these narratives but on limited information. Although sensitive to known issues, he was not told enough to realize his omission. What the narratives had in common was the motif of an endless cosmological cycling between birth and rebirth (Chapter 2). In the traditional accounts of warfare, the primary issue was not death but rather in what manner life would be maintained in perpetuity. For Hunsaker, as for Sophocles before him, the inevitability of death becomes focal. On the contrary, within Yup'ik cosmology the narratives depicting warfare are about death's impossibility not its finality. This divergence in part explains the differences between Hunsaker's and Lincoln's views regarding the motivation and meaning behind Apanuugpak's acts of violence.

Finally, in replacing traditional accounts of the beginning and end of warfare, Hunsaker also transformed the traditional and contemporary Yup'ik concepts of territoriality. In the beginning of *Winter Warrior*, Apanuugpak exclaims, "The waters do not belong to anyone." This sentiment is brought full circle when, in the final scene of the film, the young woman views with concern the portrait of her boyfriend in his National Guard uniform. Here, along with the message "war is wrong," Hunsaker attempts to make the point that with the emergence of the modern nation-state in western Alaska, the same "foreign" issues of landownership and water rights that brought on the wars of the past are resurfacing in the present.

In fact, the traditional Yup'ik Eskimos possessed a well-developed sense of territory; however, rights to land and water use were not based on, or reduced to, possession of a particular site by an individual or group at any one point in time. Rather the concept of ownership was relational; a man had a right, and in fact an obligation, to use a site because of his relationship to previous generations of people who had a defined relationship to the species taken at that same place. In other words, a man had a right to use a site not because he owned the land but because his grandparent (by name and by birth) hunted there and had a relationship with the animals of that area. A man was his grandfather incarnate, and therefore the animals that gave themselves to him were those that gave themselves to his grandfather. A man's right to resource extraction was thus relational rather than possessive. In this sense ownership was and continues to be tied to defined territories insofar as these reflect social boundaries. This traditional understanding of territoriality does not correspond to the capitalist notion of property that the scriptwriter has the Yup'ik people reject.

In the fall of 1986 I discussed with the scriptwriter the differences between his screenplay and Yup'ik history as I understood it, arguing for changes in his script that would bring it closer to the form and meaning of Yup'ik oral tradition. His answer was simple and straightforward: We were talking about two different films. From my point of view the interchange was less than satisfactory as, like the native on whom the anthropologist relies, I was put in the uncomfortable position of being asked to give information without the requisite power to control its subsequent use. Within the context of our differences, however, two issues of broad significance emerged that merit consideration here.

It should be clear that Hunsaker and I hold different views of what is important about Nelson Island. As in *Yup'ik Antigone*, in *Winter Warrior* the scriptwriter chose to focus on the universality of the human condition. This is a venerable theme in the Western tradition, and much of anthropology has been framed as an attempt to speak to this issue. My chief concern, however, is that Yup'ik Eskimos in general, and Nelson Islanders in particular, have a unique way of looking at and acting in the world. From my perspective it makes no sense to override significant and instructive differences between the seventeenth-century Yup'ik Eskimos and contemporary American culture to present the ways in which Yup'ik people were in essentials "just like us" (Fienup-Riordan 1985:9).

The dialogue between Hunsaker and me was further constrained by the fact that we have different agendas. Both of us must have the support of our peers for our work to succeed. On the one hand, to find backing for his film, Hunsaker had to convince the Sundance Institute that his script had broad dramatic appeal, not that his facts were correct. On the other hand, I must convince research agencies that there is something special but not necessarily of universal appeal about the Yup'ik people that merits detailed inquiry.

Along with and related to the different practical constraints on our work, Hunsaker and I hold very different views about the meaning of history and tradition. When Hunsaker visited Nelson Island to discuss *Winter Warrior*, in addition to gathering Apanuugpak stories, he kept his ears open to the current state of affairs. The years during which he visited Nelson Island brought dramatic challenges to the political and cultural integrity of the region. Numerous state and federal agencies had become increasingly involved in the management and regulation of the fish and game on which Nelson Islanders depend for their livelihood. New regulations challenged the islanders' ability to freely harvest the geese, halibut, herring, and musk oxen that, among other species, inhabit the area (see Chapter 8). In addition, outside pressure on these resources had also escalated. At the same time that they were feeling increased pressure on these resources, their right to the use and "ownership" of ancestral lands was threatened by the approach of 1991, when village and regional corporation land becomes transferrable under the 1971 Alaska Native Claims Settlement Act.

In the context of this political situation Hunsaker carried out his "fieldwork" on Nelson Island. Perhaps not surprisingly, native suspicion and resentment of current non-native forms of regulation colored his interviews and history lessons. Nelson Islanders told him that in the past no one had specific rights over the land or the resources, and no one could restrict another's use. In fact, this is not an accurate presentation of the past, as already indicated. However, this was the view of Yup'ik history that Hunsaker took home with him, and he developed his script based on this history. Thus the "tradition" on which Hunsaker's screenplay rests, and that may well appear to be old, is quite recent in origin and has in fact been intentionally invented by Nelson Islanders to establish continuity between their present political position and a suitable historic past. Although they desire free use of their land "as in the past," unrestricted movement and unregulated access to resources were not a part of the nineteenth-century Yup'ik way of life.

The phenomenon of "invented traditions" is not unique to Nelson Island. Hobsbawm and Ranger (1983) make it the subject of detailed inquiry. Invented tradition, as distinguished from noninvented tradition and custom, is said to be a set of practices governed by accepted rules and of a symbolic nature that seeks to inculcate certain values implying continuity with the past. Insofar as there is reference to a historic past, Hobsbawm and Ranger note, the continuity with it is largely fictitious. Moreover, this phenomenon may in part be attributed to the contrast between the constant innovation of the modern world and the attempt to find some part of it invariant. Thus, increasingly, old materials (like the Apanuugpak stories or the Bladder Festival) are used to construct invented traditions of a novel type to establish a people's legitimacy through history.

Furthermore, Hobsbawm and Ranger (1983:8) distinguish between the adaptability of genuine traditions and the "invention of tradition." They contend that where old ways are alive, traditions need be neither revived nor invented. Where they are invented, it is often not because the old ways are no longer available or viable, but because those ways are deliberately not used or adapted. In the case of *Winter Warrior*, a double invention is in process, with Hunsaker inventing a trope for the condition of modern man based on a tradition of nonownership and an absence of territorial concepts that the people of Nelson Island have themselves invented to validate their contemporary relationship to the land. Hunsaker moves from the misinterpretation of tradition to its "invention" in his claim that the people of Nelson Island regard his screenplay as acceptable history. He already has a strong following for his project.

Hunsaker vacillates between naturalizing the Yup'ik as paragons of simplicity and virtue and historicizing them as victims of Western imperialism. Nowhere is he encumbered by the specificity of Yup'ik concepts of space, time, or personhood. He has responded instead to their contemporary plea for the severing of a connection with a white man's world they view as having gone awry. Hunsaker was told essentially, "We have always been a peaceful people living in harmony with our land. Boundaries have been imposed from without, and the constraint is unacceptable." In fact, the nineteenth-century Yupiit were preoccupied with the creation of boundaries and passages in a world perceived as formless without them (Fienup-Riordan 1987). Today the Yupiit are intent on breaking externally imposed constraints and are doing so in the name of tradition.

Hunsaker was finally forced to face the claim that his "invention" conflicts with other traditions still adhered to on Nelson Island. There was danger that the bow-and-arrow wars of the past were to be fought again in the regional newspaper, the *Tundra Drums*. An exchange of letters (Hunsaker 1987; Oscar 1987) concerning the use of explicit sexual imagery in the witch-woman scene undercut local support for the project. This "paper war" was doubly ironic in that the stated goals of the film project are "to advance public understanding of a little known traditional American culture" (Hunsaker 1986a) and to be as "authentic" and historically accurate as possible. However, filmmakers (just like anthropologists), whatever else their objectives, are engaged in the process of "inventing traditions" inasmuch as they "contribute, consciously or not, to the creation, dismantling, and restructuring of the images of the past" (Hobsbawm and Ranger 1983:8).

Moreover, the push for the film is forcing more and more Nelson Islanders to expand their concept of what is and is not marketable within their own world. As in the case of the aborted construction of the old village, their oral traditions have begun to take on market value. Whereas they still value the oral traditions for what they can teach about proper living, Nelson Islanders are recognizing the monetary value they have in the contemporary world. Also, for the younger generation, the prospect of being an actor, not just a viewer, in a movie drama draws them toward what for many is the clearinghouse if not the creator of Western reality—the media.

The younger villagers are the ones most interested in acting in the film. These would-be actors are the same generation of men and women made inactive in their own culture in part by the unreality of American television. In the 1940s Nelson Islanders were more in touch with their own past than with the national present in which they were nominally included. Today, that historical reality as constructed in myth and story has dimmed to the point where its preservation on the silver screen represents true re-creation.

To date, the community continues to support the film project over the voices of individual dissidents. Among villagers, however, support remains contingent on the filmmaker's ability to find funding for his project. Although their realities are not identical, the interests of the Nelson Islanders and the filmmaker in the film overlap, and they are not at odds. Nelson Islanders are not replacing their version of history with Hunsaker's, and they retain a measure of ironic distance from cinematic concessions to Western audiences in the name of profit.

Nevertheless, winning on Hunsaker's terms may be a form of losing if stories once told to provide moral guidance and to preserve tradition become equated with monetary gain. In the film project's relationship with the community, money has talked in the past and will again in the future. Although the filming will be done in the native language, the fact that the actors will be paid in cash, in the language of venture capitalism, elicits local support for the project. Whatever Hunsaker's view of his creation and its worth, Nelson Islanders are currently content to view it as a finite resource to be harvested if and when it arrives, in contrast to the infinitely renewable resources they harvested in the past.

Beyond the invention and reevaluation of history, the question arises concerning the extent to which the collection of Yup'ik artifacts and oral tradition constitutes an invention of heritage—by the filmmaker or by anthropologists in general. By his own admission, Hunsaker's selective recording and organization of Yup'ik material is an act of creation. Although finding support within the community, the impetus for making the film comes not only from within Nelson Island but from without. The farther away the film moves, the greater the interest it elicits. The product will be an ethnic display, not an act of Eskimo self-representation.

Just as the historicism of the nineteenth century and the belief that it was necessary to collect before it was "too late" made possible the ethnological collecting associated with the "museum movement" (Cole 1985:48; Dominguez 1986:549), so the social and political climate in Alaska enables the cinematographic invention of a new Yup'ik tradition. Similarly, the collections of Eskimo artifacts and the Eskimos themselves were and remain objects of interest not because of their intrinsic value but because of their perceived contribution to our understanding of our own history. The value of *Winter Warrior* will lie not in its "true" representation of the Yup'ik Eskimos, the proverbial "others," but in the degree to which it can be read as a referential index of ourselves.

At its best *Winter Warrior* may rise above the accusation of cultural imperialism. Just as cultural order is not immediately given but constantly achieved through the process of negotiation between symbolic structures and historical circumstances, a film is a marriage between script and actors, who in this case will be Yup'ik Eskimos acting in their own language in their own time and place. Although the city council has given permission to the filmmaker to pursue his project, they do not view their agreement as writ in stone but as contingent on continued goodwill and agreement on essentials between the filmmaker and the community. The filmmaker has developed a script that both he and they view as open to alteration as they begin to play it out in the filming process. Thus, the community feels in control of the production, to the credit of all concerned.

In the enthusiasm of Nelson Islanders to use their history to talk about their present, the distinction between "authentic," lived culture and "inauthentic" invented tradition loses its force. Rather the screenplay may be viewed as performing the role of mediator in Wagner's (1986) sense, insofar as its negotiation of cultural conceptions results in a re-creation of them. *Winter Warrior* as presently conceived will not represent the traditional Yup'ik way of life any more accurately or inaccurately than *Road Warrior* represents modern American culture. Rather, like *Road Warrior, Winter Warrior* will re-present it, complete with strategic omissions and additions. Although the film may provoke the purist, it is valid in its own right. In the best anthropological tradition, the text that is the film is more than description (accurate or inaccurate) of the Yup'ik past. Rather it embodies an act of translation, of re-creation, where both Yup'ik and non-Yup'ik audiences may learn something about themselves by means of the other.

Limits exist in our ability to apprehend the other. This point has been made in myriad ways, from Sahlins's (1976) dictum that no ethnography exists without ethnology to Wagner's (1975) exegesis on the invention of culture to Clifford and Marcus's (1986) grim conclusion that constructed truths are made possible only by lies of exclusion. Accepting these limits to its own enterprise, anthropology cannot fairly condemn the filmmaker, who faces challenges similar to those of ethnographic writing, including problems of narrative and focus, of editing, and of reflexivity.

As in the case of ethnography, although we can recognize the limits of the cinematographic enterprise, we do not have to reject it in toto. With ethnography's own authority in question, anthropology's chief use is not in standing up for the accurate representation of the pure culture of the past but in clarifying the significance of action in the present. The question of the differences between the ethnographic and cinematographic enterprise appears to be a reinvention of the Mead-Freeman debate in a colder clime.[4] Following Clifford's (1986) analysis of this debate, I would argue that if anthropology's response is dismissal on the grounds of inaccuracy or inauthenticity, it misses the point of the attempt to depict the Yup'ik past so as to provide a moral lesson for the present. Just as Mead went to Samoa and Hunsaker to Nelson Island, the Yup'ik Eskimos are visiting another time within their own world to frame a present as both inherited and in the process of being reinvented.

Yup'ik Warfare and the Myth of the Peaceful Eskimo

IN THE POPULAR LITERATURE OF the twentieth century, Eskimos in general and Yup'ik Eskimos in particular have often been represented as never hostile, let alone warlike (Gordon 1906–1907:69–70; Peary 1910; Ruesch 1944:203). Comparable to the stereotype of the residents of the Arctic as living year-round in snow houses, subsisting on raw meat, and forever spoiling their children, the nonviolent character of Eskimo social interaction has been emphasized at the expense of the violence and warfare that are a very real part of their history and tradition. The Yup'ik Eskimos of western Alaska, like other Eskimo peoples, are generally understood to carefully avoid direct confrontation and the expression of hostility in interpersonal relations (Chance 1966:77–79; Foulks 1972:115; Kleinfeld 1978). Nevertheless, homicide, the publicly condoned execution of dangerous individuals, and warfare appear to have been regular aspects of eighteenth-century intra- and intergroup relations (Lantis 1946: 168–169; Nelson 1899:264, 327–329). As has been suggested for the Central Eskimos (Eckert and Newmark 1980) as well as for the Eskimos of northern Alaska and Siberia (Burch and Correll 1972), the emphasis on interpersonal tranquility was likely coupled with an extremely high homicide rate.

The following pages detail the discrepancy between the reality of traditional Yup'ik bow-and-arrow warfare and the stereotype of the peaceful Eskimo. In the process, the discussion moves from the particularity of Yup'ik history into speculative statements concerning problems of Eskimo representation more generally. To characterize the Yup'ik Eskimos as violent is no more accurate than to view them as perennially peaceful. However, to understand interpersonal violence and politically aggressive acts by Yup'ik Eskimos today, it is essential to understand the interpersonal hostilities and political alliances that were generated during the bow-and-arrow wars of the eighteenth and nineteenth centuries.

The Genesis of the Myth

Euro-Americans' popular conception of Eskimos as "naturally" peaceful in opposition to their warring selves can be traced in part to initial encounters. Comparable to their experience with American Indians, their early confrontations with Eskimos were fraught with tension in much of the Arctic and frequently deteriorated into physical violence. Most early explorers of Canada and Alaska reported tense encounters with Eskimos. During these encounters the Eskimos demonstrated what has been characterized as "realistic opportunism" (Graburn 1969b:93)—a general friendliness and willingness to trade when it suited them, mixed with a capacity to murder their guests and take what they wanted by force if they thought they could get away with it. Moreover, early explorers and traders were painfully aware of Eskimo intergroup warfare, especially insofar as it affected their work. A. K. Etolin wrote in 1840, "Trading aboard the brig *Polifem* with the savages in the North this year was very unsuccessful . . . The war now between the coastal inhabitants and the Asian shore and the inhabitants of [St.] Lawrence Island was the reason."

The stereotype of the peaceful, smiling Eskimo does not derive from this period of initial encounter. As time went on, however, hostility and suspicion were replaced by largely peaceful relations between Eskimos and Euro-Americans. As trade, rather than territorial expansion, was the primary motive for increased non-native activity in the Arctic, Euro-Americans were not disposed to antagonize or enslave Eskimos but rather desired friendly relations with them. They needed their help as guides and trappers and required their goodwill to see them through the perils of life in the Arctic.

As a result, the penetration of the Arctic during the nineteenth century was a largely peaceful process, less often disturbed by the murder and bloodshed that characterized Euro-American/native encounters in other parts of the New World. Petr Korsakovskiy recorded his initial meeting with Yup'ik Eskimos in 1818: "The local Indians [sic] greeted us joyfully and thanked us for paying them a visit" (VanStone 1988:28). Noting that they were prone to regular conflict with their Eskimo neighbors, he nevertheless experienced his hosts as "gentle, kind, generous, hospitable and merry" (VanStone 1988: 30). Although the newcomers remained on their guard, surrounding their trading stations with stockades and arming them with cannon, open confrontations between Eskimos and Russians were notable by their absence.[1]

Thus, in contrast to the experience with many Indian peoples, which increased in violence over the years, initially hostile and suspicious encounters with Eskimos were replaced by largely peaceful relations. In western Alaska, Yup'ik Eskimos killed only a handful of non-natives during the nineteenth century (Fienup-Riordan 1988d:30–31). As non-natives did not seek to dispossess them of their lands or livelihood through violent means, Eskimos did not react violently to them. Whereas the European/Indian encounter had provoked warfare and produced the image of a warlike red man, the non-native encounter with Eskimos in western Alaska not only did not cause warfare but actually brought an end to the violent interregional struggles that had characterized the region before Euro-Americans arrived.

Following Korsakovskiy, contacts with Yup'ik Eskimos in the nineteenth century elicited largely positive evaluations of their docile character. A handful of observers, including Lavrentiy Zagoskin and Edward Nelson, described the bloody wars that predated the arrival of the Russians (Michael 1967:281; Nelson 1899:264, 327–330). But as their relations with miners, trappers, traders, missionaries, and government personnel were largely nonviolent, and as the Yup'ik Eskimos preferred not to argue or resist openly even when in opposition, reports on Eskimos tended to depict them as passive to the point of lethargy (Collier 1973) and to dismiss accounts of traditional warfare as fantastic mythology (Anderson 1940:118–120).

People who knew them well knew the limitations of this characterization but did not always choose to advertise their knowledge. For example, the nineteenth-century Moravian missionary John Kilbuck recorded what are perhaps the most detailed ethnohistoric accounts of the bloody battles fought during the period of bow-and-arrow wars; however, he never published them. Instead he put them in a bread box in a Kansas bank vault for safekeeping, while in his published accounts he preferred to emphasize the latent Christian character of his Eskimo converts (Fienup-Riordan 1988d:32–34, 43–50, 390–392).

As in other hunting societies, the relatively small scale of Eskimo societies may also have contributed to the tendency to underestimate or ignore the occurrence of warfare and violence. Whites who encountered nasty natives labeled them oddballs or evil shamans and dismissed their aggressive actions as exceptions to the rule of nonviolence. For example, the Moravian missionaries attributed the killing of a native Moravian helper by his fellow villagers to an "epidemic of insanity" and viewed it as the act of a madman. It is more likely that the helper's demise was a socially sanctioned execution of an individual believed to be putting the community in jeopardy (Fienup-Riordan 1988b).

Farther north, on the Seward Peninsula, the government teacher and missionary Harrison Thornton (1890–1893, 1931) blamed the hostile response of his Inupiat parishioners on, among other things, alcohol abuse, writing in his diary that Eskimos are generous, peaceful, and friendly until they begin to drink whiskey. In fact, Thornton's own authoritative behavior probably elicited this negative response. Little suspecting that native hostility might represent a normal Eskimo aggressive reaction to his very un-Eskimo mode of interaction, he paid for his ignorance with his life.

Today in Alaska, non-natives all too often continue to consider violence in rural Alaska as without precedent in traditional non-violent Eskimo society and therefore as being "introduced," a product of "culture contact." In response to an Anchorage newspaper series detailing a recent epidemic of self-destructive violence in western Alaska, an Anchorage resident wrote describing Alaska Eskimos: "Such a happy people! If we had their gift for peaceful living the world would be a better place. And to think of the violence and trouble we have introduced them to" (personal communication, Mar. 20, 1988).

Perhaps more significant, some Alaska Eskimos agree with this interpretation. At the 1988 annual meeting of the Eskimo sovereignty group, the Yupiit Nation, Yup'ik elders were almost unanimous in their denial that violence and warfare had existed in traditional Yup'ik society. According to Willie Lomack of Akiachak, "This Yup'ik way has always been a peaceful way where no one ever fought with each other" (Apr. 20, 1988, YN).[2] Kenneth Peter, also of Akiachak, added, "They never used to kill. . . . Recently, since white men arrived, killing has started. I suspect that they have learned to do that by watching television, or by smoking pot, or by drinking alcohol" (Apr. 20, 1988, YN). Statements such as these have been dismissed by some as "hyperbolic cant" (Hippler 1974:336). On the contrary, they reflect a powerful current political attempt to represent Eskimo history and culture as distinct from and superior to its non-native

counterpart. Although non-natives deny Eskimo violence out of ignorance, the native denial represents a decision to emphasize one part
of their history rather than another.

In the continental United States the generalized image of the
peaceful Eskimo was strongly influenced by descriptions of Canadian
Inuit. Just as the Plains Indians became the Indian with a capital I,
so the Central Eskimos became *the* Eskimo. In the ethnographic literature on the Central Eskimos a native ideology of goodwill, peace-
fulness, cooperation, and equality repeatedly appears (Eckert and
Newmark 1980:193–194).

Moving further east, Greenland's Polar Eskimos reportedly lacked
not only the concept but also the word for warfare and regarded sol-
diers and officers brought up to the trade of killing as mere butchers
(Ross 1819:134–135). According to Edward Weyer (1932:168), they
could not understand why men of the same faith hunted each other
as though they were seals and stole from people they had never seen
or known: "The writer was surprised that the Europeans had not
learned better manners among the Eskimos and proposed to send
medicine men as missionaries among them. Fighting about land
seemed to him sheer greed."

At the same time that some authors described the peaceful nature
of Eskimo interaction, others noted that in fact Canadian Inuit in
general and the Central Eskimos in particular had a great propensity
for lethal violence (Balikci 1970:173–197; Hoebel 1961:88–92).
Knud Rasmussen (1932:17) wrote that no less than nine out of fifteen
men in one community had committed one or more murders of adults
and concluded that every grown man had been involved in a killing
in some way or another. Even so, these acts of violence were most
often viewed as the "natural consequences" of a society constrained
by a harsh environment and lacking formal mechanisms of social
control. These "deficits" made erratic homicide inevitable. It also im-
plied the inability of Eskimos to organize for formal warfare, an activity that was presumed to require a political sophistication that the
Eskimos were presumed to lack. Although these explanations made
sense in the central Canadian Arctic, where the population was much
smaller and much more widely dispersed than in Alaska or on the
Atlantic Coast, in Alaska they did not apply. The problem was less
with the ethnographic accounts of the Canadian Eskimos than with
the extrapolation from those accounts to all Eskimos.

Meanwhile, back in Alaska, MGM's widely viewed film *Eskimo*
(adapted from the work of Danish author Peter Freuchen (1931) and

produced in Teller in 1933) solidified the image of the smiling, nose-rubbing, gentle dwellers of the Arctic for a generation of American viewers. The Eskimo hero Mala engaged in murderous activity only in retaliation for the broken promises of a deceitful whaling captain. He killed in self-defense and because it was required for survival in a hostile environment. Like his Canadian predecessor, *Nanook of the North* (produced by Robert Flaherty in 1922), Mala was eulogized as the preeminent resourceful individual. Hence our fascination with him. His violence did not reflect an inner flaw but rather was required by the situation, which ironically was one of contact between a just native and an unjust white world. The native hero was not an Eskimo but a Western Everyman corrupted by civilization.

The same insidious pacifism pervades the closing scenes of the 1974 film *White Dawn*, based on the 1971 novel by James Houston. Throughout the film, the viewer is repeatedly confronted with how uncivilized and violent three white whalers are in comparison with their Inuit hosts. In the end they more than merit the execution they elicit. However, instead of letting the whalers rest in peace, an Eskimo turns to his companions and queries, "We were not killers of men. What caused this sad thing to happen to us?" The filmmaker could not let the act speak the truth—that a violent life merited a violent end—but instead felt compelled to declare it an exception to the rule of nonviolence. *White Dawn* was created in consultation with the Baffin Island Inuit, whom it is about and who constituted its corps of native actors. The film can thus claim to embody something of the current Inuit view of themselves. Their claim to a peaceful past may approximate the disavowal by Yupiit Nation elders of their violent history, telling us more about how they choose to be seen than how in fact they were.

Along with the relatively peaceful reception of non-natives by most Alaska Eskimos, as well as our propensity to apply stereotypic Canadian Eskimo characteristics to them, twentieth-century anthropological theory has tended to obscure rather than clarify our understanding of violence (socially sanctioned and otherwise) in Alaska Eskimo society. Culture and personality theory of the 1930s and 1940s reinforced the tendency to extend observations on Eskimo interpersonal relations to both intergroup relations and Eskimo culture in general (Lantis 1946:254). In fact, interpersonal relations within Alaska Eskimo groups were characterized largely by nonconfrontative, self-effacing behavior and restraint (see Chapter 3). The code of conduct prescribed carefully controlled thought and deed in order not to injure another's mind, let alone body. The misrepresentation of traditional Eskimo intergroup relations as nonconfrontative has in part been brought about by the false extension of these rules of interpersonal deference to intergroup relations. Even within the group, apparent nonaggression may be viewed as tactical rather than as the reflection of the absence of interpersonal hostility. An extreme example is the Yup'ik story of the young widow who showed no anger when her husband was killed, then seduced his murderer with smiles only to crush him to death in her arms.

Anthropology in the 1960s further contributed to the stereotype of the peaceful Eskimo. As the United States was torn by debate concerning the Vietnam War, anthropologists thought they could see in hunter-gatherers, including Eskimos, an originally peaceful humanity with generally low levels of violence (Lee and Devore 1968:9; Service 1966:60; Turnbull 1968:341). The generation that found fault with war in their time reacted by denying its existence among our Neolithic ancestors. This characterization, along with a number of other generalizations, reflected the position that hunting societies represented the most elemental form of the human condition. Hunter-gatherers were believed to lack not only generalized violence but also organized warfare, and Eskimos were included in these generalizations (Hoebel 1961:82; Mead 1968:216). Excepting only Pacific Eskimos, Alaska Eskimos were said to lack a well-developed warfare complex including fortified and habitable positions (Oswalt 1967:246).

Carol Embers (1978:443) subsequently tabulated warfare data from a worldwide sample of hunter-gatherers and found that only 10 percent had no or rare warfare, concluding that hunter-gatherers could hardly be described as peaceful. In 1974 Ernest Burch dealt what should have been the death blow to the view of the nonviolent Eskimo with his detailed discussion of Iñupiat warfare in northern Alaska. In the popular imagination, however, the stereotype remains. As a result, both politically aggressive acts, such as the formation of the Yupiit Nation sovereignty movement along the Kuskokwim (Chapter 9), and the distressingly high rates of interpersonal violence (*Anchorage Daily News* 1988; Fienup-Riordan 1988a:47–48) are almost universally understood as "corruptions" brought on by the onslaught of civilization and as inexplicable exceptions to the rule of nonviolence rather than as social phenomena firmly grounded in a politically aggressive and violent past.

The point here is not to replace the picture of the peaceful Eskimo with the picture of a violent one. The point is to replace a false image with one that is more readily supported by the evidence and thereby to understand more fully Eskimo social and political action today. To understand Eskimos in the past and the present we need to understand them at war as well as at peace. In western Alaska we can make a beginning by asking Yup'ik elders to orate the detailed historical narratives that are the record of their past.[3] This oratory, combined with ethnohistorical documentation, may not answer all our questions, but it can provide a beginning.

The Parameters of Traditional Yup'ik Bow-and-Arrow Warfare

On the basis of extensive research and analysis of oral and ethnohistoric accounts, it is reasonable to conclude that in the early 1800s as many as fifteen thousand people inhabited the coast of western Alaska, including the drainages of the Yukon, Kuskokwim, and Nushagak rivers. This population was organized into approximately twelve sociopolitical units that Burch (1988a:229) has aptly referred to as nations (Figure 7.1). Each of these twelve Yup'ik nations was characterized by a common language, subsistence cycle, and regular travel between villages, people "moving around like they were being poured" (Mary Worm, May 14, 1988, YN). Although tiny by contemporary standards, each nation viewed itself as socially and territorially distinct and was willing to wage war to remain so. Although interregional feasting, visiting, and trading expressed and created goodwill between the nations, violence and conflict also regularly characterized interregional exchange prior to the arrival of the Russians. To this day guests arriving from another village for a feast are in some areas referred to as "attackers."

Throughout western Alaska a single story is repeatedly cited to account for the origin of warfare. This is an old story, and narrators typically locate the incident in a village in their own region. According to tradition, two boys were playing with bone-tipped darts in the men's house. One of the boys aimed poorly and accidentally hit his companion in the eye, blinding him. The father of the offender told the father of the injured boy to go ahead and poke out one of the eyes of his son in retribution. However, the father whose son had been injured was so enraged that he poked out both the offender's eyes, blinding him completely. The other father reacted by killing the first

FIGURE 7.1 Regional groupings for the Yukon-Kuskokwim region, circa 1833.

man's son. And so it went, the violence escalating and each man join-ing sides until the entire village, and eventually the entire region, was at war.[4]

Here the origin of war is associated with blindness, a disability with devastating implications for a hunter. In fact, the opposition between restricted human vision and powerful supernatural sight was a critical element in Yup'ik cosmology, and elaborate rules circumscribed sight in the human world to empower strong supernatural vision (see Chapter 3). Given this emphasis, it is hard to imagine any more appropriate beginning for the dramatic confrontations that would follow.

Although the time when the first wars were fought is unknown, ethnohistoric and oral accounts agree that warfare had ceased by the 1830s. Ivan Vasilev described a bloody encounter between *Kiatagmiut* and *Aglurmiut* that occurred in 1816 in which the *Aglurmiut* killed as many as two hundred *Kiatagmiut*: "There were unburied heads and bones aplenty, strewn along the shore and in the woods" (VanStone 1988:91). In 1818 Korsakovskiy encountered the famous coastal warrior Apanuugpak (VanStone 1988:45), who oral accounts agree outlived warfare. By the time Zagoskin arrived in western Alaska in 1842, warfare was a thing of the past (Michael 1967:298), laid to rest by both the population decline attending the smallpox epidemic of 1838–1839 and increased trading possibilities associated with the arrival of the Russians.

As in other parts of Alaska and easternmost Asia (Burch 1988a:229), warfare in western Alaska was strictly a male activity, and young boys were trained in the arts of war from their earliest years.[5] All a young man's early training focused on making him agile, swift, and strong, traits he needed as both a warrior and a hunter. Boys generally worked hard—shoveling porches, clearing water holes, filling and carrying water buckets, activities that strengthened their bodies at the same time that the goodwill of the elders enhanced their spiritual power. Elders encouraged them to assume disagreeable jobs like emptying the urine bucket. They were instructed to rub their dirty hands over their stomachs, as the dirt would create a barrier to sickness and protect them from enemy arrows.

Food restrictions were another important part of the regimen. To make him swift and light, a young man's intake of water and oil was carefully controlled. Likewise, he should never eat the wings of ducks or geese, or he would lack endurance when he tried to paddle his kayak. Boys were also warned against eating the delicious membrane that encased a seal's internal organs, or when they were on the open tundra or ocean they would be surrounded by fog and not be able to see.

Specialized skills required for warfare included the ability to dodge missiles and use a staff to deflect oncoming arrows. The agile warrior who could accomplish these feats was used as bait to spend the arrows of the opposing group. A special jump competition (*qecgaurluteng*) performed on the last day of the annual Bladder Festival on Nelson Island publicly displayed this skill along with other shows of strength, such as climbing a rope up to the central gut skylight (Billy Lincoln, Apr. 1986, NI).

Young men also practiced the art of speedy departure. As war was often waged from kayaks, they would put their craft on wooden rollers by the bank of the river with the paddles in readiness. Then they would run to the kayak, jump in, and be off in an instant (Mary Worm, May 14, 1988, YN; Eddie Alexie, Mar. 1988, YN).

Just as the training required to make a successful hunter was in many respects the same as that required to make a skilled warrior, the tools of the hunt were also the tools of war. Yup'ik offensive weaponry (*anguyagcuutet*) was comparable to that used by the Eskimo warriors of north Alaska and Siberia (Burch 1974:5), and included the bow and arrow, spear, knife, and club. Arrowheads used in battle were more highly fractured than arrowheads used in hunting so that they would shatter in the enemy's body and leave a jagged wound. Their protective equipment was also distinctive. Coastal Yup'ik warriors used small shields made of bearded seal skin that were attached to the arms when fighting from a kayak (Billy Lincoln, Jan. 26, 1987, NI). Protective bent-wood headgear was also worn to deflect arrows, and at the end of a battle these war helmets would be worn out by the nicking of arrows (Tim Akagtak, June 21, 1984, NI).

Neither plate armor (like that used prehistorically in the Bering Strait region) nor telescoping hide band armor (used by the Chukchi and Siberian Eskimos) was employed (Burch 1974:5, 1988a:230; VanStone 1983:3–4). Rather, for easy movement the uniform of choice was a light rabbit skin or seal gut parka, belted around the middle and sometimes concealing loosely constructed mussel-shell armor.

Last but not least, Yup'ik warriors, like their Iñupiat counterparts (Burch 1974:5), took care to ensure that they had good footgear prior to going to battle, as a lame warrior soon would be a dead one. A warrior's grass boot liners were the objects of special concern and would be hung on the wall of the men's house before a raid and elaborately entertained to ensure success.

In the eighteenth century in western Alaska interregional relations were regularly punctuated with bloody encounters, usually in retaliation for a specific act or acts of aggression by the opposing group. Mounting a particular raid required both having a grievance and having the necessary force to back it up. Enmity was long-standing, and retaliation often was postponed until the aggrieved felt relatively sure of their chances of success.

The object of organizing a war party was not to acquire booty, extend territory, or defend boundaries but to exterminate the enemy. No one time of year was best suited to this end, and war parties were dispatched both on foot in winter and by kayak in summer. During periods of intense hostility between specific groups, warring factions sometimes exchanged hostages (*ilaliyak*, the one making allies) to maintain periods of safe hunting. As long as such a "guest" was present, the host village would not attack.

Although the season of the year was not specified, the number and quality of warriors that could be mustered, both from within the region and from allied groups, was a critical element in mounting a raid. Like the Iñupiat, Yup'ik warriors were fully aware of the importance of outnumbering their enemy and would retreat if they found themselves outmanned.

The element of surprise was a third important factor. Raiding warriors traveled in a single line to avoid detection and exerted extreme care during their approach. If they lit a fire, they might build it on supports over a stream so that it could be doused at the slightest noise. To avoid being taken off guard, the home village maintained lookouts and runners to warn of an approaching war party. In lowland areas, soil might be gathered to raise the ground level of the village both for easy defense and to keep watch because, as one man said, "those people had no binoculars" (Tim Akagtak, July 17, 1985, NI).[6] These mounds were visible for over ten miles and were said to have been impregnable (J. Kilbuck, "Report from Hooper Bay," 1911, p. 8, MA). Tunnels between houses and multiple exits were also built to increase chances of escape should the village be surrounded (Fienup-Riordan 1988d:48–49).

In Yup'ik as in Iñupiat warfare the ideal form of engagement was the surprise attack (Nelson 1899:327; Burch 1974:8). The aggressors approached stealthily, hoping to find their foes at home, where they could club them to death before they had a chance to rally a defense. Alternately, they might find the unsuspecting villagers gathered in the men's house in celebration or asleep. The attacking warriors would then block the entrances, set fire to the structure, and either burn the occupants alive or kill them by smoke inhalation. These neat plans did not always succeed, as in the tale of the warriors who literally laughed their way to freedom. While they were surrounded in the men's house and debating what to do, an old man among them fell off his bench head first into a bucket of urine. His companions laughed so loud that their clamor convinced the enemy that they must have a secret escape route, and the attackers left at once fearing the tables would be turned.

Although ambush was the favored form of attack, direct confrontation of two armed groups did occur. A pitched battle was usually unintentional on the part of at least one of the warring parties. In the case of two antagonistic groups living near each other on Nelson Island, a broken spear sent down the river was recognized as a sign of war, and both sides immediately prepared for battle.

Battles opened when opposing sides lined up, faced each other, and engaged in ritualized taunting. The taunting consisted of verbal sallies accompanied by a stiff-legged sideways jumping movement intended to goad the enemy into wasting their arrows. As the lines of battle closed and more and more arrows found their mark, the war cries of successful bowmen filled the air. In some areas when a warrior shot an enemy, he held his bow in his left hand and his spear in his right hand and jumped up and called out his family war cry. A final hand-to-hand encounter brought the battle to a close with the survivors of the defeated party beating a rapid retreat.

A decorative reminder of one such successful escape is the strip of caribou skin Nelson Island women sometimes sew on the shoulders of fancy parkas. Known as the "vomit design," the skin commemorates the retreating warrior who had just eaten the rich back fat of a caribou before his pursuers commenced to chase him. As he ran, he turned first to one side and then the other, emptying his stomach of its rich contents and making his pursuers' path both slippery and treacherous.

Surrender was not an option for the losers, as captives were not taken, but a single survivor was left alive to tell the tale. Although mutilation did not always follow a battle, successful warriors sometimes severed the heads and genitals of the corpses. This mutilation might have been related to the Yup'ik belief that to finally kill an opponent, especially one believed to have supernatural powers, the victor must sever the body of the vanquished at the joints. If the body were not dismembered, the spirit of the dead might successfully reanimate the corpse, and the fight would begin all over again.

FIGURE 7.2 Bow-and-arrow war ossuary located on Quluqaq Bay near Dillingham; covering rocks removed (Courtesy Matthew O'Leary).

Just as hunters carefully disposed of the remains of animals and fish, so warriors cared for the bodies of fallen adversaries. Along the coast below the mouth of the Kuskokwim, the successful combatant sometimes covered the body of his fallen enemy with rocks. If the dead were numerous, they might be gathered together and placed in a single large grave. Alternately the victors might gather all the bodies and throw them in a lake, an act comparable to the disposal of the bones of sea mammals.

The defeated warriors were not the only ones to die. All the young boys of a defeated village met the same fate and in some cases the women and girls as well. The women might be taken back to the village of the victors. Whether they were retained as slaves or wives, by all accounts their captors guarded them closely, kept them indoors, and allowed them to wear only grass insoles without boots to prevent their escape. Taking prisoners was a distinct contrast to Iñupiat practices but was similar to Aleut and Pacific Eskimo practices.

Following a battle warriors tattooed their faces and chests to commemorate the number of enemies they had killed. Great warriors could be recognized by the row of small marks extending over their eyebrows horizontally across their foreheads.

Yup'ik Alliance and Conflict, Past and Present

Now that we have noted the general features of Yup'ik warfare and some of the ways in which it was like and unlike Eskimo warfare west of the Mackenzie delta, an observation on its unique history is in order. Like those of northern Alaska and Siberia, Yup'ik war parties composed of warriors from one or more nations mounted surprise raids and took part in open battles against the warriors of other Yup'ik nations. The one constant of both Iñupiat and Yup'ik warfare was that it was intergroup rather than intragroup in character.

Although Yup'ik warfare resembled Iñupiat warfare in its international character, it appears that hostilities as well as alliances between particular nations were less transient than those described for north Alaska. According to Burch (1974:5), in northwest Alaska regional groups allied one year could be fighting one another the next. In western Alaska, however, hostilities as well as alliances between particular nations appear to have run over a long period of time, at least in the century immediately preceding the termination of interregional warfare.

Prior to the arrival of the Russians, two long-standing conflicts organized relations between the twelve Yup'ik nations. Put simply by Billy Lincoln (Aug. 1987, NI) of Nelson Island: "The Yukon area people had Hooper Bay as their enemy. And the others, like Apanuugpak bunch [*Qaluyaarmiut* and *Caninermiut*] had those who kept fleeing toward Dillingham for an enemy."

In this summary statement, the "Yukon people" included the residents of three adjoining nations: *Kuigpagmiut*, *Pastulirmiut*, and *Unalirmiut* (Figure 7.1). These nations did not fight each other but instead joined in various combinations and waged intermittent warfare with the lower coastal nations (including *Marayarmiut*, *Askinarmiut*, *Qaluyaarmiut*, and *Caninermiut*) as well as with the people of the middle Kuskokwim (*Kusquqvagmiut*) and the Big Lake region (*Akulmiut*). The lower coastal nations maintained a loose alliance in opposition to their Yukon adversaries (Hawkes 1913:2; Michael

1967:292; Nelson 1899:328). At the same time, I know of no accounts of raids or battles fought among these lower coastal groups or between the coastal nations and their tundra and riverine neighbors. Moreover, there is no indication that coastal and Yukon groups ever joined together in an alliance against a third party.

The second major long-standing conflict existed between a small but scrappy nation, the *Aglurmiut*, and the lower coastal and riverine nations, including *Qaluyaarmiut, Caninermiut, Kusquqvagmiut*, and *Kiatagmiut*. Although these groups did not regularly organize for coordinated raids against their common enemy, neither did they ever wage war against each other. Moreover, some evidence indicates that the warlike *Aglurmiut* originally migrated from the Yukon area after being defeated in an earlier Yukon/coastal encounter. Thus the history of Yup'ik warfare, roughly drawn, may have involved the long-standing opposition between two groups of allied nations rather than a large number of continually shifting alliances.

To bring the discussion back to the stereotype of the peaceful Eskimo, the failure to recognize the political alliances that were forged between Yup'ik nations during the period of bow-and-arrow wars has severely limited our ability to understand current political activity. In western Alaska today, *Qaluyaarmiut, Caninermiut, Akulmiut*, and *Kusquqvagmiut* are again joining forces in aggressive opposition to what they perceive as hostile acts by outside nations, in this case the United States and the State of Alaska (see Chapter 9). Their aggressive stance has surprised many observers who view it as inexplicably "un-Eskimo." On the contrary, it seems to me directly related to, although by no means identical with or completely explained by, the strong international political alliances of their past and impossible to understand without reference to them.

Eskimo and Indian Images at Odds

Having described Yup'ik warfare, I would like to place what I have said about the stereotype of the peaceful Eskimo in the context of the problem of the representation of native Americans generally. Along with their presentation as "naturally" peaceful in opposition to our warring selves, Yup'ik Eskimos have been represented as, among other things, perfectly adapted, dependent on the waste-free management of scarce and limited resources; preoccupied with survival and motivated first and foremost by individual need (Gordon 1906–1907:70); and lacking formal leadership, territorial boundaries, and concepts of land ownership (Vitt 1987:40). Put perhaps too flippantly, Eskimos seem to have an image problem. They are thought to be too peaceful, too clean, too ecological, and, ironically, too closely adapted to nature to conceivably coexist with their dirty, wasting, warring counterparts.[7] Moreover, Yup'ik ideology and contemporary political rhetoric have helped us into this double bind, and only a considered look at ideology in action can get us out.

The history of native/non-native relations in the United States is largely the story of white people's attempts to assimilate the Indian past in terms of their own history (Miller and Hamell 1986:315), and the history of Eskimo/white relations is no different. The image of the happy, hard-working, nonviolent Eskimo is part of our internal dialogue about the nature of natives, and facts to the contrary are all too often and easily dismissed. The stereotype of the peaceful Eskimo cannot be understood outside the context of native/non-native relations in general, and it is here that we must look to understand its origin.

American scholars have pointed out that in their depictions of Indians, non-natives employ counterimages of themselves (Bellah 1975:6–9; Berkhofer 1978:27; Pagden 1982:167). The superiority of white identity is simultaneously defined and established by reference to the negative characteristics of this group. By defining native Americans as savages and projecting onto them the sins they most abhorred, the colonizers mentally transformed their own aggressive acts against American Indian peoples into cleansing actions.[8]

White views of the American Indian are inextricably bound up with Euro-Americans' evaluation of their own society and culture, and their ambivalence about the validity of their own social values is mirrored in their valuation of Indian life (Berkhofer 1978:27). As a result, different and contradictory images of the Indian are possible, depending on the observers' valuation of their own society. While nineteenth-century Romantics saw in Indians the childlike innocence of man before the fall, Social Darwinists viewed them as irrational primitives representative of an earlier and less advanced stage of civilization. Moreover, Indians were differently regarded depending on how they treated the colonizers. Native Americans such as Sacajawea and Squanto were characterized as "good Indians" insofar as they were friendly and hospitable to the initial invaders of their land. On the other side, the resistance of Indians such as Metcom and Geronimo resulted in their being portrayed as "bad Indians" who possessed traits such as nakedness, lechery, passion, and a thirst for blood and violence.

Given the history of Euro-American/Indian interaction from the sixteenth through the nineteenth centuries in North America, the dominant characterization of native Americans as "warlike" should not be surprising, a Eurocentric categorization that continues to this day. For example, a 1974 survey of 230 kindergarteners in the suburbs of St. Paul asked children twelve questions about American Indians. The survey concluded:

> Some comments reflecting a war-like image could have been anticipated. Yet we were surprised at the relatively large number of kindergarten children who described Indians as mean or killing or shooting people. This type of comment occurred in response to every question except number 7 (Where do Indians live?). . . . Even an Indian mother's activities were described as "kills people and goes to work." (Hirschfelder 1982:8)

A survey concerning perceptions of Eskimos conducted in a Vermont elementary-school classroom elicited an equally dramatic response (Lake et al. 1984:141):

Q: Are the Eskimos different or the same as we are?
R: They are the same. . . .
Q: Are the Eskimos peaceful people or fighting people?
R: Peaceful, because they share their food.
Q: What about compared to the Indians?
R: The Indians are different, they wear paint and feathers and they are fighting, the Eskimos don't!

The characterization of Eskimos as peaceful and Indians as warlike is nothing new. According to an 1867 *Harper's* summary of Alaska, "Our new territory . . . is populated by Indians who are fierce and warlike, and by Esquimaux who are peaceful and already subjected." The cultural assumptions reflected in these observations continue to inform American popular culture to this day. For example, Alaska Airlines, one of the largest air carriers in the state, has since the mid-1970s painted a smiling Eskimo logo on the tails of its jetliners. When the company proposed changing the symbol to a mountain, the public protested, labeling the smiling Eskimo no less than "a symbol of Alaskan life" (Klahn 1988).

In its construction of the ideal (and grossly oversimplified) contrast between the warlike Indian and the peaceful Eskimo, American society vividly expresses its most prominent hopes and fears and so reveals something of itself. In our depiction of American Indian history, we explain how anarchic disorder and lack of respect for work and progress can lead only to historical oblivion (Arcand 1987). The Eskimo, however, is seen less as a contrasting persona than as an idealized image of ourselves. A robust, resourceful individualist preoccupied with survival, the Eskimo is a veritable embodiment of the Protestant ethic. If the American Indian came largely to represent the Hobbesian barbarian, whose life was brutish, nasty, mean, and short, the Eskimo was more often identified with the Rousseauian nonviolent "noble savage," pure until corrupted by civilization. Whereas American Indians were perceived as a threat, Eskimos were more often depicted as an original image of ourselves.

If one accepts that we have modeled our image of Eskimos after an idealized image of ourselves, the next question is, How in fact do we see ourselves and how do the flaws of our self-conceptualization affect our view of Eskimos? Following Macpherson (1962), the ideology of possessive individualism may be seen to underlie Western society. Society is the sum of many separate parts known as individuals, each with distinct needs and desires and each seeking to augment his or her own ends.

De Tocqueville succinctly expressed this point of view in his discussion of democracy in America when he wrote (1835:91–92):

> Aristocracy has made a chain of all the members of the community, from the peasant to the king; democracy breaks that chain and severs every link of it. . . . They owe nothing to any man, they expect nothing from any man; they acquire the habit of always considering themselves as standing alone, and they are apt to imagine that their whole destiny is in their own hands. Thus not only does democracy make every man forget his ancestors, but it hides his descendants, and separates his contemporaries from him; it throws him back for ever upon himself alone, and threatens in the end to confine him entirely within the solitude of his own heart.

According to this view a person is a dynamic yet bound center of awareness. Consequently, individual freedom is a virtue and society a constraint that is inspired by individual self-interest tempered by fear of other people. Reason dictates that people ought to get together because they cannot satisfy their individual needs unless they do. Eskimo society has in fact been described as "individualistic" in this sense because of the apparent nuclear family focus of social organization. Far from it, each person lives in a complex social web, including the living and the dead.

To take this contrast further, whereas Western society opposes the ideology of equality to the reality of economic disparity (Dumont 1970), the Yup'ik Eskimos hold to a definite social hierarchy according to age and degree of relation, while they manage to maintain a greater degree of material equality through well-established systems of redistribution and exchange. Just as it is wrong to liken their independent family groups to our individualistic society, it is also false to equate their hierarchy with social stratification and therefore conclude that in a specialized way it does just what our social classes do. On the contrary, the individualism that pervades our social relations and the complex relationships between the generations that characterize theirs constitute an essential difference.

Having contrasted Yup'ik and Western ideology, I would also contrast their respective modes of interpretation. On the Western side, anthropology enshrines our attempt to comprehend indigenous peoples; the epistemology that guides anthropologists parallels their contemporaries' work in the marketplace. If Western ideology can be characterized as possessive individualism, then anthropological analysis can in many instances be characterized as possessive signification—the abstraction of culture as a thing that people do and have, something to be known rather than a means of knowing.

An example of the limitations of this objectification of culture is the comprehension of Yup'ik ritual distribution as, first and foremost, the expression of social stratification or necessary resource distribution or both. As described in Chapter 2, a seal party, in which a woman distributes meat and gifts in honor of her husband's first catch of the season, functions to provide older people in the village with meat. Although this practical effect of the distribution is important, it should not be emphasized at the expense of meaning. To do so would present native action in reduced or literalized form. Rather, concepts that we can identify in Yup'ik cosmology may be taken as the means as well as the objects of understanding. Viewed from this angle, the seal party may be seen as an antisymbol for anthropology: It turns technique and Western artifact (cups, cigarettes, Frisbees, and toilet paper) into life and human relations, just as our comprehension of Yup'ik culture in museum collections and dance displays tends to take life and freeze it into object and theatrical act.

In the end, non-natives all too often either naturalize Eskimos as paragons of simplicity and virtue or historicize them as the victims of Western imperialism, unencumbered by the specificity of Eskimo concepts of society, history, and personhood. An original assumption of similarity (that Eskimo society works the way we think Western society does) has affected our comprehension of Eskimo history and action in the present. We have taken an idealized Western individual, dressed him in polar garb, and then assumed that we have understood the garment's maker. The result is a presentation of Eskimo society that often tells us more about the meaning we seek in our own history than in its Eskimo counterpart.

Originating partly in the history of contact, partly in the oversimplified stereotypic images we have of our own culture, and partly in our ethnocentric tendency to see similarities between cultures that are fundamentally different, the "positive" stereotype of the peaceful Eskimo can have negative social and political consequences. To continue to embrace a view of Eskimos as preeminently peaceful can only cloud our understanding of their less-than-peaceful present. Eskimos are no more naturally "passive" than American Indians are naturally "aggressive." Rather, freed from these images, we must evaluate the actions of native Americans, past and present, as those of men and women who are as historically diverse and culturally complex as their Euro-American counterparts.

Original Ecologists?: The Relationship Between Yup'ik Eskimos and Animals

FOR THE YUP'IK ESKIMOS WHO make their home in the rich coastal environment of Nelson Island, the view of animals as nonhuman persons was of central importance in the past and continues so to this day.[1] As Robert Brightman (1983:343) has pointed out for the Manitoba Cree, the conservation rhetoric about game management assumes that the obligation to limit kills was an aspect of aboriginal "respect culture." All the evidence, however, indicates that this is an incomplete understanding of the Yup'ik point of view, which sees animals as an "infinitely renewable" rather than a finite resource.[2] Although writing specifically about the Cree, Brightman's deployment of the concepts of infinite renewal, the covert personhood of animals, and the total consumption of the harvest apply throughout the Arctic and Subarctic, as my use of his language in this discussion will show.

Animals as Nonhuman Persons

Yup'ik Eskimos traditionally viewed the relationship between humans and animals as collaborative reciprocity; the animals gave themselves to the hunter in response to the hunter's respectful treatment of them as "persons" in their own right (see Chapter 4). According to this view, human and nonhuman persons shared fundamental characteristics. The perishable flesh of both humans and animals belied the immortality of their souls. All living things participated in a cycle of birth and rebirth, contingent on right thought and action by others as well as self.

For both human and nonhuman persons the soul was identified as the principle that sustained life, and it remained in the vicinity of the body for a specified time after death before going to an extraterrestrial realm to await rebirth. For sea mammals the soul had an anatomical locus (the bladder). For humans an aspect of the person was reborn in the next generation. Newborn children often received the name, and with it the soul, of a recently deceased relative. In the past, inanimate objects were also believed to possess souls. Thus, hunters decorated their implements not only to endow them with favorable attributes (as seen in the extensive use of predatory-beast motifs) and to draw the animals they hunted but to simultaneously impart life into and please the objects themselves.

Along with this belief in an essential spiritual continuity that bridged the gap between the past and the future, the Yup'ik Eskimos also believed that both people and animals possessed awareness, which allowed individuals a sense of control over their destiny. Also, this awareness was thought to be a product of experience. As a person grew to maturity and gained awareness, he or she became aware that an elaborate set of rules for living (*alerquutet* and *inerquutet*) circum-scribed interaction between persons, both human and nonhuman. At least three ideas underlie this elaborate detail: the power of a per-son's thought, the importance of thoughtful action so as not to injure another's mind, and the danger inherent in following one's own mind.

The essential similarity between human and nonhuman persons created the common ground for their interaction. Just as human hunters were capable of conscious decisions as to what and where to hunt, animals likewise were believed capable of conscious decisions that affected the success of individual hunters. For example, seals were believed to disdain the approach of a hunter who seemed care-less in either thought or action (Fienup-Riordan 1983:180). Here the character of human conduct is an important factor in the interaction; however, human action is not sufficient in itself to guarantee a hun-ter's success.

The qualities of personhood shared by humans and animals estab-lish the basis for a mutual and necessary respect. Respect is under-stood in both positive and negative terms, including love and fear. Perhaps the most often used term is *takar-* (to be shy of, respectful toward, and/or intimidated by). This term, combining both admira-tion for and fear of the person designated, is used by juniors in refer-ence to their relationship with elders as well as by humans in reference to their relationship with certain animals. It may also refer to the weather as in "the cold doesn't respect people with fancy par-kas" (Jacobson 1984:353).

One significant and ubiquitous form of respectful behavior considered important to this day is the care given to animal bones. People took great pains to remove every scrap of meat from seal bones. If they did not do so, the seals would perceive the bones as loudly singing, warning them not to give themselves to those careless people. Traditionally, these bones were either buried, burned, or submerged in a pond near the village or camp. It was believed essential that bones not be left lying around for fear they would be stepped on by people or chewed on by dogs. Moreover, the bones of food given away had to be returned to the donor. The respect shown to animal bones was motivated by the desire that the animals be able to "cover their bones" in the future—that is, return as edible game. One *qanemciq*[3] related by Tim Akagtak (July 17, 1985, NI) of Nightmute is particularly significant in this regard. He recalled a man who had saved himself from starving by thoroughly cleaning a walrus skull and placing it on a shelf in his storehouse. Five days later when the hunter went to check it, the skull was once again "full of meat."[4]

Although human/nonhuman interaction is made possible by their common possession of an immortal soul and a mind meriting respect, humans and animals are also clearly differentiated. Within the oral tradition, these differences are least evident in the *qulirat*, or traditional tales of time out of mind (for example, Lantis 1953:133–134). The mythical space/time they describe is still believed to be present, although largely invisible. In these tales, animals often lift up their beaks or muzzles, transforming themselves into human form (for example, Nelson 1899:394, 453).

The tale of Ayugutaar, a Nelson Island hunter who was visited by a wolf, described the hunter's initial encounter with the wolf (Tim Akagtak, July 17, 1985, NI):

After doing something around its head
and doing something to its mouth
when it faced him,
it became this way
taking its hood off.

In the same way awareness (*ellange-*) is sometimes equated with peeling back the skin of an animal, as when the puppies born to a Nelson Island woman who had married a dog peeled back their fur and revealed themselves to their mother in human form.

Along with depicting animal/human transformations, the *qulirat* also recall the subsequent process of differentiation, through which the physical and behavioral contrasts between humans and animals occurred. For example, the origin of the wolverine with its vicious personality is attributed to the frustration and subsequent transformation of a man following his desertion by his spirit wife (Pleasant 1981:263). In these tales, contemporary animal species are identified as descended from transformed human beings.

Perhaps the most vivid accounts of animal/human interaction, and those that best portray both the similarities and the differences between animal and human society, are tales that describe humans visiting animal society and animals living within human society. An example is the story of the boy who went to live with the seals (Fienup-Riordan 1983:177–181). On arriving in the seals' underwater home, the boy perceives his hosts as humans of differing sizes and shapes, depending on their species identity. Two hunters visiting with walrus also perceive their animal hosts as human (Fienup-Riordan 1983:236). Both tales present a covert world in which animals speak, marry, live in sod houses, take part in aspects of human material culture, and have the physical appearance of human beings. Furthermore, this world is depicted as being available to the awareness of humans under certain circumstances. Conversely, animals can enter human society, as in the case of the wolf who takes human form and comes to dwell with the hunter Ayugutaar. However, the animal nature of the wolf-man is always apparent in his propensity to crunch bones when he eats.

Although these tales depict animals as humans and describe their social interaction, they also serve to underline the differences between them. For example, in the story of the boy who went to live with the seals, emphasis is placed on contrasting perceptions by describing the seals' experience with humans from the seals' point of view. From the seals' perspective, humans who failed to live by the rules would appear distorted in one way or another:

People would be walking
and one of the men on shore
would be seen as
having a necklace of many things
such as old mukluks.
Some men were encumbered as such.

It is said that
those are the ones
who continually walk
under everything that is hanging.
    (Theresa Moses, Aug. 1987, NI)

In the same way, after drinking from a bowl or dipper people were required to make a stylized "removal motion" in which they passed their right hand back and forth across their face to clear their vision. People who failed to perform this removal motion would not be able to see animals even though they were well within view. At the same time the animals would see them as having the bowl stuck to the front of their face.

According to Brightman (1983:227), oral tradition represents the perceptible differences between humans and animals as masking underlying resemblances between them. In Yup'ik myth and story, animals thirst for fresh water and hunger for *akutaq* (literally "a mixture"). Belukha whales long to rest on dry land, and seals range themselves in their underwater *qasgiq* according to a social hierarchy comparable to their human hosts': Smaller seals sit on the lower benches while the large bearded seals, the "old men," occupy places of honor. The carcasses of the spawning salmon left on riverbanks are not their bodies but their "canoes" that they have abandoned on their journey inland (Himmelheber 1938). Just as some aspect of the human person is reborn in the next generation, so too animals experience rebirth. For example, in the story about the boy who went to live with the seals, the boy observes the arrival into the underwater men's house of the spirits of the seals killed the previous year and their subsequent departure in the spring to return to the hunters who had killed and cared for them in the past. This rebirth following their mortal demise is still a firmly held tenet of many Nelson Islanders.

On Nelson Island today, people continue to view contemporary game populations as continuous with their mythic ancestors. Moreover, animals can foretell the future. One story recalls how a woman skinning a fox discovered a tin box of snuff under the skin of its hindquarter—years before whitemen had introduced this luxury to the area. Animals are also seen to act like humans in everyday contexts, as when loons dance and mice busy themselves cleaning their "storehouses" in the spring. Not only do animals act like humans but they exhibit human sensibilities, which are also interpreted as objective signs of the hidden personhood of animals. Furthermore, contemporary accounts about hunting experiences recall the consequences (including game shortages) of a hunter's teasing or abusing his catch. These accounts presuppose both the physical renewal of the slain animals as well as their ability to recall and punish past injuries. A human hunter's daily dealings with animals continue to be structured by his awareness of the animal's covert personhood.

Even today, the view persists on Nelson Island that animals were once closer to humans and used human clothing and speech but were gradually differentiated from their human counterparts. Their possession of awareness as well as their rebirth after being killed and eaten by humans are described in the *qulirat* as essential aspects of their personhood—real yet unavailable to conventional observation. The treatment given animals by humans—the care of their bones, circumspection in discussing the kill, care and distribution of the catch—presupposes these same shared aspects of personhood. Many people still believe that animals observe what is done to their carcasses, communicate with others of their kind, and experience rebirth after death. This conceptualization of the animal as a nonhuman person underlies and sets the stage for everyday experience.

The Ideology of Production

Among the most important issues facing Yup'ik Eskimos today is the future of their relationship with their land and resources. In the past this relationship was not one of possessive ownership. Hunters believed that animals gave themselves to them by virtue of proper attitude and action in the context of both human and animal/human interaction. Hunters viewed animals as an infinitely renewable resource possessing both immortal souls and awareness comparable to that of human persons. By this view, human predation could not directly affect animal populations adversely. Rather human activity was instrumental only insofar as it was able to influence reactive decisions in the animal and spirit worlds. A hunter did not act on a finite population of animals, only on their accessibility.

To this day the representation by Nelson Island elders of the consequences of contemporary hunting and fishing activity presupposes a more or less continuous supply of animals—as long as they are given the proper respect. According to Billy Lincoln (1985, NI) of Tok-sook Bay:

> If a man kills many seals, many land animals,
> if he does not treat them well, but wastes the meat,
> they will be angry.
> In the spring the seals will come back.
> The animals will be moving everywhere.
> But that hunter will not get any,
> he will not be able to successfully hunt them.

The admonition is to conduct one's hunting in a manner that will not offend the animals taken. Moreover, such an offense does not affect the supply of animals but simply makes them hard to find. No concept of limiting the take is apparent here, only the prohibition against disrespectful treatment of the animals that present themselves.

Lincoln (1985, NI) further qualifies the character of this prescription:

> When a man is hunting.
> he is told not to let his quarry escape.
> He should try very hard to catch what he has sighted.
> He will be concerned if he stops hunting without taking it.
>
> If he stops hunting and returns to the village
> that animal will go back to his companions.
> He will tell them how he has been hunted and not taken.
> Then in times of famine
> they will hide from him.
> That hunter will not be able to find animals.

Thus, hunting is an activity (like many others) in which people's offenses come back to them in time. Avoidance of such a sanction motivates respectful hunting; however, what is significant is the view of animals carried into the present day as an infinitely renewable resource. What Lincoln is saying is substantially different from the views of those who see Alaska natives as "natural conservationists." As described by Billy Lincoln, only the availability of animals, not their existence, is within the range of human influence. The basic assumption underlying the current non-native understanding of the Yup'ik relationship between humans and animals is that the obligation to limit kills was an aspect of aboriginal "respect culture." Good evidence, however, points to this as an incomplete presentation of the Yup'ik point of view.

Over the last century non-natives have repeatedly been confounded by the combination of care and apparent extravagance in Yup'ik dealings with animals. For example, John Kilbuck, a Moravian missionary working along the Kuskokwim River at the turn of the century, decried what he viewed as an irrational and wasteful attitude toward game management. On a trip to Hooper Bay in 1911 he commented on a successful belukha drive after which only select cuts of meat were harvested. He was appalled by the natives' improvidence, remarking, "Here they are acting according to their time honored custom that the more they kill, the more whales will return the following year. Such carelessness will cost them dear the following spring" (J. Kilbuck, letter to W. T. Lopp, Aug. 12, 1911, MA). To Kilbuck's chagrin, his parishioners placed no apparent limit on their take. This "carelessness" was not restricted to the harvest. All during his career Kilbuck continued to complain that in their ceremonial distributions, the Yup'ik people acted as if there were no tomorrow. He was accurately observing the practical consequences of the idea that one's future hunting luck was partially dependent on the complete use of stores from the previous year. This practice played an important part in showing the animals that they were respected.

Kilbuck finally concluded that this apparent improvidence could be accounted for by the exigencies of the Eskimos' primitive methods of meat preservation. Here, however, the missionary betrayed an ethnocentric and characteristic functionalism. In fact, as part of the endless cycle of reciprocal exchange that they engaged in with their animal compatriots, the Yup'ik people held that the more game they consumed the more they would have. Accordingly, their winter ceremonies and elaborate gift exchanges, in which tremendous quantities of food were distributed and consumed, were both a practical way to use up leftovers and an essential act of reciprocal hosting. More than a mechanism for utilizing or rationally equalizing excess, the Yupiit considered these feasts to be the prerequisite for a successful harvest in the coming year. As such they were essential sacred acts, whatever their social cost.

Of course, the Yup'ik people worried about food shortages and limitations of their technology; but even when individual families expended great effort to provide for their future needs during one season, all their stores might be put at the disposal of the group the next. Kilbuck and his cohorts fought long and hard against what they viewed as impractical and "irrational" generosity, failing to understand the larger social need these distributions fulfilled. The failure of the game would temporarily destroy the human community (Sahlins 1986:10).

In contrast to the missionaries' deep commitment to the individual household boasting a full larder to which family members had exclusive rights, their Yup'ik converts repressed individual hunger and persisted in taking part in an incomprehensible social feasting that effectively exhausted the food at hand. Though the Yup'ik Eskimos regularly sublimated individual hunger to the larger social requirements of hospitality and social feasting, they expressed their sexuality more freely and even celebrated it as a principle of both reproduction and production—as when women bared their breasts when nursing and danced with the explicit intent of enhancing their own and their community's reproductive capacity.[5] Between their converts' mismanagement of their natural resources and perceived overindulgence of their sexual appetites, the missionaries had difficulty being sympathetic, let alone comprehending.

An understanding of Yup'ik subsistence ideology and beliefs about fertility can help explain the significance of harvesting activities observed by missionaries a hundred years ago in western Alaska. It can also help explain the miscommunication and talking past each other that characterize game management in western Alaska today. In fact, to gain perspective on current attitudes toward the harvest of fish and game, it is essential to take the Yup'ik perception of fish and game as infinitely renewable resources into account.

Limiting the Harvest: Geese, Musk Oxen, and Herring

Goose hunting in western Alaska has become a hotly debated issue. The rapid decline in the populations of cackling Canada geese, emperor geese, white-fronted geese, and brant have resulted in a prohibition against taking selected species during the early spring as well as during the summer nesting and molting seasons. Egg gathering has likewise been prohibited as have the tremendously productive bird drives, held into the late 1970s, in which men, women, and children drove thousands of molting geese and goslings across the tundra or a large lake, netted them, and dispatched them by hand.[6] Although

FIGURE 8.1 Frank Woods hunting for ducks and eggs, Nelson Island (Courtesy James H. Barker).

Nelson Islanders have cooperated with regulations limiting their hunting of selected species, their opinions about the issue dramatically contrast with those of the biologists responsible for federal oversight of the coastal waterfowl population.

Nelson Islanders admit that they do not see as many geese in the spring as in years past. They are not willing, however, to attribute this decline to overkill, either by themselves or by hunters in California and Texas who harvest from the same population of geese during their southern migrations. Although some younger Nelson Islanders find the explanation of resource decline through overkill sufficient, many reject it entirely, maintaining that fewer geese are evident because the birds are not receiving the proper treatment and respect. Some Nelson Islanders go so far as to blame the decline on the promiscuous behavior of today's teenagers. Young men and women are "always touching each other and looking at each other," and young women "run around too much outside." Also they say children are careless with their things, girls "taking their dolls just anywhere" (Frances Usugan, July 1985, NI). Moreover, I have heard older women on Nelson Island blame the decline on the prohibition against egg gathering. Traditionally, the fertility of the geese was believed to be enhanced when a woman spit in the nest and turned it upside down after gathering its contents. With the prohibition against egg gathering, this important fertility rite is no longer performed. The very act that non-natives view as essential to protecting the geese, Nelson Islanders believe contributes directly to their decline.

Nelson Island women also express concern that female biologists are doing irreparable damage to the goose population in the course of performing their scientific observations. According to Nelson Island tradition, women are forbidden from touching an empty nest lest it remain so in the future. If they find a full nest, they may touch only the eggs but never the nest itself:

And when the birds came in springtime,
they warned us not to touch their nests with our hands
before the eggs are laid
or if there are any eggs in them.
This is how the birds see:
a hand in the nest where they are going to lay their eggs.
It was because when we stick our hands inside those nests,
and if we do thus, when the bird goes back to them,

here are these hands,
So the nest would be filled with hands only.
(Theresa Moses, May 9, 1988, YN)

The majority of Nelson Island hunters adamantly oppose the activities of biologists (male and female) who have set up observation platforms in the wetlands to the north of Nelson Island to provide accurate counts of waterfowl returning in the spring. The biologists maintain that their observation strategies have been field tested in other wetland areas and could not possibly be negatively affecting the nesting geese. Nelson Islanders, however, say that in performing their observations, the biologists create trails that the foxes subsequently follow to raid the nests. Later, they say, sea gulls follow the foxes' spoor and destroy additional eggs and young (Robert Wolfe, personal communication).

In addition to having this practical (and by Western standards rational) objection rooted in what can be construed as ethno-ethology, Nelson Islanders are also profoundly disturbed by the inappropriate human activity in the bird nesting grounds and the general lack of respect shown the birds during the socially as well as biologically crucial nesting season. As far as many hunters are concerned, the scarcity of geese can be directly attributed to this carelessness, rather than to either overkill or inadvertent upset of the local ecological balance.

The Yup'ik explanation of hunting success and failure as dependent on appropriate social and ritual relations between humans and animals contradicts the idea that animal populations are manageable through selective killing. Although they grudgingly limit their takes to comply with federal regulations, Nelson Island hunters remain unconvinced that this limitation strikes at the core of the problem. Rather, offenses against the birds are the cause of their "hiding themselves from our sight," and only when such inappropriate behavior ceases will the birds return. Although they curtail their hunting during the critical nesting and molting seasons, many view limiting the catch less as a practical solution to the problem of population decline than as a moral obligation to animals that has desirable practical consequences.

The issue of how to handle the declining goose population is only one of a number of wildlife-management issues currently confronting Nelson Islanders. Another species requiring oversight is the musk oxen introduced onto Nelson Island in 1963 from nearby Nunivak

FIGURE 8.2 Musk oxen grazing on Nelson Island (Courtesy Paul Souders).

Island, which received the original herd from Greenland in 1934–1935. In the 1980s the herd grew large enough to support limited harvesting. Musk oxen have also begun to colonize the mainland and have been sighted as far north as St. Marys, on the Yukon River, and south to Quinhagak, at the mouth of the Kuskokwim River. On Nelson Island, the Alaska Department of Fish and Game makes a specific number of permits available to interested hunters. In part because of the strong opposition by Nelson Islanders to harvesting from their herd by outsiders, Fish and Game issues the permits locally on a first-come, first-serve basis. In 1986, however, eight of the thirty permits were taken by non-native, locally employed teachers who were among the first to line up on the day designated for the sale of the permits.

This incident was the cause of a significant conflict, including an attempt to prohibit the non-native teachers from hunting on native village corporation land. The teachers believed that they were acting within their rights as citizens in a free country in taking close to one-third of the available permits. When called on the issue, they justified their action on the basis of economic need. They maintained that they had as much use for the meat as any other person living on Nelson Island. Their use of an economic rationale to justify their actions is a sad commentary on their comprehension of local values and ideas about human/nonhuman relations.

For Nelson Islanders, the issue was not the meat. They would have been glad to share food with the teachers, glad to welcome them into their homes to eat, and glad to have them attend village potlucks. Sharing food of all kinds is a ubiquitous means of both establishing and affirming human relations and is usually one of the first things remarked upon by outsiders visiting the island.[7] To Nelson Islanders, the teachers were intruding into the ongoing relationship between local hunters and their prey, and this intrusion was unacceptable.

The Nelson Island attitude toward non-native hunters contrasts sharply with the attitude on nearby Nunivak Island. Although musk oxen are recent additions to the coastal fauna, Nelson Islanders are attempting to deal with them in a traditional manner. Nunivak Islanders, however, view the musk oxen as a commercial resource to be exploited. Since a permit system was introduced on Nunivak in 1975, residents have recognized the hunting of musk oxen as a means of making money through guiding, and Nunivak hunters have actively supported an open season and hunting by Caucasians. Nunivak Islanders, in fact, receive much of the meat from each kill, as most non-native hunters are interested primarily in the skin and horns. The difference in the Nelson Island and Nunivak Island response may in part be the product of the longer contact by the Nunivak Islanders with Caucasians in the management of reindeer, another introduced species on Nunivak Island. Nunivak residents have harvested reindeer as a commercial resource since the 1940s, and their successful reindeer industry may have provided a precedent for their commercial valuation of musk oxen.

The unexpected spread of musk oxen beyond Nelson Island has also been the cause of considerable conflict. Most coastal hunters abide by the Alaska Department of Fish and Game prohibition against harvesting from these scattered colonies until the herds have grown larger and become better established in their new homes. Yet hunters have sighted occasional musk oxen and have taken them illegally both on and off Nelson Island, and attempts by Fish and Game to prosecute offenders are deeply resented. Nelson Island hunters commenting on this illegal hunting articulate the Catch-22 of their situation: If they see musk oxen and kill them, they are breaking the white man's law; if they see musk oxen and let them live, they are breaking Yup'ik law. According to one seasoned hunter from Toksook Bay: "We must take what is presented to us. If we do not, our families will go hungry and the animals will stop coming near us. They will show us no respect."

For many Nelson Island hunters, a conservationist's argument that advocates reduced or controlled hunting to increase herd population makes little sense because such a measure does nothing to change the number of animals or the operation of the system as they conceive it. Having no concept of limiting the harvest, only prohibitions against waste, coastal hunters explain reductions in animal populations not by overhunting but by claiming that the animals have simply gone somewhere else.

Another resource on which conflict is presently focused is the herring fishery. In 1985 the waters adjacent to Nelson Island were opened to commercial fishing. As in the case of the management of the musk oxen, the fishery was initially limited to local use by super-exclusive regulations with highly restrictive gear limitations. In an attempt to increase both the productivity and safety of the fishery, the gear limits (primarily boat length) were raised, permitting the entry of outsiders. Predictably, Nelson Islanders resented the inroads

FIGURE 8.3 Commercial herring fishing on Nelson Island (Courtesy James H. Barker).

FIGURE 8.4 Woman drying herring for local use, Toksook Bay, Nelson Island (Courtesy James H. Barker).

made by non-native fishermen from Dillingham to Norton Sound who follow the herring runs up the coast.

Here again, the issue is simultaneously economic and moral/ideological. As far as the non-native fishermen are concerned, each person has as much right as any other to harvest the herring. After all, they say, the Yup'ik fishermen don't own the fish. For Nelson Islanders, however, rights to the fish do in fact belong to them in the sense that they have relied on the herring for generations and have a social relationship, not to mention moral obligation, to them. Nelson Islanders view rights to the herring as inalienable, conferred by knowledge of them and prior use, not by some democratic notion of individual rights and freedom.

The issue of landownership and land use is subject to the same logic. For the Yup'ik people of Nelson Island, a person has a right to use a specific site and to harvest from it by virtue of that person's relationship with previous generations of men and women who used the same site and, essentially, harvested the same animals. These animals, in turn, have returned year after year to specific sites in search of specific hunters. A contemporary Nelson Islander has a right to harvest the herring off the shores of Nelson Island because his ancestors harvested the same fish in years past. Thus, rights to both the land and its resources are understood to be relational rather than possessive. As such, they cannot be sold or legitimately usurped by nonresidents otherwise uninvolved in this cycle of reciprocity (Fienup-Riordan 1984a:74). In this view, aboriginal use is conceived as far from unregulated. As prior use gives one knowledge, knowledge of fish and wildlife gives one rights to continue that reciprocal relationship. "When they [our elders] speak out about the law pertaining to the land, they say it's a place for so and so, like for hunting, fishing, and so on. . . . They always tell us this is how it is done. They may think we don't have laws, those things are our laws!" (John 1984).

Today, perhaps the best that can be hoped for is an increased awareness on the part of non-native researchers, managers, and politicians of the meaningful organization of Yup'ik social relations, particularly human/animal relations, according to a cultural logic very different from their own. Even with such an awareness, conflict will likely continue in the arena of fisheries development and game management. Although economic in character, these conflicts are grounded in ideological differences as much as in disparate material circumstances.

Management Issues beyond Nelson Island: Sport Fishing and Walrus Hunting

Another conflict that has erupted south of Nelson Island vividly illustrates the disparity between the non-native view of animals as a finite, renewable resource that can and should be managed in a rational, scientific manner and the Yup'ik view of animals as nonhuman persons who must be shown respect. Since the 1970s recreational fishermen have flocked in increasing numbers to the banks of the Kanektok, Togiak, and Goodnews rivers. Every summer several thousand sport fishermen pay thousands of dollars each to fly into private lodges and tent camps set up by commercial guides along the rivers or have themselves flown to the headwaters and then float down to the coast, fishing as they go (Wolfe 1989:5).

These sport fishermen are predominantly non-natives. Many are avid fly fishermen, as concerned as the native residents of the region that the trophy rainbow trout, grayling, salmon, and Dolly Varden trout they encounter along the river be preserved. Most practice the catch-and-release method, whereby once a fish is taken the fisherman promptly removes the hook from its mouth and places the fish back in the water. Sport fishermen view catch-and-release fishing as sound management of the resource—a practice that will allow them to enjoy excellent fishing year after year as it does not deplete the fish stocks. Moreover, because they release most of the fish they catch (from ten to twenty a day), they see no reason why Yup'ik residents should mind their presence.

In fact, local residents do mind a great deal. They perceive both the means and the ends of catch-and-release quite differently than do the flyfishing enthusiasts. Coastal Yup'ik fishermen view fish as they do other species—as persons in possession of "awareness" and meriting respect. To hook such a person in the mouth and then replace it in the water constitutes senseless abuse, not sport. From their earliest years, Yup'ik men and women are taught that the bodies of fish must be treated with respect. Once they have taken a fish from the water, they must use every part of its body to ensure its return the following year. According to Sam Carter (May 1989, YN) of Quinhagak: "It is a warning never to place a fish back in the water once it is caught because that will cause the river to be depleted of fish. *Kelgulutenguq* [telling the others what had been done to them] the fish will disappear. And there will be no more fish. We can bury them in the land,

FIGURE 8.5 A recreational fly fisherman on the upper Goodnews River.

in a pit, for future use. But we never play around with fish. We never
catch them and put them back in the water."

To replace the fish in the water is to this day believed to "cut off"
the path of fish coming up the river. If living fish encounter injured
fish during their movement upriver, many coastal Yupiit believe that
the injured fish speak of their treatment, discouraging their relatives
from continuing their journey. If living fish encounter dead fish, they
are believed to experience them as a barrier and are prevented from
coming up the river the following year (see also Wolfe 1989:14). To
ensure against such a disaster, people carefully care for every part of
their catch—heads, bones, and flesh. Fish caught at the beginning of
the season around Chevak are cut and hung at either end of the drying racks to ensure that more fish will eventually fill the poles. On
the Yukon delta, women processing the catch give special treatment
to fish heads to encourage the fish to return to the human world the
following year:

All the Yup'ik people
hang the king salmon heads
facing away from the river
after cutting them.

And they dry them facing the current
hoping that they will come through the Yukon again.
Thinking of that happening again
they do that.

                 (Thomas Chikigak, Aug. 11, 1987, NI)

According to Quinhagak fishermen, people must never leave dead salmon and their unused parts lying around or throw them into the river. Once they have been touched by human hands, they are marked. If other fish see them in their path, they will not continue upstream but will return to the sea. Just as a bird views its nest as full of human hands if a woman has carelessly touched it, so a released fish is viewed by its contemporaries as covered with hands. In both cases, the hands are believed to terrify the nonhuman viewers, causing them to flee.

That contemporary villagers continue to view fish as nonhuman persons was vividly attested to in testimony collected by the Alaska Department of Fish and Game to ascertain the Yup'ik reaction to the new sport fishery (Wolfe 1989). Many Yup'ik residents stressed that "fish are not to be played with." From the Yup'ik point of view, catch-and-release is not sound management but an irresponsible activity that is endangering human and animal life along the rivers.

Interviews with Nelson Island elders add detail to the general proscription against "playing with the fish." According to Nelson Islanders, animals desire things they lack—seals that live in the ocean crave fresh water; belukha whales, which cannot crawl out on the ice to sun themselves, desire light and heat; and fish that swim in the river crave dry land. Yup'ik children are taught to care for the catch, placing each species according to its wishes. For older residents the maintenance of this cosmological distinction between things "of the land" and "of the sea" continues to be a critical factor in the treatment of fish and game.

As the western Alaska sport fishery has continued to grow, native resentment and resistance to this activity have likewise increased. In the summer of 1987 an angry group of villagers from Quinhagak confronted sport fishermen on the Kanektok River. Following this action, native residents went before the Alaska Board of Fisheries to protest the activities of sport fishermen along their rivers and asked the board to ban the catch-and-release fishing methods. The board did not meet their demand, but instead directed the issue to a federal/state planning group for resolution (Wolfe 1989:16).

The board's unwillingness to act was perhaps predictable, as it was in effect being asked to legislate between world views: the Euro-American view of fish as a finite resource that can and should be managed and the Yup'ik view of fish as persons who possess awareness and merit respect. Here again a sensitivity to the native point of view will not be enough to solve the problem. The differences are real, and although awareness can increase understanding, it cannot bridge the gap. The board will likely act only if Fish and Game biologists bring them quantitative, scientific proof that the catch-and-release method is in fact harming the fish population in the way Yup'ik people believe it is. Until that time, sport fishermen will be allowed to continue to "play with the fish."

On an optimistic note, whereas native/non-native interests are at odds in the majority of management issues, in some cases their interests coincide. Many contemporary Yup'ik elders view with alarm the careless actions of younger native hunters who, they believe, are no longer showing animals the proper respect. In some cases elders are as concerned by the way their children hunt animals as by the non-native attempt to prevent their hunting. Although Yup'ik elders vigorously defend the Yup'ik right to harvest animals, they do not always approve of the way the hunting is being done.[8]

Such a meeting of minds occurs over the issue of walrus hunting. The federal Marine Mammal Protection Act (1972) allows Alaska natives to hunt walrus for food and turn the ivory tusks into "authentic handicrafts," which they are allowed to sell.[9] In fact, walrus heads with carved tusks bring up to six thousand dollars in Anchorage gift shops and carved or uncarved oosiks (penis bones) eighty dollars or more. Although killing walrus for their valuable ivory with no intention of using the meat is profitable and therefore appealing to some hunters, it is illegal.

Yup'ik elders likewise decry such commercialism. Although their comprehension of waste does not require that every part of the animal be used to justify the kill, they are opposed to killing walrus specifically for their ivory with no effort made to bring the meat back to the village to share it in a traditional manner. The increasing unwillingness, particularly of young hunters, to share their catch is a problem that concerns many elders. As a result, many support the efforts by U.S. Fish and Wildlife Service officials to enforce the Marine Mammal Protection Act.

In the spring of 1989 Fish and Wildlife negotiated one of the more creative sentences ever imposed on an offender of the act, one that was positively received by a number of the culprit's contemporaries. The sixty-three-year-old patriarch Joe Clark of Clark's Point was convicted of shooting nine walrus, taking little meat, and leaving the carcasses to rot. As part of his sentence, Clark participated in the creation of a cautionary video telling other hunters not to waste meat. This seven-minute video in both Yup'ik and English was produced by Fish and Wildlife to be aired on public television and on the Rural Alaska Television Network. On screen Joe Clark says, "I believe that Eskimo hunters are the finest hunters in the world, and I am proud to be one . . . It is our privilege to hunt the walrus, and I ask that each of us hunters take a substantial part of the meat . . . It is important to respect the walrus, which we depend on even in times of abundance."

Although written by Fish and Wildlife personnel, the script accurately reflects contemporary Yup'ik hunters' view of themselves and the way they desire non-natives to see them. Yup'ik elders and Fish and Wildlife officials alike want to present Yup'ik hunters in a conservative light, if for somewhat different reasons. In June 1989 *Newsweek* published an article entitled "Off with Their Heads," in which a biologist for an environmental group reported that he had seen at least two hundred headless walrus while flying over the western Alaska coast (Beck and Anderson 1989). Fish and Wildlife Service personnel published a rebuttal in which they maintained that the article exaggerated the situation (Stieglitz 1989). Yup'ik informants likewise decried the inflammatory character of the report. Whether or not individual Yup'ik hunters engage in the kind of wasteful harvest described, both their peers and the agency responsible for regulating walrus hunting want such unrestricted hunting to appear "untraditional" and are doing what they can to present such actions as the exception to the rule.

Recognition and Resistance

The Yup'ik view of animals as unlimited in number was essentially correct through nearly all history. Although aboriginal hunters may have caused local and temporary depletion of some species, for all practical purposes most species constituted a virtually unlimited resource. Traditional Eskimo technology was among the most sophisticated in the world, but it is unlikely that the Yukon-Kuskokwim

Delta's relatively small population had any real effect on most animal populations, and thus no evidence would have contradicted this traditional view. Not until the introduction of firearms in the nineteenth century, followed by population concentration in the twentieth, did wildlife begin to become, in any real sense, a finite resource.[10] Human and animal populations were in better balance formerly. In the coastal communities the situation appears to have changed faster than people's beliefs.

Just as we looked to oral tradition to inform our knowledge of warfare and provide an alternative to the stereotype of the peaceful Eskimo, we can look to oral accounts to qualify our understanding of precisely what the Yup'ik resistance to regulatory attempts signifies. Listening to coastal Yup'ik elders today, we find fish and waterfowl largely represented as persons to be hosted, not finite resources to be managed. The availability of birds, their "desire to be seen," is viewed as a response to human activity, but their existence is not. The hunter's legal obligation to limit kills is often in direct opposition to his moral obligation to provide for his family and treat his prey with respect. To see these obligations as synonymous or compatible betrays a gross misunderstanding of the Yup'ik point of view.

The attempt in the 1980s to regulate hunting and fishing was, in fact, the first time game regulations were promoted or enforced on Nelson Island. However, people living along the Yukon River have been subject to laws regulating the salmon fishery for many decades. Throughout the Yukon-Kuskokwim Delta, resistance to regulated hunting and fishing varies among areas and may stem from many factors, including lack of prior enforcement of regulations; resistance to change; basic unfairness of regulations that prohibit hunting in the spring, when animals are both fat and abundant, while permitting it in the fall, when they are thin and less abundant; greater recreational value (even for Yup'ik hunters) in hunting than in fishing; self-interest; and, last but not least, conflict with traditional concepts of personhood.[11]

Along with problems in game management, if non-natives continue to ignore the ideological dimension of the Yup'ik relationship with animals, they are likely to misunderstand much of what they are told. For instance, in current testimony given in the villages on the future use and ownership of their land and resources, Nelson Islanders are trying to explain themselves simultaneously to us and to themselves. The result is testimony that sometimes revises the past to justify the present. In the case of game management and land use, people are in some instances presenting as tradition only a partial reflection of their past. The recognition of such intent makes it imperative to look at social action as the realization of values to sort out the origins of what we hear.

For instance, in a 1986 meeting on geese management, Alaska Fish and Game biologists who visited western Alaska were told by Yup'ik hunters that in the past no one owned the land or the animals, and no one wasted fish and wildlife. In fact, very real rights and obligations circumscribed traditional patterns of land use and resource extraction. Moreover, this resource extraction was motivated by the symbolically arbitrary and culturally specific conventional belief that animal populations fluctuated independently of human pressure on them. Yup'ik testimony, however, made reference to none of these qualifying points. Instead, it was delivered with the specific intent to object to the constraints of external regulation, and, therefore, those testifying concentrated on certain aspects of Yup'ik tradition to the exclusion of others in an effort to distinguish their view from what they see as the proprietary and impersonal view of non-natives.

In looking to the past to help us understand the Yup'ik view of the relationship between humans and animals in western Alaska today, we are faced with the question of whether the same categorical relations continue to dominate social action or whether they have become restricted metaphors with quite different meanings. Some of the current rhetoric concerning past patterns of hunting and land use may be an example of such a metaphorization of previously essential categorical relations. At present, some younger Nelson Islanders express the view that the geese are experiencing an actual population decline. Although they continue to affirm the need to respect them as essential nonhuman persons, they embrace the Western view of wildlife as a limited resource and, as such, subject to management through selective killing. Their testimony signals a fundamental ideological shift. It remains to be seen whether and when this interpretation will become dominant.

To this day, though much else has changed in western Alaska, many coastal residents view seals taken in the spring as the same animals that were killed the preceding winter. Women are still not allowed to go seal hunting, regardless of how pragmatically appealing this might be for a family in which the men are employed elsewhere in the busy village economy. Today's women are certainly less circumspect in their behavior toward men than were their grandmothers; however, young wives are still expected to limit their activity while their husbands are hunting and to be ready to care for their catch in the traditional manner.

At present, many Yup'ik people are working to reevaluate their traditional rules for living. This is a conscious effort today more than ever before. In their words, they feel that they are being "treated like tom cods, in and out with the tides." The twentieth century has brought huge changes. At the same time, they are far from dismissing their rich tradition as noninstrumental in their daily lives. It behooves those bent on writing about their culture and legislating their lives to likewise refrain from such a dismissal.

The Yupiit Nation:
Eskimo Law and Order

> We want to gather what has been
> thrown down and put the pieces back
> together. (Nick Charles, quoted in
> Alexie and Morris 1985:49)

A REVIEW OF THE LITERATURE ON
Eskimo leadership, law, and governance
reveals the most common assertion to be that they had none.[1] Diamond Jenness (1922:93) wrote of the Canadian Inuit, "One of the most noticeable features in Eskimo society almost everywhere is the absence of chiefs." John and Irma Honigmann (1965:241) echoed this evaluation: "Eskimo culture does not provide for leadership, except in limited and specific situations, and then greatly attenuates the position's responsibility and power." Gert Nooter (1976:8) indicated that the "lack of leadership" noted among the Canadian Inuit is also true in east Greenland, where "extremely little leadership" is evident. Wendell Oswalt (1963a:54) made a similar evaluation when he characterized the traditional sociopolitical situation in western Alaska as "contained anarchy": "No individual or organized group of individuals controlled any activities in the name of the community." Trader Bernhard Bendel, who traveled up the Kuskokwim River in the summer of 1870, wrote that "the Eskimos have got no chiefs and live without any form of government whatever" (quoted in Vitt 1987:40).

Probably all these observers, early and current, have been partly right and partly wrong in their classifications and interpretations. Early visitors in the North, influenced by Western political and judicial systems, looked in vain for hierarchically structured offices with clearly defined legitimation (through inheritance, election), tenure, powers, and duties. Finding instead horizontal networks and limits on individual action that might be modified by consensus, they understandably concluded that Eskimos lacked government.

Along with denying the existence of government and leadership as understood in the West, the better observers described the native alternative. For example, according to Nelson (1899:304), "The Alaskan Eskimo, so far as I observed, have no recognized chiefs *except as gain a certain influence over their fellow villagers through superior*

192

shrewdness, wisdom, age, wealth, or shamanism" (emphasis added). As we will see, the exception was the rule, and leaders were informally recognized in a number of social contexts, both public and private. In the same way, the missionary John Kilbuck simultaneously denied the existence of government as he understood it and gave tacit recognition to the Yup'ik alternative—public opinion: "The Eskimos, it would seem, never had a form of government. Public opinion furnished the rule of life. In general, every individual was a law onto himself, influenced to a greater or lesser degree by public opinion" (Fienup-Riordan 1988d:79).

Although the observation that Eskimo groups lacked formal governance is accurate, the conclusions this evaluation engendered have had a negative impact. Into the sociological gap created by the denial of an indigenous legal system, some scholars have placed its "primitive" counterpart: taboo. Adamson Hoebel (1961:70) wrote of the Eskimos that "a people more tabu-ridden would be difficult to find." Although he defended the existence of traditional Eskimo governance, he viewed it as "more religious than legal in nature" (1961:26). The implication was that once these traditional "superstitions" were taken from them following the introduction of Christianity, the Eskimos were left with nothing. Into this void, non-native forms of governance were introduced. In rural Alaska this primarily meant municipal government following statehood in 1959. All that remained was for Eskimo people to master the fine points of the state and federal systems so they would be, for the first time in their history, well governed.

Formation of the Yupiit Nation

This script is being vigorously contested by a tough-minded contingent of Yup'ik Eskimos in western Alaska. There, in 1983, the villagers of Akiachak, Akiak, and Tuluksak joined together to declare their status as a sovereign nation of Yup'ik people—the Yupiit Nation. The object of their declaration, and of the political activity that has followed, has been to reestablish self-government and local control of their land and lives. Since statehood, they have watched control of local government, education, and the land and resources on which they depend gradually shift away from the villages. The formation of the Yupiit Nation was a grass-roots attempt to arrest this erosion and in its place to reestablish "traditional" (non-Western, precontact) Yup'ik law and order.

The first major goal of the Yupiit Nation is increased control over education. Villagers have become dissatisfied with the centralized organization of education in rural Alaska, believing it to be unresponsive to the needs of individual villages. As an alternative, the three charter-member villages of Akiachak, Akiak, and Tuluksak established the Yupiit School District, which contracts directly with the state to manage primary and secondary education in the member villages. Although setting up and managing a new school district has not been an unmitigated success, it has established a precedent for increased local involvement in education.[2]

A second major goal of the Yupiit Nation has been to regain control over land and resources. Traditional Eskimo society and economy were built around a fundamental relationship between humans and animals. As they say, "The sea is our bank" and "Our land is our life." Their seasonal movement over the land to harvest fish and wildlife has been dramatically curtailed over the last two decades by increased state and federal regulation. Moreover, at the same time the Alaska Native Claims Settlement Act (ANCSA) of 1971 created native corporations and gave them title to aboriginal land, it sowed the seeds for possible loss of this title in 1991, when under the terms of the act the stock in the land could be sold. Prior to the passage of the so-called 1991 amendments in 1987, bankruptcy and stock sales posed a direct challenge to native landownership, as land is the major corporate asset. Because the economy of the region is precarious even in the best of times, loss of the land is no idle threat. If the land is lost, the people recognize that important components of their way of life will go with it. The Yupiit Nation wants to transfer land title to its tribal government to avoid any possibility of loss from economic forces. The issue of how best to safeguard their landholdings is unresolved. Whatever decisions are made in the future, at present the issue of control of the land is the rallying point around which villages are organized.

The third major goal of the Yupiit Nation, and the one that directly concerns us here, is self-government and outside confirmation of their status as a sovereign nation. The Yupiit Nation is working to establish a relationship with the federal government on a government-to-government basis, even more direct than the "limited sovereignty" enjoyed by American Indian tribes in the Lower 48. Such recognition would allow the tribal entity increased local control over education and social services, and would as well facilitate continued control of tribal lands. Above all, confirmation of tribal status would increase the ability of the Yupiit to legislate their own lives as they see fit. Progress, however, has been hampered by complex issues of statute, policy, and definition, including the federal government's refusal to consider new Indian Reorganization Act constitutions. Behind this refusal lies the general assumption that Eskimos traditionally lacked formal governance of any kind, let alone tribal or regional organization.

From the beginning the Eskimos who spearheaded the formation of the Yupiit Nation decided that the best way to achieve tribal sovereignty was to act sovereign. In 1983 the villagers of Akiachak dissolved their state-supported city government and turned power over to the tribal council. The following year they were joined by the two upriver villages of Akiak and Tuluksak. Since that time, sixteen other villages located downriver and along the Bering Sea coast have followed suit.[3] Although the Alaska Boundary Commission has still not legitimized their actions, Yupiit Nation villagers persist in asserting their tribal status.

Many non-natives view the Yupiit Nation's attempt at political revitalization as a contradiction in terms. How, they ask, can Eskimos "revitalize" traditional governance and law ways when "contained anarchy" characterized past political organization? They reject out of hand the Yup'ik bid to take control, saying that with no history of chiefs or political institutions, the Yup'ik people will be unable to govern properly. The Yupiit Nation (they believe) can be successful only insofar as it effectively mirrors non-Eskimo models of governance.

These conflicting views of the significance of contemporary Eskimo political activity rest on a basic misapprehension. Whereas many non-natives view contemporary Yup'ik Eskimos as "assimilated" natives whom we have generously helped to become more and more like us, the Yup'ik people see their own history as one of continuing efforts to control outside influences. For example, the Yup'ik Eskimos have the distinction, along with the majority of Alaska natives, of having escaped the reservation system so widely employed in the Lower 48. Most non-natives view this as a positive omission that has contributed to the Eskimos' slow but steady "acculturation." Many members of the Yupiit Nation, however, disagree. They laud the efforts of John Kilbuck to obtain reservation status for the village of Akiak in the early 1900s and regret that the federal government withheld support for Kilbuck's proposal. Ironically, Kilbuck's plan was proposed to protect, not empower, natives, whom he viewed as defenseless and prey to the evil influences of whites along the river. What some contemporary Eskimos view as enlightened empowerment was in fact paternalistic protection.

Setting the Record Straight

As a part of its efforts to confirm independent status and the right to self-government, the Yupiit Nation has sought to document the forms of governance that characterized western Alaska into the early 1900s. In 1988 they applied for and received a grant from the Administration of Native Americans (ANA) to support research on "traditional" (nineteenth-century) governance. Although the work was to be done primarily by and for members of the Yupiit Nation, provision was made for an anthropologist to guide the research and write the final report. In that capacity I was hired to help document governance from the Yup'ik point of view.

This use of anthropology to inform native political activity is increasingly common. The Yupiit Nation is not unique in its desire to document the past as a basis for attempts to affect its present status. Increasingly, anthropologists find themselves in the employ of natives who set the goals and do the fieldwork. As it turned out, the research became a vehicle to effect the local governance it was intended to describe.

My first task for the Yupiit Nation was to review the anthropological and historical record about Eskimo governance and to prepare a summary of what had been said. Report in hand, I flew to Akiachak to speak to a gathering of nearly one hundred delegates at their annual meeting in March 1988. There I was queried on the uses to which the research might eventually be put. At best, delegates met my attempt to describe what had been written by non-natives about Eskimo governance with guarded approval. They made it clear that even where the facts were accurate, the focus was off. The written record did not contain enough information on the aspect of Yup'ik governance that they considered most important—its emphasis on speaking out. To function properly, what governed the group must be continually restated.

The second stage of the project was to hire and train village researchers who would be primarily responsible for documenting Yup'ik ideas about governance. The member villages made their own choices as to who would do the work. I met with the researchers in Akiachak in April 1988 to discuss the kinds of questions that might best elicit information about the form Yup'ik government had taken prior to the introduction of the council system beginning in the early twentieth century. The questions I suggested as appropriate were not unilaterally accepted. Researchers took time to discuss what they knew about governance. Village elders from Akiachak attended and, in fact, led the workshop, lecturing the young men and women chosen to do the research on what they thought Yup'ik governance was, and was not, all about.

Following the workshop, the researchers returned to their villages, where they took formal testimony from elders locally recognized as particularly knowledgeable about Yup'ik history and tradition. During the next twelve months, twenty-four taped interviews were recorded, transcribed, and translated. The result was more than 450 pages of transcripts. I then reviewed and wrote a summary of the material that had been collected. This report was appended to the transcripts and distributed to member villages for comment and approval.

Elders' testimony addressed as much what they hoped for the future as what they remembered of the past. I will focus on this recursive aspect of their testimony. Here it is important to look at both what Yupiit Nation elders chose to say and what they omitted. Specific leaders, laws, and conflicts were neither eulogized nor detailed. Instead, elders chose to describe the principles of effective governance that they viewed as having functioned in the past and that, in their opinion, were still applicable. Their testimony also was rhetorical: They presented the problems of today as proof that ignoring the traditional framework inevitably led to disaster. Their testimony was an ideal view of the past recalled in the present in an effort to influence the future.

The value of the testimony is not its documentation of the past. Rather, its central meaning is in the present because it reports reconstructions whose focus, internal logic, and even substance are comprehensible only in reference to contemporary life. The testimony is valid on its own terms, but these terms relate only partially (and incompletely) to antiquity. The testimony of the Yupiit Nation elders is autobiographical in Paul Bohannan's (1981) sense—it is information about the present and not a historical document about the truth of the past.

In what follows, I consider four aspects of traditional Yup'ik governance as presented in the testimony: leadership, law, social control, and decision making. Throughout the discussion, one thing stands out: an emphasis on speaking out to create, maintain, and perpetuate a well-governed society. The testimony was itself a means of governance in the present. When native elders talked to young village researchers about a well-ordered society, they both described and embodied good governance as they understood it.

The Testimony: Speaking Out

TRADITIONAL LEADERSHIP

To understand the testimony on leadership in western Alaska, the reader needs to know about those being led. As described in Chapter 1, three progressively more encompassing levels of social organization could be distinguished at the turn of the century—the extended family, the village group (consisting of one or more overlapping extended families), and the regional confederation of village groups. Leadership was exerted primarily within the family and village group. Situations that required leadership at the regional level were rare, so leaders usually did not operate beyond the extended family or village level.

Parents traditionally led the extended family, which consisted of from two to four generations, including parents, offspring, and parents' parents. Married siblings of either the parents or their offspring might also be included. Within the family the men were ultimately in command: "Inside one house, this family, their father was their head . . . Their father . . . informed them about how they should live properly" (Adolph Jimmie, 15:1 YN).[4]

Among siblings, the eldest male was the recognized head: "Blood siblings were told to live as a good family, to cooperate together. Not to break each others' minds and to put the older ones as their leader. Starting from their oldest brother, all siblings should cooperate together" (Theresa Moses, 19:3 YN).

At the community level the extended family was residentially divided between a central men's house (*qasgiq*) and one or more separate dwellings in which the women and younger children lived. As the men stayed in the *qasgiq*, it was primarily the women who talked to the children within the household, gently encouraging them (*qarulluki*) toward the good. In the *qasgiq* leadership was vested in the elders, who were also the heads of extended families. "These elders used to dictate how people should live, they were intrinsically regarded with a position of leadership" (James Lott, Sr., 21:2 YN).

According to the testimony, leadership was not the exclusive prerogative of a single individual: "The elders were the leaders of these communities. . . . There were not other kinds of leaders. But the elders met together, those who were elders determined what to do if they were planning to do something. And they never specifically pointed out and said who was an exclusive leader" (Nastasia Kassel, 27:10 YN).

Though age and sex were important factors in determining a leader, they were neither necessary nor sufficient. According to the testimony, younger men who spoke well within the community might also be considered leaders: "Sometimes although one is not an elder, the one who is good at giving speeches will be the leader of them, even the elders" (Phillip 1988:5). As a leader was an individual who spoke out, elders who did not speak out did not lead:

> Those elders instructed the people and those who have "stood up on their feet" (*nangertellriit*), they teach them the way to live. . . .
> But those who never give instructions, they say that they have two minds. Even though he knows a spoken word within himself, he is like one who does not infuse life into others. And they do not work toward informing others of important knowledge. (Billy Black, 13:2 YN)

The coincidence between speaking and leading was mentioned over and over again in the testimony. "I think it was the most eloquent elder. That person was the leader of the men. . . . They had leaders who were skilled in talking with wisdom and intelligence" (Phillip Moses, 20:2–3 YN).

According to the testimony, the duty of the elders was to instruct people in the proper way to live. Leaders were teachers as well as eloquent speakers. Through their speech they "woke up the people's minds" and "made them stand up properly." Small wonder that local control of education is such a hotly contested issue in the villages today. "The leader . . . instructed his children in how to live in peace, he warned them of the consequences of living together in chaos, he let them know those things" (Kenneth Igkurak, 14:2 YN).

Although the older men were the primary leaders in the community, the duty of the elders to instruct the young people was shared by men and women alike: "The old men used to be like the leaders by the oral instructions that they gave . . . and also the old women. They were like the leaders as far as talking to the young people on how they should act" (Mary Worm, 17:1 YN).

A person who spoke out and instructed the people had to demonstrate intelligence and knowledge.

> The individual village did not have just any ordinary leaders, but only those who they regarded as not having a scattered mind. Their leaders were those who had intelligence. (Kenneth Igkurak, 14:2 YN)

> And those people . . . whom they know to be knowledgeable, they do not go against what they say. (Adolph Jimmie, 15:3 YN)

According to the testimony, knowledgeable community leaders were recognized as individuals who watched and listened to the elders, and in this way the elders ultimately determined how the community was governed. The advice of the elders was, in turn, grounded in the advice they had received from former leaders: "Those leaders before relied on the advice of the old men. They watch how the leaders conduct themselves. They watch them. And so elders are able to exercise the position of authority by the way they oversee the leaders. Just the way the elders before them exercised authority" (Joshua Phillip, 22:6 YN).

A leader was described as a person who had listened to and assimilated the teachings of the past and could replicate them exactly:

> The one who continually relies on the advice of his elders, he leads in a proper fashion. (Billy Black, 13:3 YN)

> Those are the people who are receptive to teaching. Because they live according to how they have heard, they are like weapons to their fellow men and they are leaders for them. (Joe Beaver, 31:14 YN)

Not only must the ideal leader described in the testimony listen to the elders and learn and transmit oral tradition, but he must also respond to the community as a whole. First and foremost, a leader was someone who "followed" the people: "Those who show enthusiasm in accommodating the desires of the people, they prefer those kinds of people as leaders since the beginning of time" (Adolph Jimmie, 15:3 YN). The ideal leader thus had the ability to clearly articulate what people needed and to implement their requests:

> All the villages had leaders who spoke with great wisdom. What they said was straight and true. . . . And those people whom he leads, knowing that he speaks with great wisdom, followed whatever he dictated. . . . It is that one person, by the way he spoke with wisdom, he leads his people with efficiency. (Joshua Phillip, 22:6 YN)

> [The leader] makes an effort to make people comfortable while they are with him, by what he says. He makes his relationship smooth with others.
> But if one person is prone to talk back, to both young and old, he will be like one who no one wants to go to. One is not drawn to him because of how he talks back and how he mistreats others. (Billy Black, 13:2 YN)

The ideal leader influenced the people through his actions as well as his words: "And these villages used to have a leader, who was living right and doing things right" (Billy Black, 13:2 YN). A leader was "the worker of the village" who could be relied on to help supply the community's needs: "At that time, those people of old, they chose the one who was enthusiastic about accommodating their needs. . . . That person was like the one who was the worker of the village" (Billy Black, 13:2 YN).

The ideal leader was a man of peaceful attitude and exemplary behavior: "They preferred those who were not quick tempered to be their leaders. But those who were easily irked, those whose composure breaks easily, and those who yell at someone easily, they do not prefer them at all. . . . Even if they do not consciously think to be a leader, their natural daily good conduct paves their way to be leaders" (Adolph Jimmie, 15:2 YN).

Generosity was also regularly cited as an important characteristic of the traditional community leader: "The stingy ones were never their leaders" (Adolph Jimmie, 15:2 YN).

To summarize, leadership as described in the testimony was determined by family relationship, age, knowledge and skill, wisdom and eloquence, generosity, and the ability to act and speak for the good of the community. Instead of being able to command and control others, the ideal Yup'ik leader reflected the will of the people. A good leader articulated what was commonly acknowledged rather than giving orders, and his authority was recognized only insofar as it coincided with public opinion. He was aware of the opinions of others and voiced his own opinions in relation to those of his followers. Evon Albrite (25:2 YN) of Kasigluk summed up the qualities a leader must possess:

> The leaders of the communities used to have the following traits. He knows the art of living. He is the one who imparts oral traditions. He talks to people. He taught the younger generation. He was the one who took care of the community, did good to the community, and he was a good hunter. He could be depended on. That is the person that they have as a leader and they respect him. And because he spoke with wisdom, they follow what he decreed. Those kind of people we had as community heads. They were the leaders.

Noticeably absent from the Yup'ik definition of leadership as given in the testimony was the possession of wealth. In contrast, in her discussion of leadership among the Yup'ik Eskimos of Nunivak Island, Lantis (1946:248) noted that a leader had to be wealthy and, as important, had to be able to host feasts. In testimony by Iñupiat elders, wealth was also stressed as a necessary attribute of a leader (North Slope Borough 1987:5).

Yupik elders, however, vehemently denied that a leader is necessarily a great hunter or a wealthy man. In the testimony, three words were used to designate leaders. The most common was *ciuliaq* (ancestor, from *ciu-*, forepart, area in front, time preceding). A second term for leader was *ataneq* (boss, chief, lord, from *ata-*, to be attached). A third term was *angayuqaq* (boss, chief, parent). None of these terms is comparable to the Iñupiat *umialek* (boat owner).[5]

In her description of political organization, Lantis (1946:248) noted that the term *nukalpiaq* (literally "good hunter") might also mean "chief" on Nunivak. Contemporary elders vigorously denied such a connection: "*Nukalpiat* [great hunters] were not leaders. They fed the people. They were not *ciuqliit* [plural, literally 'the first ones'] (Joshua Phillip, 22:6 YN). This denial does not necessarily mean that Lantis was mistaken in her understanding of leadership on Nunivak in the 1930s or that wealth was never an important aspect of leadership in western Alaska. In fact, other attributes of the leader, such as generosity, required the possession of ample stores, if not excessive wealth. What the denial does signify is that contemporary elders no longer consider wealth an essential characteristic of a leader. Reading back from their present focus on negotiation with the outside non-native world, they now contend that *in the past* a person's integrity and ability to speak for the people were more important than his ability to give feasts. This disjunction between the past as we know it from ethnographic description and the past as represented by contemporary elders is the first hint that what was recorded in the testimony was "discovered" history. Like its ethnographic counterpart, this history is not false but partial in what it chooses to discuss.

In the same way that they denied that a great hunter was necessarily a leader, elders also denied that powerful shamans or warriors were leaders by virtue of their accomplishments. Here again elders' statements directly conflict with standing generalizations concerning Eskimo leadership in the anthropological literature. The literature suggests that in different contexts accomplished hunters, shamans, and warriors were all leaders (Hoebel 1961:82; Nooter 1976). The father was the leader of the extended family, the elder was the leader of the community, the best hunter led in the hunt, the bravest warrior led in battle, and the shaman led on important ceremonial occasions.

Yup'ik elders denied this situational perspective. According to their testimony, warriors, hunters, and shamans did lead but not because of these talents. As in the case of the elders, only if they were knowledgeable and articulate and "spoke out for the people" were they considered leaders. Whatever practical knowledge, personal accomplishments, or special skills a person possessed, if he was not also a "voice for the people," he could not lead.

In their testimony the elders were doing two things. They were using history to establish the backdrop for their actions in the present. An understanding of their words requires an understanding of current sociopolitical problems, which led to the dismantling of the municipal governments and gave rise to the Yupiit Nation. In the past, leadership functioned primarily within the group. Leadership, rather than headship, characterized western Alaska political organization, and it was based on the respect a person commanded among his fellows rather than on a position in an organization. A leader might speak *to* the people, but he was rarely required to speak *for* the people in an intergroup encounter. Today, however, a primary function of leadership in western Alaska is to negotiate between the local native community and the larger non-native world. As a result, the ability of a leader to speak for the people has surfaced as primary.

Following the introduction of formal municipal government in the 1950s and 1960s, Yup'ik-speaking elders continued to meet in village councils and make decisions that affected internal village relations; however, the community regularly called on younger, English-speaking villagers to speak for it in relations with the non-native world. As these relations have increased in importance, especially since the passage of ANCSA and the formation of village corporations, young men and women have been pushed into positions of leadership in unprecedented ways. To all appearances a generation of elders has been effectively disenfranchised. Observers and non-native officials are all too often fooled by the seeming dynamism of younger leaders and as a result may pay inadequate attention to the halting English of the softer-spoken elders who in many cases continue to wield the real power. The formation of the Yupiit Nation is in part the elders' attempt to regain their voice. Small wonder their testimony focuses on their historical right to be heard.

Not only does the elders' testimony represent a "discovered" past in an effort to justify the present, but by speaking out they are leading in the "traditional" manner they describe. Throughout the project, elders made it clear that it was proper that they be asked such questions and that younger villagers (in this case the village researchers) listen to their answers. Even the open ears of a non-native anthropologist were acceptable.

Significantly, nowhere in the literature about Eskimo leadership is the ability and willingness of a leader to speak out emphasized. Instead, external, observable criteria are listed, including many of those mentioned above—age, family ties, wealth, and knowledge. The testimony of contemporary Yup'ik elders mentions all of these factors; however, the emphasis is elsewhere. This is not surprising. In the past family ties, wealth, and hunting knowledge were critical to community interrelations. Presently, a leader must be able not only to facilitate organization within the community but also to represent the rights and needs of that community to the outside world. Both the people's past patterns and their current frustrations explain why the ability to express local interests and needs—the emphasis on talk—is stressed in the testimony. Yupiit Nation elders gave voice to this important aspect of contemporary leadership in their contention that a leader is first and foremost someone with the ability and willingness to speak out for the people.[6]

TRADITIONAL LAWS

Law also was discussed in detail in the testimony. According to the elders, the Yup'ik people were united by a common code for conduct that emphasized personal integrity and respect for others. This system of common values applied to all Yup'ik people and acted as the moral glue holding separate groups together. Known collectively as *qaneryaraat* (oral teachings, from *qaner-*, to speak, literally "that which is spoken") and specifically as *alerquutet* (laws or instructions) and *inerquutet* (admonitions or warnings), these rules enabled a person to "stand up properly" (Mathew Frye, 18:11 YN).

The traditional system of laws was so elaborate and highly structured that it defies characterization as "informal" or "primitive." Although the laws were unwritten, they were thoroughly inscribed in people's minds and carried the same weight as any formal written code: "We have had laws from our very beginnings. The *kass'aq* [white man] thinks we have none because, unlike his, ours are not contained in books. Like the *kass'aq* we have strong laws; the strength of our law is no different from his. Our grandparents repeatedly told the law so we could learn" (Paul John, quoted in Alexie and Morris 1985:27).

Traditional rules for living were founded on the premise that all persons possessed "awareness." Such awareness both allowed people a sense of control over their destiny and required that they respect the rights of others. As young men and women grew to maturity and gained awareness, they were taught a multitude of *alerquutet* and *inerquutet* for the proper living of life:

> *Alerquun* . . . is passed on orally. They tell it so that it is strongly encouraged for people to live by. The *alerquun* gives strict guidelines for a person to live by.
> And *inerquun*, a warning. [That] which will cause bodily damage to a person or that will cause him to be irritating to his

fellow man, or cause unfavorable attention to himself, that is strongly discouraged. (Kenneth Igkurak, 14:6 YN)

As distinguished from the written laws of Western society, these rules were portrayed as changeless. In this respect they more closely resembled a moral code, like the teachings of the Old Testament, than the Western legal system. "Our positive oral traditions, . . . these true laws never change at all. . . . But those white men, after they have established laws, they say again, 'At that particular period in time this was a law, but with this other law we are changing it.' These white men change laws all the time" (Joshua Phillip, 23:9 YN).

In fact, the Yup'ik code for conduct was not unchanging. At the same time that it is presented in the testimony as timeless, the focus has shifted considerably over the last fifty years. At the turn of the century, the primary concern was the maintenance of the relationship between human and nonhuman persons. Although this relationship is still critical, increased emphasis is being placed on interpersonal relations consonant with the introduction of Christianity and its focus on Father, Mother, and Son deities as opposed to the sea, sun, moon, sky-world, and animal spirits of the past. For example, a concern for others was repeatedly mentioned in the testimony as a traditional value. Although that concern was an old positive value, it was emphasized and reinforced by the missionaries' Christian teaching. The Sermon on the Mount and the Ten Commandments focus on protecting personal relationships and serving God, not with honoring the animals, a central obligation in the traditional cosmology.

In the face of interpersonal conflict in the villages today, elders stated concern for others as a "traditional law." In the same way, in the face of a pronounced generation gap, with English-speaking young people increasingly unwilling and even unable to take the advice of their Yup'ik-speaking elders, the testimony focused on the attentiveness of young men and women in the past. According to the testimony, in the past the rules were constantly talked about and listened to by young men in the men's house and young women in the homes. Along with learning specialized skills and techniques by watching and doing, boys and girls spent hours attending to eloquently delivered oral accounts by the senior members of their community. According to the testimony, it was the duty of elders to talk about the rules and the duty of young people to listen.

They continually talked about the *alerquutet* . . . in the *qasgiq* day after day. And their young, hearing them always, lived according to what they were told to do and they know them. It seemed like they were very learned in those *alerquutet*. (Phillip Moses, 20:4 YN)

Never stopping being talked about, the oral tradition was within the *qasgiq*. (Theresa Moses, 19:5 YN)

When all the boys [and] all the men were in the *qasgiq*, they talked to them as if they were scolding them. . . . And a boy could not even move a muscle at the time someone was talking. . . . And if he moves at all the speaker yells at him not to move around but to listen. . . . And they are told to do the following while someone is speaking. The boy should always look at the mouth of the speaker. If one looks away he will not remember what he had said later on in his life. (Herman Neck, 28:9 YN)

The "power of the mind of the elders" to affect a young person's future was cited as reason both to give help to elders and to avoid their displeasure: "They have an oral directive that anyone who is an elder, they should try to make him grateful all the time. . . . Even now if I am grateful, I cannot wish anything bad toward someone who makes me grateful. But I wish him toward something that is good" (Mathew Frye, 18:3 YN).

The testimony also emphasized the importance of thoughtful action in order not to injure another's mind. "According to what their elders tell them to do and if they live according to that, they live right and proper. But those who go against what they have been told, they cannot live a long life. If they are breaking the minds of their fellow men or if one does not obey what their fellow men told him to do, that is also the reason why they do not live long" (Evon Albrite, 26:6 YN).

Another basic rule was the danger of "following one's own mind" as opposed to following the advice of the elders. "This is the worst act of breaking the rules. If a person lives using his own mind, he will not walk through life properly. He will encounter many problems. If he uses his own mind, disregarding proper advice, he is breaking the traditional ancestral *alerquutet*. . . . One will not live long if one is standing using his own individual mind" (Joshua Phillip, 22:15 YN).

Not only was it necessary to act according to the rules, but the rules themselves must be carefully and completely handed down from one generation to the next:

> I said to one who was telling a legend, "According to what you think the legends should be, omitting those parts you have forgotten, tell it like that."
> That person that I had told to do thus, answered back, "Oh my, if I made up the parts any old way like that, that legend will no longer exist! It will no longer be." . . . And then I remember what I have heard. If anyone adds on to the oral tradition, [it will cease to exist]. (Joshua Phillip, 22:14 YN)

As described in the testimony, the elders and leaders of the community were duty-bound to talk to the younger generation and instruct them. Conversely, it was the duty of the younger generation to listen carefully to what the elders said, "to listen and let your ears hear, and not use your own careless minds." To fail to listen endangered both the individual's life and well-being:

> For one they refer to as the one who cannot be told, and the one who cannot be given instructions. . . . He is going to work only to his detriment. (Billy Black, 13:5 YN)

> At that time, a long time ago, they used to put a long thin strip of wood across the door while they were talking. One of the individuals used to break that strip and rush outside. He would flee from being talked to. Probably because he will never listen at all. So when he does that, the speakers would say, "Let him be like that so that he will have very fine looking teeth at the beginning of the snowdrift." It was so that, when he freezes to death, his teeth will be showing at the spot where the snowdrift has its reason to form. They curse them in such a fashion. (Mathew Frye, 18:13 YN)

In the testimony the emphasis was on talking about the rules, not forcing people to obey them. As a result of the Yup'ik concept of mind or awareness, the mutual and necessary respect that was established between people served to guide interpersonal relations. Consonant with that principle, verbal instruction (notably from elder to junior) was acceptable, but forcing someone to follow one's advice was not.

Ironically, this law of mutual respect, and the unwillingness to interfere in another's activities, has contributed to the misapprehension that Eskimos had no laws.

This respectful attitude circumscribed human interaction. The result was that the Yup'ik people possessed a highly developed social conscience and social responsibility in the broadest sense. Yup'ik law differs from Western law in that the *alerquutet* and *inerquutet* were expressed as moral injunctions. Yup'ik law was a code for conduct that did not make the Western distinction between sacred and profane, and education in the rules for proper living framed all learning with a set of values. Conversely, the testimony directly attributed the problems of today to the failure of elders to speak about and young people to pay attention to the rules and values of the past: "But we, in our sudden infatuation with the white man, shoved our own ideals aside. We lost the strength we could have had. Now, we seem to be stuck with nothing" (Paul John, quoted in Alexie and Morris 1985:27).

Here again, as in the testimony on leadership, the emphasis is on orality. In the past the leaders were the ones who spoke and the laws were what was spoken. It is the underlying principles of these rules for living—to respect the power of a person's thought, to act thoughtfully in order not to injure another's mind, and to recognize the danger of following one's own mind—that contemporary elders want to communicate to the younger generation and see reinstated as the foundation of the Yupiit Nation. As Nick Charles stated, they want to "gather what has been thrown down and put the pieces back together." This goal they propose to accomplish not by writing the rules down as a Yup'ik counterpart to the Western legal system but by reestablishing contexts in which young people can hear the rules spoken. The Yupiit Nation workshop on traditional governance was one such context.

SOCIAL CONTROL

As described in the testimony, the Yupiit had a highly developed social conscience and sense of social responsibility. Not all people, however, followed the rules. Just as elders taught the rules by oral instruction, when someone failed to follow the rules, the first recourse was to talk to the person and warn about the consequences of thoughtless action:

If the *alerquutet* were broken, they rehabilitate that person by continually talking with him. Not scolding him, some people meet with him. They continually warn him, and if they do warn him and let him try to do what is right, he stops breaking the rules. He no longer wants to do that. They do not take him someplace, they do not futilely take him to jail. They teach him how to live right always, that is how they did it. (Theresa Moses, 19:5 YN)

When those adults do that, they talk to him like this if he disobeys or breaks the rules. People are instructed to do the following. One person should go to that person and warn him. And if he does not listen to his initial warning, then two people must go to him and again they will warn him. If he does not listen and obey those two, then lots of people meet with him then and warn him and talk to him about how he should conduct himself. By that method, they rehabilitate those people who keep messing up. . . . They do not try to break the minds of those who broke the rules, but they keep warning them not to do the things they do. . . . I have never seen anyone scolding another person but I have seen people warning other people. (Evon Albrite, 26:9–10 YN)

In the nineteenth century wrongdoing, such as not listening to the rules, was believed to result in illness and death. The human community need not interfere because the offenders had made their own punishment. Although children were not formally punished, elders maintained that the warnings were sometimes quite frightening and intimidating:

When these children break the rules, they do this: They talk to them. They talk to them. They talk to them and tell them not to do that. . . . They do not beat them but they talk to them. . . .

But they are yelling while doing so. And sometimes foam seeps out from the corner of their mouth while they are talking because they are talking with such intensity. (Herman Neck, 28:14 YN)

They consistently warned children from the beginning. But they did not scold them roughly even if they did wrong. . . . But if our child does not follow our minds or does not listen to our warning, regardless of how many times he has done it, then we scold him so that his mind will snap to reality. He is scolded to wake up his mind again. (Kenneth Igkurak, 14:8 YN)

To warn the offenders of the probable consequences of their acts in the future, speakers would cite the fate of people in the past who ignored the oral teachings: "And if he is like that, they tell him what his future will be like. And after that they tell him how he would live right if he lives according to oral tradition" (Herman Neck, 28:15 YN).[7] If talking to an offender did not work, the wrongdoer might be ignored. Conversely, if a person was wrongly accused, he was advised to ignore the false accusations.

When people broke the rules, they were warned right away. These warnings ideally focused on what they should do in the future, not what they had done wrong in the past: "But how to keep the peace was an instruction like this: Ignore those bad things but warn them on how to live in peace and harmony and do not try to argue the point with them which will encourage them to disturb the peace. But warn them so that they will live in peace with others. Even if some person goes against them, they were told not to treat them likewise" (Kenneth Igkurak, 14:7 YN).

Relatives were the ones to talk to offenders. According to the testimony, they did so in private, not in public:

They do not have a meeting on account of him. But they work on those rulebreakers in private. They do not put him on display for people to see. But in private and not letting other people know, those who are in a position to talk to him, they try to resolve his situation, that is the way they did it. (Kenneth Igkurak, 14:9 YN)

In those days, these people who are able to talk to a certain person, if they have any differences, they talk to them in private. *Cayumakluki*, it is said. They warn them how not to stand in their lives. They give them warnings. (Billy Black, 13:10 YN)

Normally, people were counseled not to retaliate against wrongdoers but to leave them alone and get them to admit the error of their ways. As wrongdoing was believed to cause illness, illness could be cured by admitting one's crimes:

And then some of the shamans asked them after they have performed medicine on them, "Now, in your past life, you haven't
fooled around with another woman? Why is your sickness this
way? Tell a little bit about yourself even though it may be em-
barrassing. Reveal a little if you have been with another woman
who is not your wife." . . .

And some people admit. . . . And the shaman would say,
"Enough said! Because you have volunteered to say by yourself,
you have saved yourself. Let me sing a song!"

And then he sings a song and makes medicine. And so that
person, even though he had been embarrassed about it, after he
has admitted to his fault, he becomes well like he had been previously. . . . If a person admits to his action, he cures himself.
(Joshua Phillip, 22:22–24 YN)

Those who committed serious crimes might be publicly shamed at
annual ceremonials such as *Kevgiq*. A person's misdeeds would be
reported to the drummers, who would make up a song such as, "If
you bring me this, then you will not have to steal it again." Teasing
cousins especially would work with the village elders and song mak-
ers composing songs about each other's misdeeds. In Yup'ik, *kingul-
lugte-* (from *kingu-*, rear, back part, time after) means to sing a
ridiculing song about someone that dredges up previous immoral or
bad acts: "It is like a public confessional. Everyone laughs when a
wrongdoer's bad ways are exposed and then the person feels a lot of
relief, like the pressure has been taken off of his shoulders" (Stebbins
Elders 1985:13).[8]

In the event of a serious infraction, such as abuse by a persistent
bully, people might either force the offender to leave the community
or move away themselves:

But they also have the following traditional law: When the
people have a notorious member and that member does not listen to what he is told whatsoever, they banish him from that
village. They let him out of the village never to regard him as
one of them.

And they do not give the following alternative. After this certain period, you can come back. But they banish him from that
village with a certainty that they do not want him to be their
village member anymore. (Kenneth Igkurak, 14:19 YN)

Here the community punished the offender by the permanent denial
of membership. The idea that in time the offender would pay for

wrongdoing was present here as well. Elders testified that for every human action, there was a reaction. No one need intervene, as the powers of the universe do not allow infractions to go unpunished.[9]

Thus, traditional social control was nonauthoritarian and indirect. Leadership based in kinship relations and the *qasgiq* organization lacked formal disciplinary power and enforcement mechanisms. For example, community leaders did not have the formal power to resolve disputes between local families, which were responsible for their own affairs. Their power was limited to persuasion by virtue of their wisdom and knowledge. Also, the idea of one person "commanding" another person to "obey" was absent. Rather a person was enjoined to "follow the rules."[10]

Powerful community sanctions compensated for the lack of formal enforcement mechanisms. Inappropriate or antisocial behavior was the subject of "talk," including warnings, gossip, and teasing. Alternatively, community members might avoid or socially ostracize the offender in other ways. Although these mechanisms of social control were indirect by Western standards, they were clearly understood by Yup'ik people and were effective correctives. Being lectured, scolded, teased, or avoided may not be classified as significant punishment in Western society, but they are legitimate forms of retribution.

As in the testimony on leadership and laws, the central place of "talk" in correcting offenders and even rectifying offenses is significant. Aggressive talk (scolding, yelling, accusing) was discouraged, while constant verbal guidance was considered critical. According to the testimony, communicating the rules for living constituted both the form and content of the interaction between elder and younger community members: "They resolve the problem by talking about it within that village. They fix it" (Herman Neck, 28:28 YN).

The testimony's emphasis on "talking it out" points up the difference between placing guilt in the Western tradition and the emphasis on working out problems in the Eskimo tradition. Whereas the purpose of litigation is to choose and isolate a guilty party in a conflict and punish that person for misdeeds, the purpose of talking to an offender and listening to that person confess transgressions is to reintegrate both parties in the conflict into the normal functioning of the community. Rather than locating the problem in the individual and separating him or her from the community, traditional mechanisms of conflict resolution emphasized interdependence within the community and brought the community into the resolution of the conflict: "They probably try to resolve that issue by looking for the best way, they did not do it by aggravating the problem but in a caring fashion so that they become of one mind, that is the only way of resolving the problem. That method where people work together in a proper fashion to arrive at a consensus. That is how they probably resolved the issues among people" (Kenneth Igkurak, 14:19 YN).

One goal of the Yupiit Nation is to reinstitute the positive aspects of traditional mechanisms of social control by establishing tribal courts to adjudicate civil offenses, litigate adoptions, and publicly "talk out" minor problems within the community. The fact that since the 1930s social control has largely been taken out of the community's hands is at present a source of deep resentment and continuing frustration.

DECISION MAKING

As with all other aspects of governance, the testimony on decision making emphasized "talk" to arrive at "one mind." Decision making was largely by consensus within a fundamentally egalitarian and nonauthoritarian social order. Whenever a village activity was to take place, the men ordinarily met together to plan it:

> A long time ago when they were going to make a decision on what to do, what they were thinking about, they got together. . . . And·they went ahead and did that when they had one mind together. (Carl Will, 16:5 YN)

> They meet together and talk about it when they are invited by one particular village and thus they go to that place. They cooperate together, meet and talk to each other. (Theresa Moses, 19:8 YN)

> Those elders and only the men just stand around outside and meet, and there may be so many elders and those who are not old yet. And like that they decide on what they should do. Those elders who are middle aged just stand around any place outside. They never meet formally but they just meet outside and they go to their peers and decide what to do. So when they are going to go or if they are going to move, they keep telling others that is what they should do. (Nastasia Kassel, 27:19 YN)

As in the testimony on traditional law ways, consensus in decision making derived from the power of the human mind. When people came to a consensus it was called *amllerutaq* (from *amller-*, to be much, numerous, enough). Once consensus had been reached, it was dangerous to go against it (*pairrsaqevkenaku*, do not go to meet it). As in interpersonal relations, the danger of disagreeing with the group derived from the power of the human mind to negatively affect that which goes against it. If people were to disregard group opinion and follow their own minds, negative attitudes toward them might develop in the rest of the people. To avoid such an eventuality, people paid careful attention to the opinions of others. When a problem needed to be resolved, community leaders met and stated their views. Ideally they made no decision until all had been heard, and continued talking until they reached a consensus.

Yup'ik mechanisms of social control and decision making have changed in some ways since the early 1900s and in some remain the same. Shinkwin (1984:359) suggests that the disappearance of the *qasgiq* in the early twentieth century introduced a degree of political disorganization, especially in the larger traditional communities where the *qasgiq* had provided a setting in which elder male heads of large families could discuss matters of community concern and exert control over younger community members. She suggests the possibility that without the *qasgiq* the strength of local family organization may have increased. Hippler and Conn (1973:31), however, maintain that traditional social control was weak at best and that the introduced council system provided a new and beneficial mechanism for decision making and social control.

We can consider a third possibility: that Yup'ik communities experienced neither a decline in traditional social control with the loss of the *qasgiq* nor an increase in social control with the introduction of the council during the historical period. In some cases the *qasgiq* organization was not so much abandoned as replaced by the judicial role of the council, which exerted social control similar in function if not in form to that exerted by the *qasgiq* (for example, Lantis 1972:49). Even today, Euro-American observers often are struck with the "traditional" character of modern village government and decision-making processes, especially in the communication style. Coincident with past patterns, meetings are opportunities for discussion whether or not any decisions are made. This discursive character of decision making is the foundation that the Yupiit Nation would build on.

Arguing from Past to Present

The most striking feature of traditional Yup'ik law and order, as described by members of the Yupiit Nation in 1988, was its constant, competent discourse. First and foremost, leaders were attentive listeners and knowledgeable speakers. The laws that ordered their lives were known collectively as *qaneryaraat*—that which is spoken—and instruction in these laws constituted both the form and content of a vast amount of social interaction, especially between older and younger community members. Moreover, social control and decision making both turned on speech—voicing opinion, administering warnings, listening to advice.

Although the anthropological literature on traditional Eskimo law and governance refers to the importance of speech in the establishment, transmission, and maintenance of the social order, the emphasis is on governance as a fact rather than as an act, a thing they had (or did not have) rather than a way of doing things, an organizational form rather than an arena for speech. As new forms of governance and community organization have been introduced, non-natives have viewed their acceptance as presaging the inevitable "replacement" of traditional governance. Yupiit Nation members do not necessarily agree. Although the form of organization may change (from *qasgiq* to council and now to a confederation of villages united into a single Yupiit Nation), they contend that regional government can remain "traditional" if it maintains its past emphasis on discourse.

In the Yupiit Nation testimony the primary focus is on the importance of speaking out in the past. This emphasis is also apparent in contemporary political activity. Yupiit Nation meetings are typically attended by representatives from a majority of member villages. This is no small accomplishment, as upriver and coastal communities are separated by as much as one hundred miles, and intervillage travel depends on good weather. Once the village representatives have arrived, meetings consist of two to four days of vigorous debate from nine o'clock in the morning until eleven or twelve at night.

From the opening invocation until the meeting closes with a formal benediction, participants speak only Yup'ik. Any written material distributed to delegates appears in both Yup'ik and English. At a 1989 meeting of the regional elders' committee, the organizers in Akiachak printed out a welcome banner on computer paper that read "Welcome Yupiit Nation Regional Committee of Elders" and hung it over the speakers' table at the front of the room. During the meeting the banner was roundly criticized as unacceptable because it had been written in English.

Yupiit Nation meetings are, first and foremost, an arena for Yup'ik speech. The primary speakers—the leaders—are acknowledged by deference. With few exceptions, elders are given the first opportunity to speak and are rarely interrupted, no matter how long they talk. People are shocked when non-native bureaucrats in attendance appear to challenge an elder's words during a public meeting. As with discussion within the traditional men's house, few women attend.[11]

At these meetings the leaders of the Yupiit Nation do as much listening as talking. Deference governs who speaks first, longest, and is most influential, but everyone has an opportunity to talk. This bold speaking may not appear particularly bold to non-native observers, as the Yupiit consider acting rashly or abruptly immature. Discussion can, however, be heated. The common generalization that Eskimos do not express emotions freely and are nonconfrontational is belied by the often impassioned debate that takes place. The anger is usually directed out (for example, at outsiders in positions of power) or indirectly meant for others. Although all the issues may not be resolved, the discussion continues until everyone has had a chance to speak. Yupiit Nation meetings are a powerful vehicle for expression, reminiscent of New England town meetings. Primarily, they are occasions for people to hear each other's opinions and express or modify their own.

Although an agenda is published, the floor is open to extended comments by delegates at any time. While one topic is being discussed, a second or third issue may also be addressed. When a speaker takes the floor, he continues uninterrupted for up to thirty minutes until he has said his piece. The next speaker may wish to address another part of the debate. Comments on the content of the first speaker's talk may follow on and off for hours. What might appear to a non-native as a meeting with a frustrating lack of focus is in fact an open forum in which each individual who so chooses can be heard. Conversely, non-natives attending a meeting may assume that statements made are definite decisions when they are not.

To date, the major accomplishments of these meetings cannot be measured by political recognition, as outside acceptance of the Yupiit Nation is slow. Neither can their success be gauged by economic development and increased control of federal and state funding, which in some cases has been withheld pending confirmation of tribal status. Where the Yupiit Nation has already been successful is in the restoration of a voice to its members as well as in the provision of a context for oral expression. The Yupiit Nation meetings are a regional forum for talk about the form and meaning of local government, in the past as well as the future.

This contemporary emphasis on speech, both in the Yup'ik representation of their past as well as in their contemporary political activity, is often perplexing to outsiders. For Eskimos to speak out aggressively on any topic is by definition "untraditional" from the non-native point of view. The stereotypical Eskimo is happy and easy going, and by extension passive. Few non-natives know anything about the Yupiit Nation, and those who do know of its existence often cannot recognize its activity as legitimate. What could be more anomalous than for the quintessential peaceful people to meet and talk radical politics? Yet, in fact, this new Eskimo political activism makes perfect sense.

Looked at one way, the Yupiit Nation wants to return to a traditional nineteenth-century form of governance. Under the ANA grant my mandate was not to write a history of Yup'ik governance, recording the ways in which it had and had not changed over the last one hundred years. Rather I was told specifically to write a clear account of people's views of past patterns of governance, so that they might be used to guide the members in the governing of a new Yupiit Nation.

Looked at another way, the Yupiit Nation is a radical innovation. In the past, Yup'ik governance and law were played out in the context of kindred and community. The personal encounter that was the trademark of governance took place at the local level. Insofar as the Yupiit Nation's goal is to restore traditional Yup'ik governance at a regional level, it is a contradiction in terms. Traditional governance was characterized by a high degree of autonomy beyond the level of the local group, whereas the formation of a nation implies regional unity and the delegation of authority.

In the end, the Yupiit Nation is new and innovative in its strident bid for regional control, yet at the same time traditional in its emphasis on discourse. The issue of recognition presents a problem of translation, part of the history of the negotiation of the difference between Eskimos and non-Eskimos. Observers falsely assume that Eskimos must either remain traditional, holding on to their past, or become modern. Must this be an either/or decision? The Yupiit Nation seems to be both—people seeking global recognition of their unique character as Eskimos. They neither totally reject nor blindly acquiesce to historical changes. Rather they come together to speak about the possibilities of the future. In this sense, their meetings are acts of "consideration" in which the past is called to serve the future and the future is held accountable to the past (Clifford 1988:289).

Yupiit Nation villages are not the only Yup'ik Eskimo communities actively engaged in speaking about and considering the place of their past in their future. Farther north along the coast, the village of Chevak is actively involving elders in teaching in the schools. They have also established a theater group that has written plays based on their traditional view of the world and has performed the plays for local as well as international audiences (Chapter 10). Nor are Yupiit Nation meetings the exclusive or only effective arena for speaking out. In the coastal village of Toksook Bay (a member of the Yupiit Nation), a weekly meeting takes place at the community hall in which elders lecture young men and women on traditional rules for living that they consider critical to survival in the world today.[12]

In the *qasgiq* meetings at Toksook, the school and performance group at Chevak, as well as the meetings of the Yupiit Nation, community leaders are increasingly taking the initiative to speak out. As in the testimony on traditional governance, they idealize the past in an effort to shape the future. In so doing, they are commenting as much on the present as on the past. Statements about "tradition"— what it did and did not entail—constitute an attempt to regain control in the twentieth century, and they should be appreciated as such. The testimony on traditional governance is part of a widespread tendency to argue from "was" to "ought" (Kirkpatrick 1988). When elders laud the context and content of "traditional" governance, they do so as commentary on the problems of today.

Through statements about their past, including their representation of traditional Yup'ik governance as active "speaking out" as opposed to silent acquiescing, they create a common history on the basis of which they can make claims for the future. If, instead, they were to continue to allow themselves to be led from without, they would be left with nothing:

> They want people to go for training so they will know how to fill out forms to ask for monies. This is the way our state is making fools of us. They are continually giving us money trying to make us lose our Yup'ik heritage. When 1991 comes around, the government will lay its hands palms down and we will end up in

the shadow where we will suffer. It is time for us, before it is too late, to stretch out our Yup'ik hands and put our young people on the palms and revive the powerful, ancestral laws, now, before 1991. Let us try to reduce their problems before we are all gone. (Paul John, quoted in Alexie and Morris 1985:29)

Questions of Eskimo identity and power permeate the testimony, as they do the meetings, of the Yupiit Nation. By recalling a unique history, the speakers attempt to carve out a place for modern Eskimo lives, "lived within and against the dominant culture and state."

Eskimos are famous for their ability to successfully adapt to changing environmental circumstances while strengthening their cultural integrity. Like many other peoples "pronounced dead or dying by anthropologists and other authorities," the Yupiit are actively searching out new ways to be different. As Clifford (1988:338–341) points out, metaphors of continuity do not account for the complex historical processes of appropriation, compromise, and revival that inform the activity of a people no longer living in isolation but "reckoning themselves among the nations." By "risking themselves in novel conditions," Yupiit Nation members seek to "reproduce themselves historically." In this sense the "traditional" character of their political activity as "speaking out" is a product of both reinvention and survival.

Conclusion: The Invocation of Tradition

THE YUP'IK ESKIMOS ARE perhaps the least known and most "traditional" of Native Americans. At the dawn of the twenty-first century, many Yup'ik people continue to speak their aboriginal language, harvest fish and game for sustenance, and engage in elaborate ritual distributions of the bounty the land and sea provide. Yet they have also undergone dramatic changes during the last one hundred years. They use computers to write their language, and the latest in communications technology transmits their words statewide. All-terrain vehicles, high-caliber rifles, and thirty-foot fiberglass boats are the tools of the modern hunt. At villagewide feasts, Pampers and soda pop are as likely to be distributed as dried fish and *akutaq*.

Keeping these innovations in mind, I have described aspects of the rich cosmology of the Yup'ik people as it continues to be played out in western Alaska today. Of necessity, I have lingered on the Yup'ik view of their past and what they choose from it to support their view of themselves in the present.

Just as Yupiit Nation testimony was characterized by the constant invocation of an ideal past to discuss current problems, contemporary public discourse in many contexts in western Alaska abounds in historical tropes that comment directly on the present. According to elders, the past was quiet and peaceful as opposed to the noise and confusion of modern times.

> I often hear it said that young people are changing. It isn't their fault. Long ago, old men would say that the world would become noisy and people would quit loving each other. I don't hear anyone teaching anymore. (John Avakumoff, quoted in Alexie and Morris 1985:9)

> When *Nunacuarmiut* got a school, they became noisy. . . . Because of *kass'at* [white people], where is that peaceful and

221

harmonious way that people used to live by! (Nastasia Kassel,
27:20 YN)

In the past, they say, food left one full and strong, not empty and
weak: "The old way of life is fading away, and the food which makes
us strong is going too" (Jessie Oscar, quoted in Alexie and Morris
1985:13). The intake of fluids was circumscribed, and as a result the
Yup'ik people were more fit and disciplined in facing the rigors of the
environment: "They were light and agile because the boys did not
indulge in water. . . . Now I'm drinking all I want to—coffee, tea, water all the time" (Joe Beaver, 31:12 YN).

People were generous and helped one another freely without thinking of pay: "The beautiful, quiet, Yup'ik lifestyle, along with its ideals
of helping one another and sharing is lost with the past. Yesterday it
was said that these days one will fetch neither ice nor water without
pay" (Mike Albert, quoted in Alexie and Morris 1985:21).

Land was open to all, devoid of boundaries: "There were absolutely
no boundary lines. No one claimed to own any portion of the land.
No boundary lines whatsoever. No one claimed to own land before
the coming of the white man" (Philip Moses, 20:9 YN).

The weather was even better: "Back then, when we were young,
the weather was not like it is today. The environment is changing. . . .
The wind is beginning to blow continuously; we are just like it" (Mike
Angaiak, quoted in Alexie and Morris 1985:23).

In the past the elders led by what they said, and the younger generation listened and followed their advice. "In the community, the
leaders were made up of the old men. When they are told by them
how to do a certain action, they would do that thing according to
what they said" (Mathew Frye, 18:1 YN). Moreover, leaders were local and known, not distant and unaccountable. "Those leaders of the
communities were not separated from the rest . . . because they all
knew the way of life and *alerquun* [the law], too. They had leaders
who were not somewhere else but who lived right there in the village.
And he did not flaunt his authority. But they encouraged their young
to observe their ways" (Herman Neck, 28:21 YN).

If we take these statements at face value, they seem to add support
to the image of the stereotypical Eskimo as quiet, peaceful, generous,
and respectful until corrupted by civilization. Alternately they may
be seen to reflect the well-worn theme throughout human history of
people harkening back to a golden past. The words of Yup'ik elders

are on one level no different from the recollections of many contemporary non-native grandparents who contrast the peaceful rural world they knew in their youth to the complexities of urban life in the 1990s.

Yup'ik elders arguing from "was" to "ought" in fact invoke the past to talk about present problems. More than being merely an idealization of the past, these historical tropes are a rhetorical attempt by the Yupiit to publish themselves in opposition to the noisy, nasty non-native world. According to Mary Beaver (30:10 YN), "People are now getting noisy at this present time because white men are increasing in number. They are increasing and they are in need of reasons to be noisy; they make noise all because of this state of Alaska. We do not go to their land and work on things that will create noise. But we stay here where we grew up."

In western Alaska the bridge between the past and future is forged in the present as Yup'ik people grapple with their individual and social roots. As history establishes the backdrop for what they do today, their "rediscovery" (and redefinition) of history is shaped by their present situation. In their statements about the past, elders are not merely reciting memories out of context. Rather their statements are enactments, and an understanding of their words requires an understanding of the current sociopolitical dilemma that gave rise to them.

Part of the consciousness-raising associated with the passage of the Alaska Native Claims Settlement Act of 1971 and its aftermath, a diffuse yet nonetheless important cultural reformation is in progress in much of western Alaska. Here the term *reformative* is used in David Aberle's (1982:319–320) sense: The locus of desired change is supraindividual, and the desired change is partial rather than total. The substantial changes many Yup'ik people are seeking in the political system are neither cataclysmic nor immediate. In an important sense the movement has restorative elements that place it in contrast to many other transformative and reformative movements. Today, the major issues that animate Yup'ik residents are regaining control of their land, resources, and local affairs; improving economic conditions; and maintaining Yup'ik language and values. Although these issues are not new, the degree to which they focus public debate is unprecedented.

In the fall of 1988 the Toksook Bay Traditional Council issued a position paper that exemplified this desire to return to an ideal past. Although the text said nothing that had not been said in the village before, it was the first expression of these ideas that was written down by community members and published in a statewide newspaper explicitly for the non-native audience. The public character of the statement was as striking as the content. The paper began: "The Yupik traditional customs, standards and values have been passed down from one generation to another with the same aspects and techniques which our ancestors have used over and over again, and we want this to continue on through generations for the benefit of our descendants and their descendants thereafter" (Toksook Bay Traditional Council 1988).

Like many other indigenous peoples, the Nelson Island elders presented their tradition as timeless in opposition to the protean character of the non-native world. "This new way of life is completely different from ours and those ever changing laws and regulations from State of Alaska and United States government made us mixed up morally" (Toksook Bay Traditional Council 1988). Laws were likewise presented as changeless:

> You see, our ancestors did not have to change any of their laws and customs that have been passed down from their ancestors because the law was the land. . . . Today, many laws and regulations are ever changing and new. (Toksook Bay Traditional Council 1988)

Over and over again, the contrast was emphasized between the ideal past of the Yupiit and their circumscribed and dependent position in the present. In that ideal past, people moved freely over the land:

> Our ancestors didn't have to have boundaries . . . because they all consider the land as something that everyone can share. . . . Today, as a result of corporation land selections and Native allotments, we are told not to trespass here and there. (Toksook Bay Traditional Council 1988)

Hunting was regulated only by need: "Our ancestors were hunters all year around. . . . Today, as a result of the Migratory Bird Treaty Act, we are being told that we can only hunt geese in certain time of the year or fish in certain time of the year. . . . All these ridiculous laws and regulations . . . are dividing the Yupiks" (Toksook Bay Traditional Council 1988).

The once "dominant" Yup'ik culture has become subordinate, leaving the younger generation "scattered like reindeers without herders."—"In viewing all of these visible problems, we are very concerned and are sympathetic to our children because they are like orphans without parents and they are scattered like the reindeers without herders. We find that we must take the steering wheel and try to make our people realize that our own way of life is love and sharing, not hate and fighting" (Toksook Bay Traditional Council 1988).

The central meaning of these statements applies to the present. The focus and internal logic of this ideal reconstruction are comprehensible only in reference to contemporary life. The elders' primary goal is not to provide an objective report for some impersonal posterity but to make a highly charged statement about the authenticity of a uniquely Yup'ik way of life as it was lived in the past and continues to be lived in the modern world.

This same contrast between the ideal Yup'ik past and its degraded contemporary counterpart was portrayed in *Homesick for a Dream*, a play presented in Anchorage in spring 1989 by Chevak's Tanqik Theatre. Tanqik (literally "bright light") is an all-Yup'ik performance group whose members range in age from six to sixty. It was established in 1984 in the village of Chevak through the collaboration of Joshua Weiser (a longtime theater arts director in rural Alaska) and John Pingayak (the Yup'ik director of the cultural heritage program at the Chevak high school).

From beginning to end the dramatic force of the production relied on the juxtaposition of the best of the Yup'ik past with the worst of the Yup'ik present—the powerful rhythmic beat of a skin drum compared with the jarring blare of a ghetto blaster; the quiet laughter of children playing traditional string story games compared with the dazed look of teenagers suffering from an overdose of video games; the loving hugs and smiles shared in the traditional sod house compared with the verbal abuse and drunken fights rocking the walls of the new prefabricated houses.

As the play unfolded, a Yup'ik teenager described a dream she had, "a dream for which at this very moment, I am homesick." She simultaneously described and enacted her dream, in which she gradually shed the accouterments of the modern world and returned to the sod house inhabited by her ancestors: "It was as if something was pulling me back to another place in time, to a memory that was deep within me, to a past life. . . . I closed my eyes and had a dream unlike any that I'd ever had before—a dream filled with the spirits of my ancestors" (Davidson 1989).

FIGURE 10.1 Chevak's Tanqik Theatre (Courtesy James H. Barker).

Inspiration for this play came from real experience as well as re-membrance. Each spring, as part of the Kashunamiut School Dis-trict's cultural heritage program, Chevak high school students spend a week on the tundra living in a traditional semisubterranean sod house. Rock music, video games, and basketball are left behind as the students spend time sitting quietly on the hard-packed dirt floor listening to village elders recount the *qaneryaraat* (oral teachings) of their ancestors. Sleeping on skins and grass mats, eating dried fish and seal meat, and listening to the Yup'ik language by the light of a seal-oil lamp, the young people immerse themselves in the sights and sounds that characterized life along the Bering Sea coast into the 1930s. The school district hopes that experiences such as these, circumscribed as they are, can provide students with the grounding in their past that they feel young people need to enable them to step firmly into the future.[1]

During their stay in the *qasgiq*, Chevak students are enacting (however briefly) the life rhythms and learning style described by the Yupiit Nation elders. *Homesick for a Dream* carries these experiences one step beyond the village. Like the testimony of the Yupiit Nation, the Yup'ik performance presents them to the world at large and invokes them as evidence for their special identity.

As in other performances by the Tanqik Theatre, in *Homesick for a Dream* the ideal past is used simultaneously as a foil to point out the emptiness of the present and as a springboard into the performers' vision of a fuller future. Although cognizant of the impracticality of a wholesale return to the nineteenth century, the play actively asserts the possibility of reestablishing selected aspects of that history—specifically the clear vision and spiritual integrity that many Yup'ik people today feel they have sacrificed in their encounter with the Western world.

The Tanqik Theatre's performance bears out the stated goals of the group as published in their printed program. Moreover, this selective reformulation of tradition coincides in important respects with the non-native ideal view of Eskimos. The program reads:

We continue our language.
We cherish our families.
We love our children and teach them the ways of the land.
We share with those in need.
We pass on our oral history, stories, and dances to our children.
We respect others and their differences.
And above all we help, listen to, and respect the keepers of our
    traditions—our Elders!
                            (Chevak Tanqik Theatre 1989)

Like the members of the Yupiit Nation, the Chevak performance group and high school cultural heritage program are engaging in a selective, idealized reconstruction of their past. Also like the Yupiit Nation, they are actively taking their new view of themselves and displaying it to non-native audiences throughout the world. At the same time that representatives of the Yupiit Nation have visited the Lower 48 and the Hawaiian Islands to meet with organizations representing indigenous peoples outside of Alaska, the Tanqik Theatre has performed throughout Alaska and in Hawaii, Canada, New Zealand, Australia, the Fiji Islands, and the Soviet Union.

The reformation sought by the Toksook Bay elders, the Yupiit Nation activists, and the Chevak performers can be seen as an expressed desire to return to the "old ways." In political and economic terms, the "old ways" refer to the 1920s, which was after many positive technological improvements had been introduced into western Alaska but before the Yup'ik people had experienced subordination to federal and state government control and the dependency that it entailed. This reformation is also presently embodied in the rhetoric against oil development and in favor of subsistence rights at public hearings; the revival of intra- and intervillage winter dance festivals; the hosting of local and regional elders' conferences; and the increased awareness of and concern for the preservation and use of the Yup'ik language and oral tradition. In all this activity one finds a deep concern for and commitment to the natural environment and the way of life it supports. Such activity reveals the desire of the Yupiit, often frustrated, to keep control of their land and their lives.

As yet these trends have not coalesced into a single, concerted, unified regional movement. However, the numerous small and large arenas in which issues of native cultural identity and political control are articulated indicate an increased awareness of and value placed on being a Yup'ik Eskimo in the modern world. The previous four chapters in this book are, in fact, a direct outgrowth of this reformative movement and would never have been written without it. The testimony on Yup'ik leadership, warfare, and the relationship of humans and animals was gathered as part of recording projects dedicated to preserving and communicating contemporary Yup'ik people's remembrances of their past in an effort to inform their future. In particular, the Nelson Island Oral History Project and the Yupiit Nation's Traditional Law and Governance Project provided rich material for these reflective discussions. They also provided the inspiration insofar as they articulated the desire of Yup'ik people to be understood as possessing a unique past, an essential part of which they are actively trying to carry with them into the future.

FIGURE 10.2 Elders testifying at Emmonak offshore oil-lease hearings, 1981 (Courtesy James H. Barker).

Euro-Americans attend performances of the Tanqik Theatre in part to be entertained by the exotic and in part to understand the history and traditions of "real" Eskimos. They are confronted, however, with Eskimos seeking recognition by non-natives of a new image of themselves. Unless these performances, political as well as dramatic, are viewed with this often unstated purpose in mind, the observer may miss the point.

Into the present day, many outsiders have viewed the Yup'ik people as culturally bankrupt, as having lost their original and authentic past in their forced encounter with the non-native world. At the beginning of the twentieth century, Euro-Americans decried the Eskimos' loss of cultural integrity. For example, George Gordon (1906–1907:80) described the "corruption" of the Yup'ik artistic tradition in the name of profit: "The acquaintance of the Eskimo artist with our illustrated literature could not fail to leave its mark on his artistic productions, . . . and although his work is not always improved by this external influence, . . . he cultivates the habit for he finds that it pays. At present, the carving of the Eskimo is degenerate."

At the end of the twentieth century, the Yup'ik Eskimos remain the

FIGURE 10.3 Toksook Bay Dancers at St. Marys, 1982 (Courtesy James H. Barker).

quintessential "people in peril." According to Pulitzer Prize-winning journalists, they are drinking themselves to death; under the influence of alcohol they are committing suicide and engaging in family violence at rates that rival the worst in the world (*Anchorage Daily News* 1988). The unpleasant truth of these facts cannot be denied. At the same time, many Yup'ik people are actively seeking alternate ways of dealing with the rapid technological and social change and the political and economic dependency that beset them. Although one response has been alcoholism and withdrawal, another response, so far underreported in contemporary writing about western Alaska, has been a variety of dramatic innovations, some of which I have described here.

Contrary to non-native claims that "traditional Yup'ik culture" is either dead or dying, Yup'ik Eskimos continue to realize distinctively Yup'ik, although not necessarily "traditional," ways of being. As demonstrated in the Nelson Island seal parties, the *Selaviq* celebration of Orthodox communities, the masked dances of the Bethel dance group, and the meetings of the Yupiit Nation, Yup'ik culture has undergone radical innovation. In different ways, previously independent views have married and produced children related to both parents but undeniably unique. These "new traditions" are simultaneously unprecedented and unmistakably Yup'ik.

The Yup'ik present is no simple reflection of the past. As James Clifford notes (1988:339), it is just as problematic to say that the Yup'ik way of life survived as it is to say that it died. Although the rhetorical character of their testimony might lead us to believe otherwise, the Yupiit are no more blindly holding on to an outdated past than they are forsaking that past to just as blindly embrace "modernity." Like other indigenous peoples the world over, they are engaged in a complex process of invention, innovation, and encounter. Contrary to the view that would see them as either traditional or modern, many Yupiit are, in the words of Chevak's Tanqik Theatre (1989), striving to be both: "With the strength that comes from education and knowledge, we learn to deal with the future, at the same time, we stand firmly planted in our cultural roots."

Notes

1
Introduction: Eskimos, Real and Ideal

1. All Yup'ik terms are given in the standard orthography (Reed et al. 1977) and have been italicized to set them apart from names given in missionary or conventionalized map transcription.

2. Exceptions were the descriptions written by Dionise Settle and George Best, who accompanied Frobisher as naturalists specifically to make observations (Hakluyt 1589:211–230, 250–283).

2
The Ideology of Subsistence

1. An *uluaq* is a woman's traditional semilunar knife set in a handle opposite the arc-shaped edge. It is also sometimes referred to as *ulu* in English from the Iñupiaq name for this type of knife (Jacobson 1984:391).

2. Since the passage of the Alaska Native Claims Settlement Act (ANCSA) in 1971, regulatory control over land and sea resources has become as big an issue as landownership and the closely related issue of the retention of subsistence hunting and fishing as priority activities. The d(2) section of ANCSA mandated legislation passed in 1980 as the Alaska National Interest Land Conservation Act (ANILCA). Although ANILCA is nearly 450 pages long, it sets down only general guidelines for the U.S. Fish and Wildlife Service to follow in managing land. The Fish and Wildlife Service has begun to implement broad provisions of the bill, and its regulations will ultimately determine the bill's success or failure. As they say on the delta, "You can't eat a regulation;" but, what's worse, regulations can make it so you can't eat, period.

Legislative actions and administration policies have already begun to tie the concept of subsistence use as a priority activity into the fabric of management—for example, the issuing at a reduced fee of resident permits to hunt musk oxen on Nelson Island. Yet the villagers' continuing concern is

234 / NOTES TO PAGES 50 – 53

that when resources dwindle and competition from other users increases, the political process will undercut their subsistence rights. As political battles in Alaska have made abundantly clear, their fears are justified (see Chapter 8).

3
The Mask: The Eye of the Dance

1. Although mask-making declined on Nelson Island and along the Kuskokwim drainage, masks were made continuously on Nunivak Island, where there was no missionary until the late 1930s. Even after the coming of the missionaries, Nunivak carvers made masks for sale regularly in the 1940s and 1950s, although they did not make them for local use in dances (Margaret Lantis, personal communication). Mask-making also continued in other parts of the region such as the lower Yukon Delta and along the Kuskokwim, as discussed and illustrated by Himmelheber (1953).

2. A metaphor for this period of cultural suppression can be found in a traditional tale told by Maggie Lind of Bethel, relating how Crane got his blue eyes. According to Maggie, once while berry picking, Crane took out his eyes and set them on a nearby mound to watch for danger. While he was bending over the tundra, someone stole them, and Crane then replaced them with blueberries. In a retelling of the event, Flintoff (1984) extrapolated, "That's what happened to the masks. Someone stole their eyes. Eyes were no longer needed to see with." Traditional forms remained, although functionally transformed.

3. *Ellam yua* (literally "the person of the universe or weather") is the Yup'ik counterpart of Sila, or *Silap inua*, described for the Inuit. According to Weyer (1932:389), this spirit possesses less fixed and definite traits and functions than those ascribed to other supernatural entities: "Sometimes spoken of as masculine, sometimes as feminine, Sila pervades the natural world, as Ruler of the Elements. . . . *Silap inua*, literally 'the person of the air,' suggests that the spirit is not simply an essence or an abstract power, but the personification of these characters."

4. Nelson Islanders, at least through the 1940s, might tie a string joining the wrist of a child to a door or house post. One young man recalled this treatment. He attributed it to the fact that his elder siblings had all died in infancy, and that his parents were taking extra precautions to ensure his survival.

5. In 1889 Edith Kilbuck noted the manner of disposal of a female shaman suspected of killing several children: Her own husband clubbed her to death, severed all her joints, and burned her with oil (see Chapter 4).

6. On the distribution of the nucleated circle as such, see also Smith and Spier (1927). Given the connection between shamanism and vision imagery for the Yup'ik Eskimo area, it is noteworthy that eyes have also been found in the palms of carved wooden hands used by Tlingit shamans.

7. Extracted by Weyer from Thalbitzer's "The Heathen Priests of East Greenland," in *Verhandlungen des XVI Amerikanisten-Kongresses* (Vienna, 1908), 447–464.

8. In a number of contexts, the snowy owl (*anipaq*) was associated with acute powers of observation. For example, traditionally warriors were some-times said to pretend to be owls. *Anipaunguarvik* (Owl Village, literally "a place to be like an owl") was located at a point on the Kashunak River where warriors traditionally watched for the approach of their adversaries during the bow-and-arrow war period. Birds in general, especially the loon, often figure as guardians endowed with supernatural sight in Yup'ik oral tradition.

9. This practice of ritual scarification has also been observed among the Siberian Yup'ik Eskimos. Bogoras (1904:408) noted that "the man who gave the last stroke, if this happens to be his first whale or bear, has the skin near all his joints pierced with the tattooing-needle, leaving a simple but indelible mark."

According to Henry Collins, as cited in Schuster (1951:17), among the Es-kimos of St. Lawrence Island in the Bering Sea, "men are tattooed on wrists, elbows, shoulder-joints, back of neck, middle of back, hips, knees and ankles with one prick in commemoration of some event—killing a whale, polar bear, *mukluk* (bearded seal) or being a pallbearer." Moore (1923:345) asserts that these tattoos consisted of "two small dots near together at each shoul-der, wrist and elbow, the cervico-dorsal and lumbo-sacral areas, and at the knee and ankle." Bogoras (1904:256) records that among the maritime Chuk-chee of northeast Siberia, tattooed joint marks once served as a tally of homicides.

Finally, Schuster (1951:18) concludes:

> These tattooing customs, when aligned with the custom of applying eye-shaped markings to the joints in the decorative arts of adjacent areas to the south, . . . strongly suggest that the single dot, as used in such tattooing, is itself the rudiment of an eye motif. The simple one-dot tattooing of the joints among the Bering Strait Eskimo and the Chukchee might very well be the survival of a primitive practice under-lying the artistic tradition of joint marking in areas farther, and per-haps even much farther, to the south on the American continent. On the other hand, . . . such tattooing of the joints shows a surprising simi-larity to tattooing practices prevailing among certain peoples in the South Pacific.

10. Dark circles also appear as goggles on Bering Sea Eskimo nineteenth-century objects. The goggles identify beings as supernatural, are puns for masking, and refer to the state of transformation (Fitzhugh and Kaplan 1982:194–195).

11. Other instances of culturally appropriate and inappropriate direction-ality are also apparent in Yup'ik daily life. For example, when making *akutaq* (a traditional mixture of berries, snow, and oil), one must always move one's hand around the inside of the bowl in a clockwise direction. Likewise, when

braiding herring, grass should begin to be crossed right over left, and when dancers begin a performance, they always start on the right side. The precise significance of these rules, as well as their connection with traditional encircling actions, is at this point unclear.

12. This story is also the explanation for the blue mark found at the base of the spine on Yup'ik babies. It is said to be the bruise marking the spot where the old woman kicked the child out of the womb.

13. An exception that immediately comes to mind is the individual dances traditionally performed by men standing outside the *qasgiq* in late summer, sometimes as a welcome to guests, and labeled *puallauq* by Paul John of Toksook Bay. Steven Jacobson (1984:296) defines the base *pualla-* as "to stand up and dance (of men at an Eskimo dance doing an Iñupiaq-style dance)."

14. Carved and incised story knives were traditionally, and still are occasionally, used by Yup'ik Eskimo girls to draw designs in mud or wet sand as they tell each other stories. As the story is related, the orator draws with the tip of her knife stylized designs that depict the events recounted in the tale. If an ivory knife is not available, a child may use a wooden stick or metal butter knife (Ager 1974; Oswalt 1964).

15. Both Lavrentiy Zagoskin (Michael 1967) and Nelson (1899:33) noted evidence of this same alteration when they described the hunter capped by the crown of the hide of his prey or alternatively wearing behind on his belt a wolf or wolverine tail to which was sewn the tip of a wolverine muzzle.

16. The circle of rotting masks found at the mouth of the Yukon Delta in 1980 by a group of villagers from Sheldon's Point who were on a berry-picking expedition exemplifies this attitude. The masks were not left to rot because they were valueless but because traditionally their value lay in their construction and use rather than in their possession. Villagers subsequently took the masks—all that was left of a long-ago event—back to the village and sold them to the Anchorage Museum of History and Art.

4
The Real People and the Children of Thunder

1. For instance, Paul John (personal communication) described as a distinct category people who talk or answer back as soon as they hear something. Those who act in such a way are considered reprehensibile because they bounce their pain and anger back to the speaker without regard for the effect of such rash verbalization. Instead, people should carefully weigh in their minds what has occurred before they respond to a situation with either an act or a word.

2.   But the other side of it
           when it is included in the *alerguun* [instruction],
           if he is dealt back with kindness and compassion
           it might be beneficial

at the time he is having a hard time and he does not feel
he is considered something good by the other.

Breaking his mind,
thinking to pay him back,
it is not good to do that.
They used to say in those days,
even if he did or said things to people,
we were not to follow his mind and be unkind to him.

(John 1977)

3. When discussing indirection, one should bear in mind that what appears to one person as indirect may be very explicit for another.

4. Note that this ideal of awareness is antithetical to the state of drunkenness.

5. This controlled use of language carried into the twentieth century. One of the Kilbucks' grandchildren described running out the back door, yelling "Shut!" as it closed behind her, followed by "up" under her breath, as her own small rebellion against her parents' strict control of her speech (personal communication).

6. "A case of this very kind we know of, for the witch was an old woman that we had with us part of one Winter when she was sick. They said she had killed several children; which had enraged the whole village, and her own husband clubbed her to death, severed all her joints and burned her with oil" (E. Kilbuck 1889:533).

Another, even more pitiable incident, occurred about one week ago, and not far from here. Some one tied a helpless little child of about two years down to the water's edge at low tide. Its cries attracted the attention of a passer-by, who found the water already nearly up to its neck. The man took it to his home and took good care of it. It was recognized as a Neposkiogamute [Napaskiak] child, whose mother had died, the father leaving it in the care of an old woman at Mumtrkhlagamute [*Mamterilleq*]. The child is sickly and doubtless was too much of a care for her. The only surprise the people have about it is that any one should want to drown or kill a boy; their girls are often killed, but seldom a boy. (E. Kilbuck 1887:598–599)

An old woman was brought down the river last week who was insane and very hard to care for. When strangers refused to keep her, her nephew took her back and deliberately froze her to death. He had offered pay to some one if they would kill her but as no one would do it for him he did it himself against strict orders from Mr. Lind *not* to take her life. Such cruel things are hard to believe of those who are of the average standing amongst our people. None of the natives seem the least surprised nor do they seem to think less of him who did the very act. (E. Kilbuck, journal, Dec. 2, 1888, MA)

7. To this day the Yupiit, as well as other Alaska natives, are the subject of negative stereotyping that derives from cultural differences in communication styles and concepts of appropriate interpersonal interaction (Scollon and Scollon 1980).

8. Cutting of any kind was carefully controlled in nineteenth-century Yup'ik cosmology and was prohibited during ritually dangerous times, as when the spirits of the animal and human dead were entering or exiting the human world. Ironically, John's own father, William Kilbuck, wore his hair long.

9. Unfortunately for John, his openness to Yup'ik morality (specifically his adulterous relations with native women) led to his dismissal from the ministry in 1899. After ten years away from the Kuskokwim, he and his wife returned to Akiak, where he continued to work as both a missionary and a teacher until his death there in 1922 (Fienup-Riordan 1991).

10. This name may be a Yup'ik derivation from the Russian word for play or performance (*igra*). It may also have originated as the Russianized variant of the Yup'ik word *itrukar(aq)*, designating a small gift brought to get into a dance or feast (Jacobson 1984:178). Over the years the Kilbucks used it to refer to a number of distinct events, including *Petugtaq*, *Kevgiq*, and *Ingulaq*.

11. The twentieth-century Kilbuck family tradition of never letting guests depart empty-handed and encouraging them to eat heartily at their table looks suspiciously like this nineteenth-century Yup'ik pattern.

5
Selaviq: A Yup'ik Transformation of a
Russian Orthodox Tradition

1. The Russian Orthodox Churches in the Soviet Union and Alaska are unusual in that they continue to follow the Christian Ecclesiastical calendar, which was adopted from the Julian calendar by the ancient church. As a result, the Nativity Feast falls on January 7 of the secular, Gregorian calendar, which in most parts of the world replaced the Julian calendar in the seventeenth and eighteenth centuries

2. Nunacuarmiut had a population of 40 in 1880 (Petroff 1884:16), which had increased to 146 by 1900 (U.S. Bureau of the Census 1901). The influenza epidemic of 1919 negated subsequent population increases. In 1930 the population was less than 100 and in 1939, only 66 (U.S. Bureau of the Census 1942).

3. Father Epchook was a native of the Yukon of mixed Russian-Eskimo extraction. He was educated in the Russian Orthodox seminary at Unalaska in the Aleutian Islands. After several years in Nushagak as well as on the Yukon as a deacon, he was ordained a priest and subsequently served at Kwethluk from 1926 until 1962.

Father Guest was raised in the Akulmiut area and later educated at Sitka.

He first served as a church reader in Kasigluk and was ordained a priest in 1954. He subsequently spent thirty years traveling from Nicolai on the upper Kuskokwim to the coastal communities of Kwigillingok and Eek and is credited with designing and constructing seventeen churches and chapels in Alaska (Oleksa 1987:254).

4. According to Bel'kov's Journal of Worship Services, on December 17, 1878, Russian Mission parishioners asked his permission "to make stars for the holiday." Bel'kov agreed on condition they learn the *Selaviq* songs to accompany the starring, which to his surprise they did, and they subsequently celebrated Russian Mission's first *Selaviq*.

5. According to Russian Orthodox iconography, the shape of the building recalls a ship, signifying that the church is the vessel of salvation. The believers are the passengers who, after stormy and rough journeys, are saved by Christ through the Holy Church.

6. More than being merely pictorial representations, the icons are conceived as windows into the spiritual world. According to Mousalimas (1988:4), these visible images not only remind the faithful of the heavenly company but also act as a channel to this sanctified energy, thus allowing the worshippers to participate in the existence of the images' prototypes. Although icons remain distinct from that which they represent, in some measure they participate in that sacred reality as a "meeting point" between heaven and earth.

7. This directionality refers to the beginnings of the Orthodox Church. In fact, Russian Orthodoxy entered Alaska from the west.

8. The church is further organized on the north-south axis, along which the iconostas is built. This icon screen is penetrated by three doorways, one on the north, another on the south, and the third in the very center, where the east-west axis intersects. This central or "Royal Door," through which the "King of Glory" (the Eucharist) passes, leads to the throne, or altar table, directly behind the screen.

9. Among the Aleuts, each family has its own star, kept at home but brought into the church each Christmas season by a selected young man of the family to be consecrated anew by the priest in a special service. There is no such ceremony in the Soviet Union; this is strictly an Alaskan elaboration (Lydia Black, personal communication).

10. In 1976 the voters approved a constitutional amendment to establish an Alaska Permanent Fund with revenues from mineral developments on land owned by the state. The dividend program was enacted in 1982. The dividend check for each resident was $826.93 for 1988 as the fund approached assets of ten billion dollars.

11. Father Alexie was born in Kwethluk and was educated for the priesthood at St. Herman's Seminary on Kodiak. After his ordination he served first in Chuathbaluk and subsequently at Napaskiak. In western Alaska the Orthodox clergy have always been predominately native. Aleut priests worked in the region from 1843, and after 1920 nearly all priests were either Yup'ik Eskimo or Aleut (Black 1984b). According to Oleksa (1987:361), twenty-three of the thirty ordained clergy in Alaska in 1987 were na-

tives, with the non-native priests serving primarily in the larger urban centers.

12. Russian Orthodox churches lack pews because church canons strictly prohibit sitting on Sundays ("On the Lord's day, we pray standing"). Sunday (in Russian, "Resurrection Day") is a day of rejoicing and thanksgiving and is considered to be a likeness of the future age, in which there will be no kneeling or prostrations, acts that are done only in penitence.

13. The all-night vigil service originally held on the eve of the Nativity was eliminated in the 1950s.

14. These *pelatuuq* (scarves, from Russian *platok*) mark a woman as married. As noted in Chapter 4, Moravian missionary Edith Kilbuck gratified her parishioners by accepting the gift of a "Russian wedding cap," which she wore to signify her married status (letter to her father, Dec. 1889, MA).

15. "Many years" is an exclamation of goodwill delivered during the liturgy on any joyous occasion to convey God's blessing.

16. This "icon corner" actually extended over an entire wall and included numerous small icons and visual representations of Christ, as well as depictions of saints and holy men. The icon corner was ideally located on the east wall. When the house was not oriented east/west, the icons were hung on the wall facing the entrance to greet people as they came into the room. In modern-day Kasigluk, the home as well as the church provides a sacred context for secular day-to-day life.

17. In the priest's house, as well as in all the subsequent houses, a decidedly American component of *Selaviq* was also visible. Families in Kasigluk decorated their homes in much the same manner as people in any other town in the United States during the Christmas season. Inside the houses commercial Christmas cards were pinned to the walls or strung across the living room. Christmas trees had been set up and decorated, and the presents underneath included Nintendo sets, tricycles, and Barbie dolls as well as sealskin boots, new parka covers, and hand-sewn beaver hats. The life-size plastic Nativity sets and colored lights set up outside the houses gave the village a festive appearance.

18. Twice during the Epiphany season the Great Blessing of the Water is performed: on the first day inside the church and, weather permitting, on the second day outdoors at a lake or stream (Oleksa 1987:67).

19. As noted, Orthodoxy constructs a world in which there is overlap between home and church. Rather than being seen as opposites, their difference is a matter of degree. Both home and church contain "windows" or passages to heavenly reality in everything from postcard icons tacked to the wall of a house to the iconostas's "Royal Doors." Similarly, traditional Yup'ik cosmology presented the world as permeable to an unseen, spiritual reality at multiple points. The scrap of food or drink of water thrown on the floor of the traditional woman's house would find its way to the spirits of the dead as surely as the clothing used to dress the namesake in the formal Feast for the Dead performed in the central men's house. The traditional men's house, like the church, was the focal point of contact between the human and spirit worlds without being the exclusive arena of such encounters.

20. The congregation also circles the church three times to the right on

Holy Friday and again on Easter Sunday carrying Christ's shroud. During funeral services in many villages, the coffin may be carried around the church before proceeding to the cemetery, a ceremony that parallels the Holy Week procession with the shroud.

21. The parallel between the Orthodox and the Yup'ik ritual requirement to move in the direction of the sun's course is somewhat ambiguous. In Orthodox ritual, this movement is always translated "to the right." In Alaska, however, the sun moves lower on the horizon than in more southern latitudes. In the winter it rises in the southeast and sets in the southwest, and at the height of summer rises in the northeast, makes a low arch, and sets in the northwest. As a result, although Orthodoxy and nineteenth-century Yup'ik cosmology agreed that the sacred circuit should be made in the direction of the sun's course, for the Orthodox this translated as movement to the right whereas for the Yup'ik Eskimos it may have signified movement either to the left or right, depending on the season.

The issue of directionality is further complicated by differences in vantage point during the ritual act. For example, whereas contemporary *Selaviq* participants perceive the star as spinning to the right, from the star-bearer's point of view the star is moving to the left.

22. Anyone who has visited western Alaska will recognize how very un-Yup'ik it is to leave curtains open at night. Even where no house or person is in sight, residents routinely close curtains over every window of the house at dusk and keep them closed until daylight, to keep "bad things" at bay.

6
Robert Redford, Apanuugpak, and the Invention of Tradition

1. As of fall 1989, this project was still under way. It has involved primarily a group of Nelson Island men and women working to record traditional narratives and oral history from the oldest living Nelson Islanders. Some of these accounts are now being transcribed into Yup'ik and translated into English for use by students in the local elementary and high schools.

2. Anthropologists continue to debate the extent to which writing and for that matter filmmaking are inevitable corruptions (for example, Derrida 1973, 1974; Ong 1977, 1982). Although something may be sacrificed in such textualization, what is lost is not the power of a culture to re-create itself, which is at issue here (for example, Sahlins 1985; Wagner 1975).

3. A science fiction magazine published a story about Nelson Island. In it a man awakens in a traditional Eskimo village, dresses himself in fur clothing, and leaves the sod house to walk down the beach. His destination, however, is not a kayak but the modern village of Toksook Bay. He had paid cash to experience the past. His time was up and he was returning home.

4. Whereas Margaret Mead (1928) selectively described aspects of Samoan culture to demonstrate that the stressful adolescence of American teenagers was not a universal phenomenon, Derek Freeman (1983) marshaled

examples of Samoan anxiety and violence to show where Mead's conclusions were wrong. Freeman's criticism talked past the value of Mead's initial enterprise and ignored the fact that his account of the "real" Samoa was as much a framed construction determined by his point of view as Mead's had been before him.

7
Yup'ik Warfare and the Myth of the Peaceful Eskimo

1. Only once, in 1839, was the Russian-American Company post at Russian Mission attacked and a number of inhabitants murdered by natives of the Kuskokwim or the lower Yukon. The native dissidents then traveled to Kolmakovsky on the Kuskokwim, but the post had been warned of their approach and no damage was done (Michael 1967:81, 236–237, 252, 275, 300).

2. Yup'ik narrative is referred to by orator, date, and archival collection. Full transcriptions and translations are included in Fienup-Riordan (1989).

3. The Yup'ik Eskimos categorize war stories as history rather than myth. Although time has distanced us from the original accounts, substantial agreement exists between narratives of traditional warfare recorded in the nineteenth century and those still part of the oral repertory of the 1980s. This continuity, along with the widespread agreement concerning particular historical events among elders living in the region today, allows us to rely on these oral accounts as a source of information.

4. This origin-of-war tale has elements of a probably ancient (pre-1000 A.D.) Inuit story. In one variant, a visitor cast a spear and accidentally killed a member of the host community (or sometimes one of the host's dogs) and fighting ensued. The Netsilik Eskimos told Rasmussen (1931:117) that such an event caused the legendary Tunrit to abandon the home of their ancestors. A Greenlandic version uses it to explain the origin of war with the Norse (William Workman, personal communication).

5. Yup'ik strategy and tactics were similar in most important respects to that reported for the Iñupiat by Burch (1974, 1988a), and his work should be consulted for a point-by-point comparison.

6. Siting game and periodic flooding were also the impetus for establishing settlements on high ground. Mounds were not always constructed for defense; they were just as often the result of natural processes, including long occupancy (Nelson 1899:249, 327).

7. "As a stock the Eskimo have adapted themselves perfectly to their environment. . . . This specialized development of the Eskimo renders them unfit to meet the shock of intimate contact with an aggressive civilization" (Gordon 1906–1907:70).

8. The initial contrast is created by establishing a distance between us and them: They are more primitive, closer to nature, prehistoric, inefficient, and backward. They are like children in comparison with our mature, adult

selves. Moreover, these Indians are dead, killed in a process of national expansion in which only the strongest survived. The American Indian was too extreme, too violent, and too sexy, and he died (Arcand 1987).

8
Original Ecologists?: The Relationship between Yup'ik Eskimos and Animals

1. These beliefs were probably widespread in western Alaska into the first decades of the twentieth century, and they continue in effect in many parts of the region today. Examples in this particular discussion have been drawn primarily from Nelson Island.

2. The following discussion is indebted to the fine doctoral work of Robert Brightman, particularly for his development of the concept of animals as infinitely renewable: "The spiritual idea governing decisions about how many animals to kill was that hunting did not affect animal populations since the latter were an infinitely renewable resource" (Brightman 1983:384).

Many contemporary discussions of the human/animal relationship among hunter-gatherers in general and Alaska Eskimos in particular focus on describing subsistence harvesting techniques and their practical results (for example, Nelson 1969; Nelson, Mautner, and Bane 1982; Wolfe 1979, 1981). Although the relationship between ideology and adaptation has been detailed for hunter-gatherers in other parts of the world (for example, Meggitt 1962; Munn 1973) and a beginning made in the sub-Arctic (Brightman 1983; Kretch 1981; Martin 1978; Nelson 1983), ecological approaches to the study of subsistence practices have until recently dominated research on Eskimos. According to this perspective, "foraging strategy, settlement patterns, and material techniques are considered predictable from a principle of energy-efficient least effort . . . or from biological need satisfaction" (Brightman 1983:414). At present, optimal foraging theory is a particularly influential approach, asserting that "hunter gatherer survival and reproduction are maximized when productive techniques optimize the net rate of energy capture per unit of time and/or energy expended" (Durham 1981, cited in Brightman 1983:421).

The ecological/adaptation focus within the literature has largely relegated the consideration of symbolic aspects of the hunt to the background. As applied in western Alaska, this theoretical approach has produced useful information concerning the ways in which Yup'ik Eskimos understand the biological "facts" of animal behavior. As Sahlins (1976:208) has repeatedly pointed out, however, the utility of these conclusions is limited by the fact that so-called natural factors often become significant by virtue of cultural selection.

Consideration of animals as finite, renewable resources can never be more than partial as the way animals are valued crosses the analytical and often arbitrary border between ideology and practice.

3. A *qanemciq* is a narrative based on the narrator's personal knowledge, either direct or transmitted by persons to whom living men and women can trace a relationship.

4. The numbers four and five figured prominently in Yup'ik ritual, representing among other things the number of steps leading to the underworld home of the dead.

5. The performance of the marriage dance (*ingulaq*) during the Bladder Festival on Nelson Island provided a strong image of the complementarity between the production of game and the reproduction of life. While literally enacting the successful hunt, the bride held her skirt below the waist and rhythmically "fluffed it up to ward off old age and let her have children."

6. Although these goose drives have excited horror in many conservationists, Yup'ik hunters have viewed them pragmatically as the best way to harvest the most meat. They see no need to limit the harvest as long as they do not waste what they take.

7. Conversely, one of the first things Nelson Islanders remark about nonnative population centers such as Anchorage is that in those places people do not freely share food.

8. Mather (1986:51) provides a clear example of the concerns of many contemporary village elders:

> A couple years ago I went to the village of Stony River and I happened to talk to an older woman there and while we were walking on the path, we ran across a moose hide that was just thrown and being trampled on the path and being torn up by dogs. So she and I picked it up and put it away into the trash can. And then she says, "You know, we don't have very much moose up here anymore. It's because people are not respecting our game. Look at this skin. It's just being trampled on. We don't treat our moose that way, and that is why the moose population is going down."

9. The implementation of this act has not been without controversy. In the infamous "Teddy Bear Case," a Tlingit and an Aleut were cited for producing "unauthentic" items from sea otter fur, including teddy bears and fur flowers. Because the use of sea otter pelts has been illegal since the mid-1700s, it would be difficult to say what an "authentic," traditional use would be. The actions of the native artisans were simultaneously modern and traditional—modern in the form they chose to take and traditional in the adaptation of known techniques to new uses (Kancewick 1989).

10. "With the advent of the white hunters in large numbers and the general introduction of firearms, the sea and land mammals have become scarce, and the Eskimo find themselves in a position where an adequate supply of their staple food can no longer be obtained. Their natural food supply, in short, is rapidly being cut off" (Gordon 1906–1907:70).

11. Thanks to Calvin Lensink of U.S. Fish and Wildlife for bringing these points to my attention.

9
The Yupiit Nation: Eskimo Law and Order

1. Remarkably little has been written about the traditional forms of governance and law ways of western Alaska. The best information occurs in a long article on leadership and factionalism on Nunivak Island by Margaret Lantis (1972) and in brief discussions of traditional governance by Fienup-Riordan (1984a), Lantis (1946:247–251), Nelson (1899:287, 292–309), Oswalt (1963a:54), and Shinkwin (1984). The Inuit of northern Alaska, Canada, and Greenland fare little better than the Yupiit in a review of the literature on this topic. Although traditional governance is given limited consideration in a number of ethnographic accounts (including Burch 1975, 1980:264–267; Chance 1966:62–70; Jenness 1922:93; Spencer 1959:97–124; VanStone 1962:101–106), it is the focus of attention in only a handful of works (Dahl 1985; Graburn 1969a; Hippler and Conn 1973; Hoebel 1941, 1963; Hughes 1966; Nooter 1976; Pospisil 1964; Ray 1967; Van den Steenhoven 1962; Wenzel 1979).

2. In the Yupiit School District, a new Yup'ik-oriented reading program is getting national attention for the way it mixes easy-to-understand reading material with contemporary educational methods. Village leaders, teachers, and a California educational consulting company developed a program that starts as soon as children enter school. The results were quick. In three years the district's reading scores rose from the fifteenth percentile nationally to above the fiftieth, according to superintendent Brad Raphel.

3. In 1988 Yupiit Nation member villages were: Akiachak, Akiak, Tuluksak, Atmauthluak, Kasigluk, Nunapitchuk, Napakiak, Napaskiak, Toksook Bay, Nightmute, Newtok, Chefornak, Kipnuk, Kongiganak, Kwigillingok, Tuntutuliak, Quinhagak, Goodnews Bay, and Togiak.

4. The testimony cited in this chapter derives primarily from the transcripts of interviews with village elders on traditional law and governance that were carried out by the Yupiit Nation in 1988. References are to transcript number and page.

5. Nelson (1899:304) recorded two additional terms for leader used at the mouth of the Yukon Delta and northward along the coast: näs-kuk (*nasquq*, literally "the head") and äñ-aí-yu-kŏk, literally "the one to whom all listen" (probably *angayuqaq*, parent, boss). Like their Kuskokwim counterparts, these terms emphasize the speech rather than the wealth of the person so designated.

6. "Chief" Eddie Hoffman, the late native leader of Bethel, is an excellent example of the sort of person the elders had in mind. He had wealth, but many people were wealthier. He was old, but many were older. He was

knowledgeable and had a large, extended family, but here too he was like many other long-time Bethel residents. Hoffman stood out from his contemporaries in one important respect: He was outspoken. And when he spoke, he spoke for the people. His tombstone reads, "The cannon we pulled out when all else had failed."

7. An example of such a warning is the story mentioned previously of the man who went out of the *qasgiq* while the speaker was talking and as a result ended up frozen to death with "fine looking teeth at the beginning of the snowdrift" (Mathew Frye, 18:13 YN; see also Herman Neck, 28:15 YN; James Lott, Sr., 21:10 YN; and Joshua Phillip, 23:3–7 YN). This story recounts the past consequences of an individual's not listening to the rules. It also serves as a warning to a present offender of the probable future consequences of improper behavior.

8. The Stebbins elders (1985:13–14) went on to compare traditional ceremonies with the modern judicial system:

> The meaning of the potlatch is just like a court with a judge or a lawyer. . . . It is to teach the young people to respect their elders, to listen to them and obey the laws and follow their elders, their instructors, just like they would a judge.
>
> It makes people keep on remembering and obeying the old laws of the land. To show how important it is to obey the laws of the village. It makes people aware that they have to live within the laws all the time because people watch and tell what other people do wrong in the village. It causes the people to control their emotions and actions.

9. In the case of murder, the victim's family practiced blood revenge and was obligated to retaliate (Nelson 1899:292).

> At the time, killing occurred because of one's subsistence catch or because of another's wife . . . and also by warfare. At that time when people lived like that under those situations, brothers and sisters practiced the art of retaliation. (Adolph Jimmie, 15:10 YN)

> Even though they know that they were murderers, they left them alone. And they told the murderer not to be like that because he would eventually meet up with someone who will retaliate even though he may be strong and a swift runner. Some persons will eventually do the same to him. (Joshua Phillip, 23:8 YN)

This eye-for-an-eye ethic was a far cry from the "unchecked violence" that some observers report as characterizing traditional Eskimo society (for example, Hippler and Conn 1973:22). In fact, fear of reprisal was probably an important and effective deterrent in nineteenth-century intragroup relations.

10. The Yup'ik base for "follow" is *maligte-*, from *malik*, literally "companion, thing taken along."

11. Women do however get heard, but indirectly in their homes. Although informally delivered, their speech has an impact that is far from negligible.

12. These *qasgiq* meetings (as they are called) began following a sudden storm in January 1989 during which several young hunters from the village lost their way. Most of the boys knew enough to stay in one place and wait the storm out. One boy, however, attempted to find his way home and as a result froze to death. Community leaders decided that the way to guard against such tragedy in the future was to renew their efforts to educate younger community members in traditional survival skills.

10
Conclusion: The Invocation of Tradition

1. As with many high school church retreats, students' enjoyment of the week is in part a response to the contrast between the time spent in the *qasgiq* and everyday village life. The long-term impact of the week is muted by the fact that at its close students return to the life they left behind.

References

Archives and Unpublished Tape Collections

MA Moravian Archives, Kilbuck Collection, Boxes 1–10, 1885–1922, Bethlehem, Pa.

NI   Nelson Island Oral History Project, Toksook Bay, Nelson Island, Alaska. Interviews taped between 1985 and 1989.

YN Yupiit Nation Traditional Law and Governance Project, Akiachak, Alaska. Interviews taped in 1988–1989. Transcribed and translated by David Chanar.

Articles and Books

Aberle, David. 1982. *Peyote Religion among the Navaho*. Chicago: University of Chicago Press.

Ager, Lynn Price. 1974. "Storyknifing: An Alaskan Eskimo Girls' Game." *Journal of the Folklore Institute* 11(3):187–198.

Agibinik, Emily. 1973. "Russian Orthodox Christmas." *Theata* (Student Orientation Services, University of Alaska, Fairbanks) 1(1):91.

Alaska Journal (Anchorage). 1984. "The Alaska-Yukon-Pacific Exposition of 1909: Photographs by Frank Nowell." Summer, 8–14.

Alexie, Oscar, and Helen Morris, eds. 1985. *The Elders' Conference 1984*. Bethel, Alaska: Orutsararmiut Native Council.

Ali, Elizabeth, and John Active. 1982. "The Bethel Native Dancers in Performance." Bethel Council on the Arts, Bethel, Alaska. Printed program.

Aloysius, Bob. 1986. "Ordination Speech." *Tundra Drums* (Bethel, Alaska) 15(7):17.

Anchorage Daily News. 1988. "A People in Peril." Jan.-Feb.

Anderson, Eva G. 1940. *Dog Team Doctor*. Caldwell, Idaho: Caxton.

Arcand, Bernard. 1987. "The Other Is Dead." Paper presented at the 86th Annual Meeting of the American Anthropological Association, Chicago.

Arnold, Robert D. 1978. *Alaska Native Land Claims*. Anchorage: Alaska Native Foundation.

Austrup, Eivind. 1896. "In the Land of the Northernmost Eskimo." *Fortnightly Review*, Mar., 466.

Balikci, Asen. 1970. *The Netsilik Eskimo*. Garden City, N.Y.: Natural History Press.
———. 1984. "Illustres Sauvages." *LeMonde Aujourd'hui*. July 15–16.
Beck, Melinda, and Carry Anderson. 1989. "Off with Their Heads." *Newsweek*. June 5.
Bellah, Robert N. 1975. *The Broken Covenant: American Civil Religion in Time of Trial*. New York: Seabury.
Berkhofer, Robert F., Jr. 1978. *The White Man's Indian: Images of the American Indian from Columbus to the Present*. New York: Knopf.
Black, Lydia, ed. 1984a. *The Journals of Iakov Netsvetov: The Yukon Years 1845–1863*. Kingston, Ont.: Limestone Press.
———. 1984b. "The Yup'ik of Western Alaska and Russian Impact." *The Central Yupik Eskimos*, ed. Ernest S. Burch, Jr., supplementary issue of *Etudes/Inuit/Studies* 8:21–43.
Boas, Franz. 1897. "The Decorative Art of the Indians of the North Pacific Coast." *Bulletin of the American Museum of Natural History* 9:123–176.
Bogoras, Waldemar. 1904. "The Chukchee." In *Memoirs of the American Museum of Natural History*, ed. Franz Boas, vol. 11. Reprint. New York: AMS Press, 1975.
Bohannan, Paul. 1981. "Unseen Community: The Natural History of a Research Project." In *Anthropologists at Home in North America*, ed. David Messerschmidt, pp. 29–44. Cambridge: Cambridge University Press.
Bradley, John Hodgdon. 1968. *World Geography*. Boston: Ginn.
Brightman, Robert Alain. 1983. "Animal and Human in Rock Cree Religion and Subsistence." Ph.D. diss., Department of Anthropology, University of Chicago.
Burch, Ernest S., Jr. 1974. "Eskimo Warfare in Northwest Alaska." *Anthropological Papers of the University of Alaska* 16(2):1–14.
———. 1975. *Eskimo Kinsmen: Changing Family Relationships in Northwest Alaska*. American Ethnological Society Monograph 59. San Francisco: West.
———. 1980. "Traditional Eskimo Societies in Northwest Alaska." *Senri Ethnological Studies* 4:253–304.
———. 1984. "The Central Yupik Eskimos: An Introduction." *The Central Yupik Eskimos*, ed. Ernest S. Burch, Jr., supplementary issue of *Etudes/Inuit/Studies* 8:3–19.
———. 1988a. "War and Trade." In *Crossroads of Continents*, ed. William Fitzhugh and Aron Crowell, pp. 227–240. Washington, D.C.: Smithsonian Institution Press.
———. 1988b. *The Eskimos*. Norman: University of Oklahoma Press.
Burch, Ernest S., Jr., and Thomas C. Correll. 1972. "Alliance and Conflict: Inter-regional Relations in North Alaska." In *Alliance in Eskimo Society*, ed. Lee Guemple, pp. 17–39. Seattle: University of Washington Press.
Chance, Norman A. 1966. *The Eskimo of North Alaska*. New York: Holt, Rinehart & Winston.
Charles, Nick, Sr. 1983. "Life History." Taped interviews with author. Bethel, Alaska, June. Rasmuson Library, University of Alaska, Fairbanks.

Chevak Tanqik Theatre. 1989. Performance brochure. Chevak, Alaska: Kashunamiut School District.

Christopher, Robert. 1988. "Narrators of the Arctic." *American Review of Canadian Studies* 18(3):259–269.

Clifford, James. 1983. "On Ethnographic Authority." *Representation* 1(2): 118–146.

———. 1986. "On Ethnographic Allegory." In *Writing Culture: The Poetics and Politics of Ethnography*, ed. James Clifford and George E. Marcus pp. 98–121. Berkeley: University of California Press.

———. 1988. *The Predicament of Culture: Twentieth-Century Ethnography, Literature, and Art.* Cambridge: Harvard University Press.

Clifford, James, and George E. Marcus, eds. 1986. *Writing Culture: The Poetics and Politics of Ethnography*. Berkeley: University of California Press.

Cole, Douglas. 1985. *Captured Heritage: The Scramble for Northwest Coast Artifacts*. Seattle: University of Washington Press.

Cole, William E., and Charles S. Montgomery. 1967. *High School Sociology*. Boston: Allyn & Bacon.

Collier, John. 1973. *Alaskan Eskimo Education*. New York: Holt, Rinehart & Winston.

Collins, Henry. 1984. "History of Research before 1945." In *Handbook of North American Indians*, vol. 5: *Arctic*, ed. David Damas, pp. 8–16. Washington, D.C.: Smithsonian Institution.

Comaroff, Jean, and John Comaroff. 1986. "Christianity and Colonialism in South Africa." *American Ethnologist* 13(1):1–22.

Crantz, David. 1767. *The History of Greenland*. 2 vols. London: Brethren's Society.

Curtis, Edward S. 1930. *The North American Indian, Being a Series of Volumes Picturing and Describing the Indians of the United States, the Dominion of Canada, and Alaska*, vol. 20. Reprint. New York: Johnson Reprint, 1970.

Dahl, Jens. 1985. "New Political Structure and Old Non-fixed Structural Politics in Greenland." In *Native Power*, ed. Jens Brøsted, Jens Dahl, Andrew Gray, Hans Christian Gulløv, Georg Henriksen, Jørgen Brøchner Jørgensen, and Inge Kleivan. Oslo: Universitetsforlaget.

———, ed. 1989. *Keynote Speeches from the Sixth Inuit Studies Conference, Copenhagen, October 1988*. Copenhagen: Institute for Eskimology, Copenhagen University.

Dall, William Healy. 1870a. *Alaska and Its Resources*. Reprint. New York: Arno Press, 1970.

———. 1870b. "On the Distribution of the Native Tribes of Alaska." *Proceedings of the American Association for the Advancement of Science* 18: 263–273.

———. 1877. "On the Distribution and Nomenclature of the Native Tribes of Alaska and the Adjacent Territory." In *Contributions to North American Ethnology*, vol. 1, Pt. 1: *Tribes of the Extreme Northwest*, pp. 7–40. Washington, D.C.: Government Printing Office.

———. 1884. "On Masks, Labrets, and Certain Aboriginal Customs, with an Inquiry into the Bearing of Their Geographical Distribution." In *Bureau *of American Ethnology Third Annual Report, 1881–1882,* pp. 67–203. Washington, D.C.: Government Printing Office.

Damas, David. 1984. "Introduction." In *Handbook of North American Indians,* vol. 5: *Arctic,* ed. David Damas, pp. 1–7. Washington, D.C.: Smithsonian Institution.

Davidson, Art. 1989. "Homesick for a Dream." *Alaska Magazine,* Oct., pp. 31–33, 58.

de Poncins, Gontran. 1941. *Kabloona.* New York: Reynal & Hitchcock.

Derrida, Jacques. 1973. *Speech and Phenomena.* Evanston, Ill.: Northwestern University Press.

———. 1974. *Of Grammatology.* Baltimore: Johns Hopkins University Press.

Dominguez, Virginia R. 1986. "The Marketing of Heritage." *American Ethnologist* 13(3):546–555.

Drebert, Ferdinand. 1959. *Alaska Missionary.* Bethlehem, Pa.: Moravian Book Shop.

Dumont, Louis. 1970. *Homo Hierarchicus: The Caste System and Its Implications.* Chicago: University of Chicago Press.

Durham, William H. 1981. "Overview: Optimal Foraging Analysis in Human Ecology." In *Hunter-Gatherer Foraging Strategies,* ed. B. Winterhalder and E. A. Smith. Chicago: University of Chicago Press.

Eckert, Penelope, and Russell Newmark. 1980. "Central Eskimo Song Duels: A Contextual Analysis of Ritual Ambiguity." *Ethnology* 19:191–212.

Egede, Hans P. 1745. *A Description of Greenland.* London: C. Hitch, S. Austen, J. Jackson.

Eliade, Mircea. 1964. *Shamanism: Archaic Techniques of Ecstasy.* Trans. Willard R. Trask. Princeton, N.J.: Princeton University Press.

Embers, Carol R. 1978. "Myths about Hunter-Gatherers." *Ethnology* 17:439–448.

Etolin, A. K. 1840. "Communications Sent to the Company's Main Office, September 27." *Records of the Russian-American Company, Correspondence of the Governor's General,* vol. 19, no. 150, 194–195. National Archives (microfilm, University of Alaska Fairbanks).

Fienup-Riordan, Ann. 1977–1987. Transcripts and translations of interviews with Yup'ik elders. Tapes 1–99. Unpublished manuscript compiled for the Nelson Island Oral History Project. Prepared with the support of the Alaska Humanities Forum, Anchorage.

———. 1982. *Navarin Basin Sociocultural Systems Baseline Analysis.* Alaska Outer Continental Shelf Socioeconomic Studies Program Technical Report 70. Washington, D.C.: Government Printing Office.

———. 1983. *The Nelson Island Eskimo.* Anchorage: Alaska Pacific University Press.

———. 1984a. "Regional Groups on the Yukon-Kuskokwim Delta." *The Central Yupik Eskimos,* ed. Ernest S. Burch, Jr., supplementary issue of *Etudes/Inuit/Studies* 8:63–93.

———. 1984b. "Yup'ik Dance." In *1984 Festival of American Folklife,* ed. National Park Service. Washington, D.C.: Smithsonian Institution.

———. 1985. "The Uses and Abuses of Anthropology in Alaska." Distinguished Humanist Address. Alaska Humanities Forum, Anchorage, Feb.

———. 1986a. "The Real People: The Concept of Personhood among the Yup'ik Eskimos of Western Alaska." *Etudes/Inuit/Studies* 10(1–2):261–270.

———. 1986b. *When Our Bad Season Comes: A Cultural Account of Subsistence Harvesting and Harvest Disruption on the Yukon Delta.* Monograph Series 1. Aurora: Alaska Anthropological Association.

———. 1987. "The Mask: The Eye of the Dance." *Arctic Anthropology* 24(2): 40–55.

———. 1988a. "Alakanuk Village Description." In *Village Economics in Rural Alaska.* Alaska Outer Continental Shelf Environmental Studies Program Technical Report 132. Washington, D.C.: Minerals Management Service, U.S. Department of the Interior.

———. 1988b. "The Martyrdom of Brother Hooker: Conflict and Conversion on the Kuskokwim." *Alaska History* 3(1):1–26.

———. 1988c. "Robert Redford, Apanuugpak, and the Invention of Tradition." *American Ethnologist* 15(3):442–455.

———, ed. 1988d. *The Yup'ik Eskimos as Described in the Travel Journals and Ethnographic Accounts of John and Edith Kilbuck, 1885–1900.* Kingston, Ont.: Limestone Press.

———. 1989. "Eskimo War and Peace: The History of Yup'ik Warfare and Interpersonal Violence." Anchorage. Manuscript.

———. 1991. *The Real People and the Children of Thunder: The Yup'ik Eskimo Encounter with Moravian Missionaries John and Edith Kilbuck.* Norman: University of Oklahoma Press.

Fitzhugh, William W., and Susan A. Kaplan. 1982. *Inua: Spirit World of the Bering Sea Eskimo.* Washington, D.C.: Smithsonian Institution Press.

Flintoff, Corey. 1984. *Eyes of the Spirit.* Video documentary of 1982 mask-making workshop. Bethel, Alaska: KYUK Radio Station.

Foulks, Edward F. 1972. *The Arctic Hysterias of the North Alaskan Eskimo.* Washington, D.C.: American Anthropological Association.

Freeman, Derek. 1983. *Margaret Mead and Samoa: The Making and Unmaking of an Anthropological Myth.* Cambridge: Harvard University Press.

Freuchen, Peter. 1931. *Eskimo.* New York: Grossett and Dunlap.

Friday, Joe. 1985. Interview. Trans. Louise Leonard. Feb. 19. Lansburg Productions, San Francisco.

Gordon, George Bryan. 1906–1907. "Notes on the Western Eskimo." *Transactions of the Free Museum of Science and Art* (University of Pennsylvania) 2:69–101.

Graburn, Nelson H. 1969a. "Eskimo Law in the Light of Self and Group Interest." *Law and Society Review* 4(1):45–60.

———. 1969b. *Eskimos without Igloos: Social and Economic Development in Sugluk.* Boston: Little, Brown.

Hakluyt, Richard. 1589. *The Principal Navigations, Voyages, Traffiques and Discoveries of the English Nation in Twelve Volumes,* vol. 7. Reprint. New York: Augustus M. Kelley, 1969.

Hamilton, J. Taylor, and Kenneth Gardner Hamilton. 1967. *History of the Moravian Church, 1722–1957.* Bethlehem, Pa.: Moravian.

Harper, Kenn. 1986. *Give Me My Father's Body: The Life of Minik the New York Eskimo.* Frobisher Bay, N.W.T.: Blacklead Books.

Harper's. 1867. "Our New Northwest." 35 (July 1867):185.

Hawkes, Ernest William. 1913. *The "Inviting-In" Feast of the Alaska Eskimo.* Geological Survey Memoir 45, Anthropological Series 3. Ottawa: Canada Department of Mines.

Himmelheber, Hans. 1938. *Eskimokünstler, Teilergebnis einer ethnographischen Expedition in Alaska von Juni 1936 bis April 1937.* Stuttgart, Germany: Strecker und Schroder.

———. 1953. *Eskimokünstler, Ergebnisse einer Reise in Alaska.* 2d ed. Eisenach, Germany: Erich Roth-Verlag.

Hippler, Arthur E. 1974. "Some Alternative Viewpoints of the Negative Results of Euro-American Contact with Non-Western Group." *American Anthropologist* 76:334–337.

Hippler, Arthur E., and Stephen Conn. 1973. *Northern Eskimo Law Ways and Their Relationship to Contemporary Problems of "Bush Justice."* Fairbanks: Institute of Social, Economic and Government Research, University of Alaska.

Hirschfelder, Arlene B. 1982. *American Indian Stereotypes in the World of Children: A Reader and Bibliography.* Metuchen, N.J.: Scarecrow Press.

Hobsbawm, Eric and Terence Ranger, eds. 1983. *The Invention of Tradition.* Cambridge: Cambridge University Press.

Hoebel, E. Adamson. 1941. "Law Ways of the Primitive Eskimos." *Journal of the American Institute of Criminal Law and Criminology* 31:663–683.

———. 1961. *The Law of Primitive Man: A Study in Comparative Legal Dynamics.* Cambridge: Harvard University Press.

———. 1963. "Community Organization and Patterns of Change among North Canadian and Alaskan Indians and Eskimos." *Anthropologica* 5:3–8.

Honigmann, John J., and Irma Honigmann. 1965. *Eskimo Townsmen.* Ottawa: Canadian Reseach Center for Anthropology, Saint Paul University.

Houston, James. 1971. *The White Dawn.* New York: Harcourt Brace Jovanovich.

Hughes, Charles. 1966. "From Contest to Council: Social Control among the St. Lawrence Island Eskimos." In *Political Anthropology,* ed. Marc J. Swartz, Victor W. Turner, and Arthur Tuden. Chicago: Aldine.

Hunsaker, Dave. 1986a. "New Feature Film Focuses on Yup'ik Legends." Anchorage, Nov. 24. Press release.

———. 1986b. *Winter Warrior.* Dancing Bear Productions, Juneau.

———. 1987. "Letter to John Oscar." *Tundra Drums* (Bethel, Alaska) 15(43):2, 23.

Jacobson, Steven A. 1984. *Yup'ik Eskimo Dictionary.* Fairbanks: Alaska Native Language Center, University of Alaska.

Jenness, Diamond. 1922. *The Life of the Copper Eskimos,* vol. 12. Report of the Canadian Arctic Expedition, 1913–1918.Ottawa.

Jochim, Michael. 1976. *Hunter-Gatherer Subsistence and Settlement.* New York: Academic Press.

John, Paul. 1977. *Quliraq.* Recorded on Feb. 14 at Toksook Bay, Nelson Island, Alaska. Trans. Louise Leonard and Ann Fienup-Riordan. Anchorage.

———. 1984. Interview with Charles Haecker, Aug. 10, Toksook Bay. Nelson

Island 14(h) (1) Site Survey. Realty Office, Bureau of Indian Affairs, Anchorage.

Kan, Sergei. 1987a. "Introduction. Native Cultures and Christianity in Northern North America: Selected Papers from a Symposium." *Arctic Anthropology* 24(1):1–7.

———. 1987b. "Memory Eternal: Orthodox Christianity and the Tlingit Mortuary Complex." *Arctic Anthropology* 24(1):32–55.

Kancewick, Mary. 1989. "Tradition Is Hip: A *Nalukataq* Lesson for a *Tunnaq* Lawyer." Anchorage. Manuscript.

Kane, Elisha Kent. 1856. *Arctic Explorations.* 2 vols. Philadelphia: Childs & Peterson.

Kilbuck, Edith. 1887. "Journal to her Father, October 1, 1887." *The Moravian* 33(38):598–599.

———. 1889. "The Alaska Mission: Letter from the Kuskokwim, February 20." *The Moravian* 34(34):530–533.

Kilbuck, John Henry. 1886. "Annual Report, June." *The Moravian* 31(30):473.

———. 1890. "Journal. December 12, 1888." *The Moravian* 35(4):57.

Kirkpatrick, John. 1988. "From Was to Ought: Arguments from Tradition in Modern Hawaii." Paper presented at the 87th Annual Meeting of the American Anthropological Association, Phoenix.

Klahn, Jim. 1988. "Airline Keeps Smiling Eskimo." *Anchorage Daily News,* Jan. 22, C-1.

Kleinfeld, Judith. 1978. *Eskimo School on the Andreafsy.* New York: Praeger.

Kretch, Shepard, III, ed. 1981. *Indians, Animals, and the Fur Trade.* Athens: University of Georgia Press.

Lake, Ahnna, Linda Peerce, Jacqueline Grémaud, Jacques Leroux, Guy Tessier, with Asen Balikci. 1984. "Le Stéréotype des Esquimaux chez les Elèves du Niveau Primaire." *Etudes/Inuit/Studies* 8(2):139–144.

Lantis, Margaret. 1946. "The Social Culture of the Nunivak Eskimo." *Transactions of the American Philosophical Society* (Philadelphia) 35(3):153–323.

———. 1947. *Alaskan Eskimo Ceremonialism.* American Ethnological Society Monograph 11. Seattle: University of Washington Press.

———. 1953. "Nunivak Eskimo Personality as Revealed in the Mythology." *Anthropological Papers of the University of Alaska* 2:109–174.

———. 1972. "Factionalism and Leadership: A Case Study of Nunivak Island." *Arctic Anthropology* 9(1):43–65.

———. 1984. "Nunivak Eskimo." In *Handbook of North American Indians,* vol. 5: *Arctic,* ed. David Damas, pp. 209–223. Washington, D.C.: Smithsonian Institution.

Lechat, R. 1976. "Evangelism and Colonialism." *Eskimo,* n.s. 33(11):3–7.

Lee, R. B., and I. Devore, eds. 1968. *Man the Hunter.* Chicago: Aldine.

Lenz, Mary. 1986. "Alaska Native Teens Are Nation's Highest Risk Suicide Group." *Tundra Drums* (Bethel, Alaska). 14(50):4, 5.

Lyon, George F. 1824. *The Private Journal of Captain G. F. Lyon.* London: John Murray.

Macpherson, Crawford Brough. 1962. *The Political Theory of Possessive Individualism.* Oxford: Clarendon Press.

Malaurie, Jean. 1982. *The Last Kings of Thule*. Trans. Adrienne Foulke. Chicago: University of Chicago Press.

Martin, Calvin. 1978. *Keepers of the Game: Indian-Animal Relationships and the Fur Trade*. Berkeley: University of California Press.

Mather, Elsie. 1985. *Cauyarnariuq [A Time for Drumming]*. Bethel, Alaska: Lower Kuskokwim School District.

———. 1986. "Alaska Natives and Literacy." Transcripts of round-table discussion held in Kodiak, Alaska. Alaska Humanities Forum, Anchorage.

McGinniss, Joe. 1980. *Going to Extremes*. New York: Knopf.

Mead, Margaret. 1928. *Coming of Age in Samoa*. New York: Morrow Quill.

———. 1968. "Alternatives to War." In *War: The Anthropology of Armed Conflict and Aggression*, ed. Morton Fried, Marvin Harris, and Robert Murphy, pp. 216–228. New York: Natural History Press.

Meggitt, M. 1962. *Desert People*. Sydney: Angus & Robertson.

Meyendorff, John. 1979. *The Byzantine Legacy in the Orthodox Church*. Crestwood, N.Y.: St. Vladimir's Seminary Press.

Michael, Henry N., ed. 1967. *Lieutenant Zagoskin's Travels in Russian America, 1842–1844*. Toronto: University of Toronto Press.

Miller, Christopher L., and George R. Hamell. 1986. "A New Perspective on Indian-White Contact." *Journal of American History* 73(2):311–328.

Moore, Riley D. 1923. "Social Life of the Eskimo of St. Lawrence Island." *American Anthropologist* 25(3):339–375.

Morrow, Phyllis. 1984. "It Is Time for Drumming: A Summary of Recent Research on Yup'ik Ceremonialism." *The Central Yupik Eskimos*, ed. Ernest S. Burch, Jr., supplementary issue of *Etudes/Inuit/ Studies* 8:113–140.

Mousalimas, S.A. 1988. "Continuity and Discontinuity in Belief Systems in Southern Alaska." Paper presented at the 15th Annual Meeting of the Alaska Anthropological Association, Fairbanks.

Munn, Nancy D. 1973. *Walbiri Iconography: Graphic Representation and Cultural Symbolism in a Central Australian Society*. Ithaca, N.Y.: Cornell University Press.

Murdoch, John. 1892. "Ethnological Results of the Point Barrow Expedition." *Ninth Annual Report of the Bureau of Ethnology for the Years 1887–1888*. Washington, D.C.: Smithsonian Institution Press. (Reprinted 1983.)

Neatby, L. H. 1984. "Exploration and History of the Canadian Arctic." In *Handbook of North American Indians*, vol. 5: *Arctic*, ed. David Damas, pp. 377–390. Washington, D.C.: Smithsonian Institution.

Nelson, Edward W. 1882. "A Sledge Journey in the Delta of the Yukon, Northern Alaska." *Proceedings of the Royal Geographical Society*, n.s. 4:669–670.

———. 1897. *Report upon Natural History Made in Alaska between the Years 1877–1881*. Arctic Series of Publications III. Washington, D.C.: U.S. Army Signal Service.

———. 1899. *The Eskimo about Bering Strait*. Bureau of American Ethnology Annual Report for 1896–1897, vol. 18, no. 1. Washington, D.C.: Smithsonian Institution. (Reprinted 1983.)

Nelson, Richard K. 1969. *Hunters of the Northern Ice*. Chicago: University of Chicago Press.

———. 1977. *Shadow of the Hunter*. Chicago: University of Chicago Press.

———. 1983. *Make Prayers to Raven*. Chicago: University of Chicago Press.

Nelson, Richard K., Kathleen Mautner, G. Ray Bane. 1982. *Tracks in the Wildland: A Portrayal of Koyukon and Nunamiut Subsistence*. Fairbanks: Cooperative Park Studies Unit, University of Alaska.

Nooter, Gert. 1976. *Leadership and Headship: Changing Authority Patterns in an East Greenland Hunting Community*. Leiden: E. J. Brill.

North Slope Borough. 1987. "North Slope Borough Elders' Conference on Traditional Law." Barrow, Alaska, June 1986. (Typescript.)

Oleksa, Michael J. 1987. "The Orthodox Christian Mission and the Development of the 'Aleut' Identity among the Native Peoples of Southwestern Alaska." Ph.D. diss., Orthodox Theological Faculty, Presov, Czechoslovakia.

Ong, Walter J. 1977. *Interfaces of the Word*. Ithaca, N.Y.: Cornell University Press.

———. 1982. *Orality and Literacy*. London: Methuen.

Oscar, John. 1987. "Letter to Dave Hunsaker." *Tundra Drums* (Bethel, Alaska) 15(42):2.

Oswalt, Wendell. 1963a. *Mission of Change in Alaska: Eskimos and Moravians on the Kuskokwim*. San Marino, Calif.: Huntington Library.

———. 1963b. *Napaskiak: An Alaskan Eskimo Community*. Tucson: University of Arizona Press.

———. 1964. "Traditional Storyknife Tales of Yuk Girls." *Proceedings of the American Philosophical Society* 108(4):310–366.

———. 1967. *Alaskan Eskimos*. Scranton, Pa: Chandler.

———. 1979. *Eskimos and Explorers*. Novato, Calif.: Chandler & Sharp.

———. 1990. *Bashful No Longer: An Alaskan Eskimo Ethnohistory, 1778–1988*. Norman: University of Oklahoma Press.

Pagden, Anthony. 1982. *The Fall of Natural Man: The American Indian and the Origins of Comparative Ethnology*. New York: Cambridge University Press.

Parry, William E. 1828. *Journals of the First, Second and Third Voyages for the Discovery of a North-West Passage*. 5 vols. London: John Murray.

Peary, Robert E. 1898. *Northward over the Great Ice*. New York: Frederick A. Stokes.

———. 1910. *The North Pole*. New York: Frederick A. Stokes.

Petroff, Ivan. 1884. *Report on the Population, Industries, and Resources of Alaska. Tenth Census of the United States, Special Report*, vol. 8. Washington, D.C.: Government Printing Office.

Phillip, Joshua. 1988. Interview with Robert Drozda, July 1. Tuluksak 14(h)(1) Site Survey. Realty Office, Bureau of Indian Affairs, Anchorage.

Pleasant, Charlie. 1981. "The Man Who Turned into a Wolverine." In *Yupik Lore: Oral Traditions of an Eskimo People*, ed. Edward A. Tennant and Joseph N. Bitar. Bethel, Alaska: Lower Kuskokwim School District.

Pospisil, Leopold. 1964. "Law and Societal Structure among the Nunamiut Eskimo." In *Explorations in Cultural Anthropology*, ed. Ward H. Goodenough, pp. 395–431. New York: McGraw-Hill.

Pratt, Kenneth L. 1984. "Classification of Eskimo Groupings in the Yukon-

Kuskokwim Region: A Critical Analysis." *The Central Yupik Eskimos*, ed. Ernest S. Burch, Jr., supplementary issue of *Etudes/Inuit/Studies* 8: 45–61.

Rasmussen, Knud. 1927. *Across Arctic America: Narrative of the Fifth Thule Expedition*. New York: Putnam's.

———. 1931. "The Netsilik Eskimos: Social Life and Spiritual Culture." *Report of the Fifth Thule Expedition 1921–24*, vol. 8, no. 1–2. Copenhagen: Gyldendalske Boghandel, Nordisk Forlag.

———. 1932. "Intellectual Culture of the Copper Eskimo." *Report of the Fifth Thule Expedition*, vol. 8. Copenhagen: Gyldendalske Boghandel, Nordisk Forlag.

———. 1933. "Explorations in Southeastern Greenland: Preliminary Report of the Sixth and Seventh Thule Expeditions." *Geographical Review* (New York) 23(3):385–393.

Ray, Dorothy Jean. 1967. *Eskimo Masks: Art and Ceremony*. Seattle: University of Washington Press.

———. 1981. *Aleut and Eskimo Art: Tradition and Innovation in South Alaska*. Seattle: University of Washington Press.

Reed, Irene, Osahito Miyaoka, Steven Jacobson, Paschal Afcan, and Michael Krauss. 1977. *Yup'ik Eskimo Grammar*. Fairbanks: Alaska Native Language Center, University of Alaska.

Richards, Brad. 1984. "Eskimo Hunters of the Bering Sea." *National Geographic* 165(6):814–834.

Rosaldo, Renato. 1986. "From the Door of His Tent: The Fieldworker and the Inquisitor." In *Writing Culture*, ed. James Clifford and George E. Marcus. Berkeley: University of California Press.

Ross, John. 1819. *A Voyage of Discovery*. London: John Murray.

Ruesch, Hans. 1944. *The Top of the World*. New York: Harper & Brothers.

Rydell, Robert W. 1984. *All the World's a Fair*. Chicago: University of Chicago Press.

Sahlins, Marshall. 1976. *Culture and Practical Reason*. Chicago: University of Chicago Press.

———. 1981. "Alaska: Towards the Twenty-First Century." Lecture given at Alaska Pacific University, Anchorage, May.

———. 1985. *Islands of History*. Chicago: University of Chicago Press.

———. 1986. "Social Science; or the Tragic Western Sense of Human Imperfections." Hillsdale Lecture given at the University of Wisconsin-Madison, Apr. 30.

Schiller, Paula. 1981. "Shadow of the Hunter." *Tundra Times* (Anchorage) 17(15):16.

Schuster, Carl. 1951. "Joint Marks: A Possible Index of Cultural Contact between America, Oceania and the Far East." *Royal Tropical Institute* (Amsterdam) 39:4–51.

Scollon, Ronald, and Suzanne B. K. Scollon. 1980. *Interethnic Communication*. Fairbanks: Alaska Native Language Center, University of Alaska.

Service, Elman R. 1966. *The Hunters*. Englewood Cliffs, N.J.: Prentice-Hall.

Shaw, Robert Dane. 1983. "The Archaeology of the Manokinak Site: A Study of the Cultural Transition between Late Norton Tradition and Historic

Eskimo." Ph.D. diss. Department of Anthropology, Washington State University.

Shinkwin, Anne D. 1984. "Traditional Alaska Native Societies." In *Alaska Natives and American Laws*, ed. David S. Case. Fairbanks: University of Alaska Press.

Shinkwin, Anne D., and Mary Pete. 1984. "Yup'ik Eskimo Societies: A Case Study." *The Central Yupik Eskimos*, ed. Ernest S. Burch, Jr. supplementary issue of *Etudes/Inuit/Studies* 8:95–112.

Smith, Barbara Sweetland. 1980. *Russian Orthodoxy in Alaska: A History, Inventory, and Analysis of Church Archives in Alaska with Annotated Bibliography*. Anchorage: Alaska Historical Commission.

Smith, Dorothy A., and Leslie Spier. 1927. "The Dot and Circle Design in Northwestern America." *Society of Americanists*, n.s. 19:47–55.

Sokolof, Archpriest D. 1899. *A Manual of the Orthodox Church's Divine Services*. Jordonville, N.Y.: Holy Trinity Russian Orthodox Monastery. (Reprinted 1968.)

Spencer, Robert F. 1959. *The North Alaskan Eskimo*. Smithsonian Institution Bureau of American Ethnology Bulletin 171. Washington D.C.: Government Printing Office.

Stebbins Elders. 1985. *The Stebbins Potlatch*. Nome, Alaska: Kawerak.

Stieglitz, Walter O. 1989. "Letter to the Editor of Newsweek." *Tundra Times* (Anchorage) 26:2, 12.

Tanner, Adrian. 1979. *Bringing Home Animals: Religious Ideology and Mode of Production of the Mistassini Memorial Cree Hunters*. New York: St. Martin's Press.

Thornton, Harrison Robertson. 1890–1893. Diaries. Peary-MacMillan Arctic Museum and Arctic Studies Center, Bowdoin College, Brunswick, Maine.

———. 1931. *Among the Eskimos of Wales, Alaska 1890–1893*, ed. Neda S. Thornton and William M. Thornton, Jr. Baltimore: Johns Hopkins Press.

Tocqueville, Alexis, de. 1835. *Democracy in America*. Trans. Henry Reeve. London, 1875.

Toksook Bay Traditional Council. 1988. "Elders Issue Position Paper on Culture." *Tundra Times* (Anchorage) 26:11.

Turnbull, Colin. 1968. "Comments on Primitive Behavior and the Evolution of Prefarming Societies." In *Man the Hunter*, ed. R. B. Lee and I. Devore, pp. 321–334. Chicago: Aldine.

U.S. Bureau of the Census. 1901. *Twelfth Census of the United States, 1900*, vol. 1, pt. 1. Washington, D.C.: Government Printing Office.

———. 1942. *Sixteenth Census of the United States, 1940*, vol. 1. Washington, D.C.: Government Printing Office.

Usugan, Frances. 1982. *Quliraq*. Recorded by the author on Nov. 3 at Toksook Bay, Nelson Island, Alaska.

Van den Steenhoven, G. 1962. *Leadership and Law among the Eskimos of the Keewatin District, Northwest Territories*. The Hague: Uitgeveij Excelsior.

VanStone, James W. 1962. *Point Hope: An Eskimo Village in Transition*. Seattle: University of Washington Press.

———. 1967. *Eskimos of the Nushagak River, An Ethnographic History*. Seattle: University of Washington Press.

———. 1983. "Protective Hide Body Armor of the Historic Chukchi and Siberian Eskimos." *Etudes/Inuit/Studies* 7:3–24.

———. 1984a. "Exploration and Contact History of Western Alaska." In *Handbook of North American Indians*, vol. 5: *Arctic*, ed. David Damas, pp. 149–160. Washington, D.C.: Smithsonian Institution.

———. 1984b. "Mainland Southwest Alaska Eskimo." In *Handbook of North America Indians*, vol. 5: *Arctic*, ed. David Damas, pp. 224–242. Washington, D.C.: Smithsonian Institution.

———. 1988. *Russian Exploration in Southwest Alaska: The Travel Journals of Petr Korsakovskiy (1818) and Ivan Y. Vasilev (1829)*. Rasmuson Library Historical Translation Series IV. Fairbanks: University of Alaska Press.

VanStone, James W., and Ives Goddard. 1981. "Territorial Groups of West-Central Alaska before 1898." In *Handbook of North American Indians*, vol. 6: *Subarctic*, ed. June Helm, pp. 556–561. Washington, D.C.: Smithsonian Institution.

Vaughn, Mary Ann Woloch. 1983. *Ukrainian Christmas*. Munster, Ind.: Ukrainian Heritage Co.

Veniaminov, Ivan. 1840. *Notes on the Islands of the Unalaska District*. Trans. Lydia Black and R. H. Geoghagan. Ed. Richard Pierce. Kingston, Ont.: Limestone Press, 1984.

Vitt, Kurt H., ed. 1987. *Bernhard Bendel, 1870 Kuskokwim Expedition*. Bethel, Alaska: Moravian Seminary and Archives.

Wagner, Roy. 1975. *The Invention of Culture*. Chicago: University of Chicago Press.

———. 1986. *Symbols That Stand for Themselves*. Chicago: University of Chicago Press.

Weber, Caroline. 1890. "Diary, December 10, 1890." *The Moravian* 36:787.

Wenzel, George. 1979. "Inuit and Local Control: The Case of Somerset Island." *Etudes/Inuit/Studies* 3(2):19–26.

Weyer, Edward Moffat. 1932. *The Eskimos: Their Environment and Folkways*. New Haven, Conn.: Yale University Press.

Winterhalder, Bruce. 1981. "Foraging Strategies in the Boreal Forest: An Analysis of Cree Hunting and Gathering." In *Hunter-Gatherer Foraging Strategies*, ed. B. Winterhalder and E. A. Smith. Chicago: University of Chicago Press.

Wolfe, Robert J. 1979. "Food Production in a Western Eskimo Population." Ph.D. diss., Department of Anthropology, University of California at Los Angeles.

———. 1981. *Norton Sound/Yukon Delta Sociocultural Systems Baseline Analysis*. Technical Report 72. Anchorage: Subsistence Division, Alaska Department of Fish and Game.

———. 1989. "'The Fish Are Not to be Played With': Yup'ik Views of Sport Fishing and Subsistence-Recreation Conflicts along the Togiak River." Paper presented at the 16th Annual Meeting of the Alaska Anthropological Association, Anchorage.

Woodbury, Anthony C. 1984. *Cev'armiut Qanemciit Qulirait-llu: Eskimo Narratives and Tales from Chevak, Alaska*. Fairbanks: Alaska Native Language Center, University of Alaska.

Index

Page numbers in *italics* refer to illustrations.

Printed in the United States
60533LVS00002B/1-60

9 780813 515892